Whittlin', Whistles, and Thingamajigs

Whittlin',

Stackpole Books

Whistles, and Thingamajigs

The Pioneer Book of Nature Crafts and Recreation Arts

by Harlan G. Metcalf

WHITTLIN', WHISTLES, AND THINGAMAJIGS

Published by STACKPOLE BOOKS
Cameron and Kelker Streets
Harrisburg, Pa. 17105

Printed in the U.S.A.

Library of Congress Cataloging in Publication Data

Metcalf, Harlan G
Whittlin', whistles, and thingamajigs--the pioneer book of nature crafts and recreation arts.

Bibliography: p.
1. Handicraft. 2. Nature study. 3. Games.
I. Title.
TT157.M47 745.59'2 74-8630
ISBN 0-8117-1882-2

To Peg, my wife,
whose understanding,
love, and inspiration
made this book possible

Contents

Foreword

THIS BOOK IS NEEDED AND TIMELY. IT NOT ONLY HAS A MESSAGE for those who aspire to create beautiful and useful objects from materials found in nature; there is also a wealth of how-to-do information about many of the basic crafts that were a part of cultures that preceded the twentieth century, but which can serve today's needs in new and unique ways, as well as help to link cultures with one another. Here is a book that helps to preserve some of the authentic values of the "good old days."

The book has another distinction and uniqueness: it is authored by a person who is as skilled in the arts herein portrayed as the craftsmen of the past. Another important feature of the book is that the author has tested the quality of the native materials he recommends by extensive research and experimentation over a period of many years.

It has been said of Harlan G. Metcalf that he has more skills and knowledge about the kind of outdoor-related interests and pursuits described in this book than any other person. Furthermore, he is a nationally recognized leader in outdoor education and recreation and served long and well in his chosen profession. Thus, the book has the creative touch of the artist, the designs of a craftsman, and the authority of a professional. By improving the skills of the leaders of youth in the kinds of human endeavor that take form from the creative spark in the heart, the pages of this book will help bring rewarding experiences for countless numbers who live in these times.

JULIAN W. SMITH
Director, Outdoor Education Project
of the American Association for Health,
Physical Education and Recreation

Acknowledgments

THE AUTHOR WOULD LIKE TO EXPRESS HIS GRATITUDE TO several people. First, to his wife, Margaret Wyer Metcalf ("Peg"), who took most of the pictures, did much of the editing, endured her husband's many muddy field trips and his disposition during the preparation of the book, and gave him constant encouragement and inspiration at all times; next, to his parents, Rev. and Mrs. Paul Harlan Metcalf, who started his interest in and love for the outdoors, and finally to the following, who further stimulated his love of nature by letting him tag along with them on many of their nature exploration trips: cousins Francis M. Root and John Goldsbury and uncle Thomas Nelson Metcalf. The author is also indebted to Dr. Julian W. Smith for his constant encouragement and the inspiration of his leadership.

Introduction

WILL HISTORY SAY OF THE PEOPLE OF THE UNITED STATES THAT they had the daring and technological know-how to reach and walk on the moon but failed to use their God-given intelligence to find ways to keep their own land and planet inhabitable by human beings? It is evident that the degradation of our environment has reached such proportions that the survival of our children and their children to come is at stake. Somehow people everywhere must be persuaded to take the steps necessary to make their continued existence on earth possible. But how can this be done?

Love is the key. People do not consciously destroy or pollute the things they love, but rather preserve, protect, and nurture them. The more people learn to love the natural world around them, the better will be the chances of protecting all life on earth. One of the best ways of inculcating this love is to teach as many citizens as possible (especially youngsters) the art of making useful and/or beautiful objects from natural materials by hand or with hand-made tools without depleting the supply of those materials.

The question of depleting natural resources is an important one. Many of the nature crafts activities described in this book utilize the shoots and limbs of trees and parts of other plants, in the process of which sound conservation principles must be followed. To find out which wild flowers and plants of your state are protected, contact your state department of conservation. Learn to recognize these plants, protect them, and encourage others to do the same. Also be sure to use only those plants that grow most abundantly in your section of the country. Be especially careful with edible plants. Certain wild foods, such as the bulbs at the base of adder's tongue *(Erythronium americanum)* and spring beauty *(Claytonia virginica)*, should be taken only in an emergency survival situation because they could easily become extinct if they were all uprooted. If you must pick one such plant from a group, take only one and leave at least four untouched within a three-foot radius.

More specific conservation measures to be followed in regard to certain plants will be discussed in those places in the book where the plants are dealt with.

In teaching nature crafts, one must not only be cognizant of sound conservation procedures but must possess the necessary skills in working with the natural materials. It is our purpose in these pages to provide teachers, camp counselors, and recreation leaders with the information they need to develop skills in nature crafts which they will enjoy passing on to children and others who, in turn, will experience the thrill of creative activity.

One example of such creative activity might be making a basket from cattail leaves, giant bulrushes, or spruce roots. The fact that American Indians before you have fashioned such baskets does not make it any less a creative effort on your part. Indeed, it is hard to find and practice any nature craft which America's first inhabitants did not master, but even today people of all ages can experience the zest of thinking the thoughts of the American Indian after him and making the same kinds of cordage, whistles, bows and arrows, etc. that he made.

But one need not limit himself to making those artifacts familiar to the American Indian. Dare to try something different. Make something using native materials that no one else has used before. You'll get more satisfaction from making it whether anyone else does or not. You'll learn many things and get ideas for new nature crafts projects.

In learning nature crafts one activity just naturally leads to another. This "leading on," as William Heard Kilpatrick, the noted educational philosopher, pointed out, is a major characteristic of good education. An educational activity should "lead on" into many new and varied activities in never ending, ever widening circles of new experiences. As an example, take the following situation.

A group of children with their leader are strolling in the woods when they hear a high-pitched, clear whistle featuring two notes of the major scale, *re* and *do*, and repeated every five to ten seconds. The leader stops the group, calls their attention to the sound, and asks them what they think it is. After the children have given their answers, right and wrong, the leader imitates the sound and is answered from the forest. The leader continues to whistle at regular intervals and is answered quicker and louder each time until a bird smaller than a sparrow appears and flies about the leader's head as both bird and leader continue to answer the other's call. Then the bird hears a similar call from the woods and flies off after making a few dry noises.

The children ask what kind of bird it was and why it answered the leader's call. The leader first asks the children to describe the bird. The answers he gets include the information that the bird had a black cap, a black bib, and white cheeks. The leader reminds the children that just before the bird flew off it made a dry, insectlike noise that sounded something like "chick-a-dee-dee-dee." One child guesses correctly that the bird was a chickadee, and the leader volunteers the information that it was called a black-capped chickadee. He then explains that the high two-note whistle which attracted the bird is the chickadee's spring mating call and that the bird flew toward the leader's call hoping to find a mate. When the bird discovered his mistake, he gave his alarm call of "chick-a-dee-dee-dee." The leader also mentions that several other birds, such as the tufted titmouse, respond to their well-imitated mating calls and that both the titmouse and the chickadee belong to the titmice family. In answer to other questions the leader explains how chickadees help us human beings by eating insects that damage food crops. He also tells how to attract chickadees by putting suet in bird feeding stations and suggests that those who want to learn more about the chickadee can do so by consulting books in the school and local library.

One child wishes out loud that he could whistle as high and as clearly as a chickadee. The leader then remarks that some American Indian tribes made whistles from small branches and shoots of certain trees and shrubs that could almost exactly duplicate this bird's call. He asks if any of the children would like to see how it was done; all enthusiastically voice approval. The leader tells the group what trees make good whistles and how to recognize them. Then he lets the youngsters have the fun of finding the desired trees by themselves. Some of the trees selected are sugar maples and others are willows. In connection with the former, the leader tells his charges that the sap, when boiled long enough, yields maple syrup and sugar; and he promises to take them to a farm next spring to see it done. In connection with the latter, the leader informs the youngsters that one species of willow, the purple willow, is good for making baskets and fishing creels as well as whistles. The leader also demonstrates good conservation practice by showing the group how to assure a future supply of willows. He sticks the crown of the shoot from which he has cut a section for making a whistle back into the ground several yards from the place where it was cut, explaining in answer to the children's questions that the shoot will soon sprout new roots and start a new clump of willows.

After cutting a few suitable shoots and branches of sugar maples and willows, the leader makes a whistle or two, at the same time showing the youngsters how to use a pocket-knife properly and safely. Then he lets some of them make whistles under his close supervision.

The whistles made are of two types: the "slide-trombone" type, capable not only of making the two-tone call of the chickadee but of playing entire tunes, and the single-tone type. The leader shows how to vary the pitch of the trombone-type whistle by sliding the plunger inside the bark up and down. He tells the children that the length of the air column in a whistle determines its pitch and explains that sliding the plunger under the bark down lengthens the air column and thus lowers the pitch while sliding the plunger under the bark up shortens the air column and raises the pitch. The leader also demonstrates how to imitate the mating call of the chickadee by making two single-tone

Two shoots of purple or basket willow *(Salix purpurea)*. **Note the long narrow leaves. These turn a purplish tint as they dry. For making whistles use shoots thicker than the ones shown, with a diameter no smaller than 3/8 inch and no larger than 7/8 inch.**

whistles with air columns of differing length and blowing the whistles alternately. This episode provides an excellent opportunity to interest the children in the physical principles underlying the phenomenon of pitch, and the leader suggests that when the youngsters return to their school, they look up in a physics text the explanation of pitch and what governs it.

The above situation illustrates perfectly the "leading on" quality of good education. Hearing the mating call of the chickadee led on into many skills and areas of knowledge which it made more meaningful: ornithology, botany, forestry, conservation, handcrafts, the safe way to use a knife, and physics, to name a few. The same situation also illustrates how children and people of all ages learn by doing. Activity exercises the mind. We would have nothing to think about if we had not been doing things from the beginning of our lives. Activities, moreover, are the building blocks of experience. The importance of experience becomes apparent when one realizes that he thinks only in terms of his own experiences and those of other people, gleaned from observing, hearing, and reading about them. It follows, therefore, that the greater the quantity and variety of an individual's experiences, the better is the quality of his thinking and, one might add, of his education. The key part played by experience in education was underscored by John

Dewey, who conceived of education as the continuous reconstruction of experience in such a way that one develops increasing understanding and control of himself and of his environment.

Of course, youngsters and people of all ages do not as a rule plunge into activities because they are educational or good for them. People just naturally like to do things, especially things that are fun—and nature crafts activities *are* fun! One of the reasons why the author wrote this book is that he would like today's kids to enjoy some of the same simple nature-based skills and activities that he enjoyed when he was a kid—things like carving and blowing a wooden whistle and making and using a slingshot. Many of these skills seem to be unknown or forgotten today, which is a real pity because they were, and are, much more imaginative, creative, and stimulating than such modern-day pursuits as watching television.

The author hopes that the readers of this book will not content themselves with mastering the nature crafts skills outlined in its pages, fascinating though they are, but will use the book as a self-starter for devising satisfying and creative nature-based activities of their own. Happy adventuring!

chapter 1

Whistles and Horns: Nature's Own Musicmakers

IN THE AUTHOR'S BOYHOOD ONE QUALIFICATION FOR BEING A good father, grandfather, or uncle was one's ability to make a slip-bark whistle that would really whistle. Either the standards for selecting these close relations nowadays are slipping or whistle-making has become a lost art.

BEST TREES FOR MAKING WHISTLES

During the spring, when the sap is running and there is plenty of moisture from spring rains, excellent whistles can be made from a wide variety of trees. The author's favorite tree for making whistles is the striped maple, also called moosewood, moose maple, or goosefoot maple. Other suitable trees are sugar maple, mountain maple, red maple, willow, alder, dogwood, elder, viburnum, poplar, and basswood.

Residents of southern states can make good whistles of the single-tone type from bamboo. In northern states where bamboo is lacking, a good substitute is Japanese knotweed *(Polygonum cuspidatum)*, also known as false bamboo or Mexican bamboo. This can be planted on a campsite or the edge of a school forest. It has a beautiful white, lacy, many-flowered bloom through August and most of September. It is very hardy, and grows

Fig. 1-1. Japanese knotweed or false bamboo *(Polygonum cuspidatum).*

and spreads rapidly. The stalks may grow in one summer to an outside diameter of 1-1/2 inches and reach a height of 8 to 10 feet. The stalks or shoots have bamboolike joints and sections (see Fig. 1-1). It is not as straight as real bamboo and the woody outside is not as strong. However, it will make very good whistles. Once this plant gets started it will develop into a grove of many shoots which could "take over" and become a nuisance. Therefore, it should be closely supervised and used often by the nature crafts counselor to keep it under control.

Undoubtedly there are many other species of trees and shrubs that will yield satisfactory whistles in the spring. As a rule, however, it is easier to make slip-bark whistles from willow and/or some member of the maple family. Because it grows near water the bark of willow can be made to slip for whistle purposes not only in the spring but during the summer months through late August. (Alders and dogwoods growing on lakeshores or streambanks also make good slip-bark whistles from spring through August for the same reason.) A disadvantage of willow shoots, however, is the fact that their buds and leaves spiral alternately around the shoots or branches, leaving only 3/4 inch to 1 inch of a clear smooth area for making a whistle. Since this is not enough, you must make the willow whistle over a 2-1/2-inch to 3-inch area regardless of the roughness caused by leaf scars, buds, and bruises. Directly underneath the willow bark at the sites of buds and leaf scars, small woody protuberances or nodules will be found. If these are too large or sticking out into the bark too far, they will tear the bark in the slipping process and hence ruin the chances of making a whistle. Willow is generally abundant; so take care to select the smoothest shoots possible.

On the other hand, the striped maple and all other maples have opposite buds, leaves, leaf scars, etc.; and if the shoots are well nourished and fast-growing there will be clear, vertical spaces of from two to five inches in length between the leaves or scars, which will minimize chances of injuring the bark during the slipping process.

CONSERVATION OF WHISTLE-MAKING TREES

Willows appear to be generally abundant throughout most of the United States, but if everyone cut willows carelessly they would soon be gone. Probably the best way to maintain an abundance of willows on public and/or private property is to take the upper branches or the crowns of the willow shoots and stick their butt ends down into the moist soil as far as you can so they will take root and live to produce more willow whistles in a few years. Camp directors who do not have an abundant supply of willows should secure rooted shoots of willow (possibly from the state department of conservation) and plant them in appropriate places along the shores of their lakes and streams, so they can have a good supply of these excellent whistle-making trees.

Although any species of willow will make whistles, it is suggested that basket or purple willow (*Salix purpurea*) be planted, since annual shoots or branches of this tree can be used for making fishing creels and many other types of baskets as well as for whistles.

Plant several different patches of willows at some distance from each other so that different areas can be used each year. This way, you can prevent one place from taking all the punishment of collection at one time.

In hiking through hardwood forests one frequently finds a very dense grove of tightly clustered sugar maple saplings one inch to two inches in diameter, often as close together as six to ten saplings to a square yard. This would be an excellent place to cut a branch or two for making whistles, a walking stick or two, a Boy Scout stave, or some green sticks for outdoor fireplace fixtures, as the thinning out will assist the growth of the remaining saplings.

When looking for striped maple from which to make whistles, take one only from a place where three or more plants are growing. One or two good branches an inch or more in diameter will make eight to fifteen whistles. Do not cut striped maple for any purpose when it borders on either side of a woodland trail or road. This makes an ugly scar. Use trees ten yards or more from the trail. Places cut generally resprout and make more browse available for deer.

In regard to basswood or linden, do as the Indians did; use only the "sucker shoots" that sprout out from the base of the trunk. Some of the best inner bark of basswood can be secured from a circular stand of sucker shoots surrounding a dead basswood stump. There might be as many as six to eight of these shoots, each one three to six inches in diameter. In this case select one or two shoots each year, and leave one or two standing to grow into the fine varied-use timber that basswood is.

HOW TO MAKE A SLIP-BARK WHISTLE

The selection of the proper shoots, branches, or sections of shoots of a particular species of tree is just as important as the choice of species itself. For example, in selecting striped maple, look for a tree or clump of shoots growing in a particularly damp area, which has pure white stripes in brilliant contrast to the green bark, rather than dull gray or yellowish white stripes. Furthermore, select for the whistle a long section of smooth bark and straight wood below one set of opposite branches and the adjacent section of opposite branches below this for the handle (see Fig. 1-3). The mouth section of the whistle should always be made at the upper end (end that was closer to the sky) of the chosen section. This end will always be the smaller in diameter, so that the loosened bark can slip off it without splitting.

The ease with which the whistle can be made is in direct proportion to the shortness of time needed to get the bark to slip. The following procedure is both the first step in making a whistle, and a test to show whether or not the bark will slip easily.

With your jackknife, the essential tool for making whistles, choose a spot on the straight section which is to be the base or lower end of the bark to be slipped, and make a transverse cut which completely circles the section cleanly through the bark. Make a similar cut one-eighth of an inch below the first cut, being sure in both cases that the knife cuts cleanly through the inner as well as outer bark. Next insert the point of the knife-blade into the one-eighth-inch collar of bark and pry outward and off. If the collar or ribbon of bark comes off the wood immediately and cleanly in one piece, you can be sure that the section of bark from which the whistle is to be made will slip, when properly tapped, and a whistle can be made. If, however, the test collar of bark is dry and sticks to the wood, you will not be successful in making the whistle. So to save time and frustration, throw this section away and find a moister one in which the test collar of bark comes off freely (see Fig. 1-2).

At the other end (upper or mouth end) approximately three or four inches from the test collar, shape the embryo whistle to fit the mouth so that the upper lip can rest lightly on the bark of the top side of the mouth end, and the lower lip is against an upward slanting cut of the wood on the bottom side of the mouth end.

Remember that the length of the whistle, or more properly, the length of the column of air that will be found in the hollow bark of the completed whistle will determine the tone or pitch of the instrument. The shorter the whistle (and the column of air), the higher will be the pitch; conversely, the longer the column of air in the whistle the deeper or lower will be the pitch. Although it is fun to experiment with long whistles of the lower

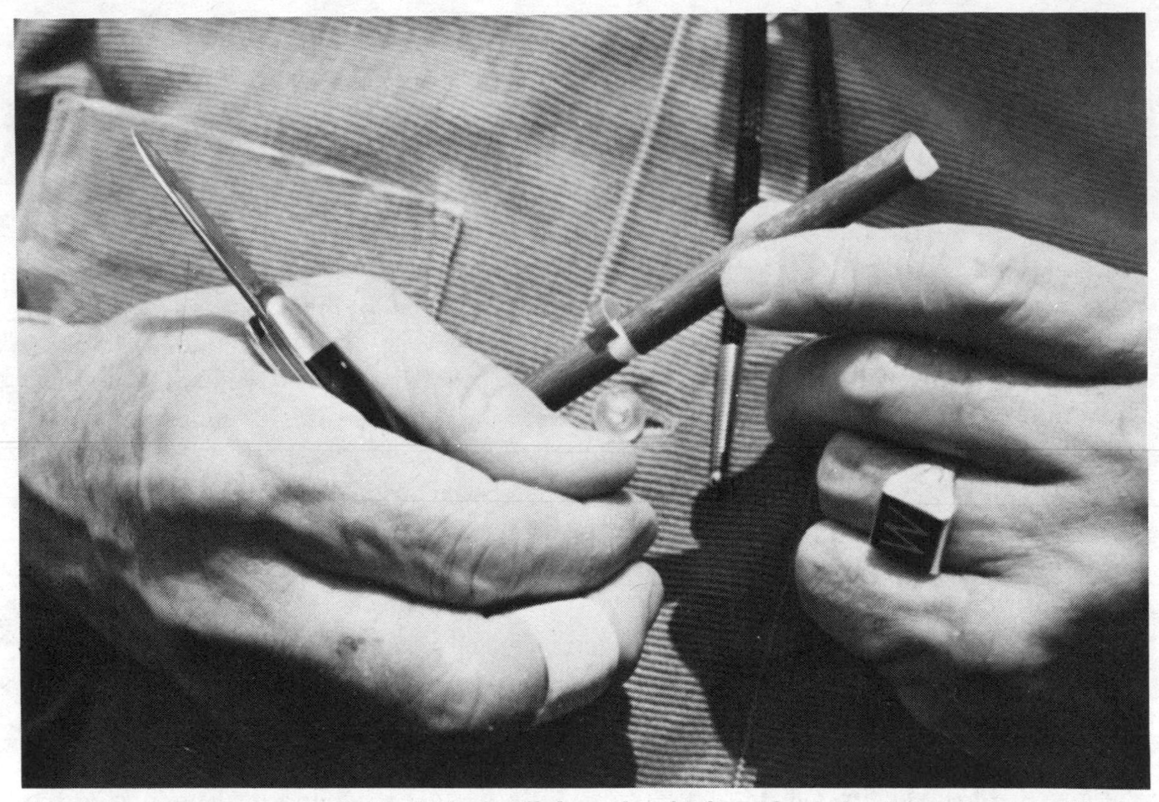

Fig. 1-2. Successful test as to whether the bark will slip and a whistle can be made. The 1/8-inch ring of bark is coming off clean in one piece. The slanting cut at the upper end of the branch section will be the underside of the mouth end of the whistle.—*Photograph by A. O. Haugen.*

pitch, they take more energy to blow and produce a disappointingly weak noise. In general the shorter, higher-pitched whistles are more satisfactory. To start with, the author recommends an air column within the whistle not more than 1-1/2 to 2-1/2 inches long. The diameter of the shoot to be used for making the first whistle should be not less than three-eighths of an inch, or more than seven-eighths of an inch. If the diameter of the wood is less than three-eighths of an inch, when one tries to make the bark slip after tapping, there is danger of twisting the wood fibers instead of loosening the bark.

The next procedures in making the whistle in their proper sequence are: tapping the bark, slipping the bark, adjusting the bark, cutting the window, removing the bark, cutting away wood to make the air column, and replacing the bark. A comment or two on each of these steps is in order.

Place the part of the shoot to be made into a whistle on a smooth hard surface (flat-topped tree stump, fallen tree minus its bark, workbench, or piece of hardwood board across your lap); at the same time hold the handle end of the whistle with the fingers of your left hand (lefthanded readers should reverse "left" and "right" in these directions) so you can twirl it around, rotating every spot on the surface of the outer bark to the top where it can be tapped. Place the closed jackknife in the right hand with the flat back of the knife handle down. Then tap the bark surface solidly and continuously with the knife handle, taking care not to cut into the bark surface by letting an angular corner or edge of the back of the knife handle hit the bark. Give additional, light taps on the bark at the mouth end and lower end. When every part of the bark has been thoroughly and carefully tapped from end to end once or twice, it should slip.

To slip the bark hold the stick vertically with the embryo whistle uppermost in the left hand and the handle of the whistle in the right hand. Now grip the stick tightly with wrists flexed; then with strong extension of the wrists twist the handle in a clockwise direction and the bark in the left hand in a counterclockwise direction. You will feel the bark slip suddenly, generally making a light noise at the same time. Next slide the bark back into the exact position it was in before it was slipped. This is easily done by watching the mouth end of the whistle, where a slanting cut was made for the lower lip.

The next step described is a small one not generally done or known. Slide the bark straight down about one-sixteenth of an inch so that it covers a part of and makes narrower by one-sixteenth of an inch the white girdled area where the test collar of bark was removed (see Fig. 1-3, Step B).

Carefully holding bark and wood together in this position with the left hand, place the whistle, top side up, on the table or bench and proceed to cut out the window by making two cuts (see Fig. 1-3, Step C). Make the first cut three-fourths of an inch to one inch from the mouth end perpendicular to the long axis of the whistle and on the top, going straight down through the bark and a little bit of the wood. Start the second cut directly below the first cut at a distance approximately the same or slightly less than the diameter of the stick used. This cut should angle down to meet the bottom end of the first cut. The second cut of the knife cleanly removes a small shield-shaped piece of bark and the smaller similarly shaped section of wood beneath it. It is important that this small section of wood be cleanly removed, for if allowed to remain it will tend to slip up and split the bark from the window down when the bark is removed.

Next, slip the hollow cylinder of bark in which the window has been cut completely over the mouth end, and place it in a safe place where it will not be crushed or blown away by the wind (see Fig. 1-3, Step D).

Resting the stick on solid wood support, and holding the knife edge perpendicular to the long axis of the whistle exactly on top of the first straight down cut for the window, press down so that this cut is deepened by approximately one-sixteenth of an inch. Then placing the knife edge down lower on the top surface of the naked wood and about one-half inch above the place where the collar of bark was removed for test purposes, make a cut slanting the edge of the knifeblade downward and forward. Using the left thumb on the back of the blade, push it upwards or forward until it meets the deepened first cut made and thereby removes a thin slice of wood an inch and one-half to two inches long. Further deepen the first cut and take out another long sliver of wood. Continue these two cuts, alternately deepening and scooping out the long slivers of wood until you have gone below the pith and as much as three-fourths or even four-fifths of the wood in the center of the whistle has been cleanly cut out (see Fig. 1-3, Step E). Next, carefully cut a shallow

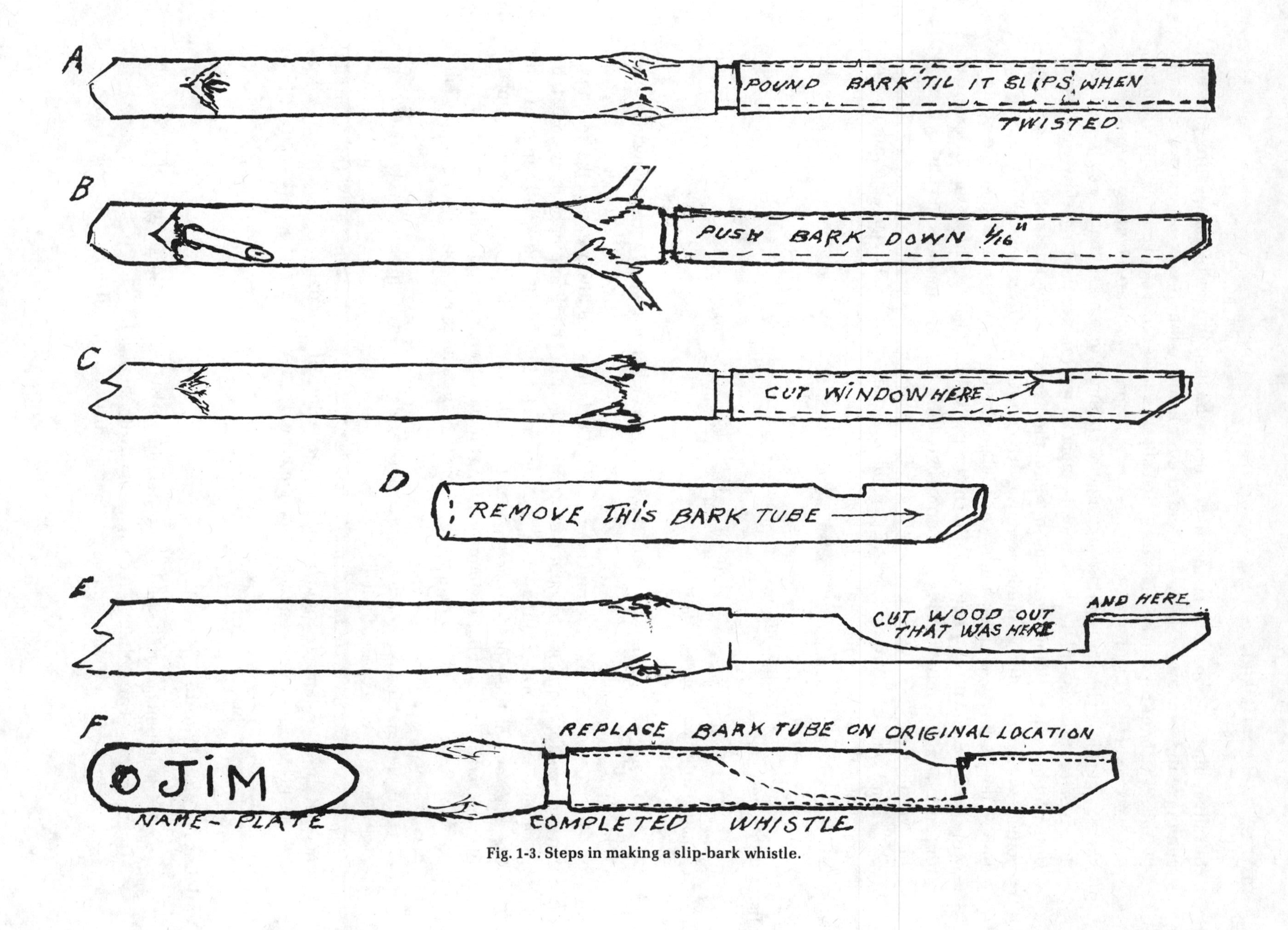

Fig. 1-3. Steps in making a slip-bark whistle.

flat sliver of wood about one-sixteenth of an inch thick off the top of the area from the beginning of the window to the mouth end of the whistle so that it makes a narrow channel through which the air can be blown when the bark is replaced (see Fig. 1-3, Steps E and F).

Before replacing the bark on the remodeled inner wood area of the whistle, dip the wooden part in water, or put it in your mouth, turning it around so that the saliva will act as a lubricant for easing the bark back in place. Then replace the bark slowly and carefully into its exact original position, so that at the mouth end the edges of bark and wood coincide at every point. If the bark is properly adjusted in its original position as it was before the bark was slipped, a thin white ledge or corner about one-sixteenth of an inch wide just underneath and below the open window will be visible. This is the lower end of the air channel, where the blown air drops over the ledge into the enlarged hollow area of the whistle.

The whistle is now complete. Try it out. Experiment with different amounts of force in blowing air to see which yields the best tone.

Mistakes to Avoid

The following are a few mistakes frequently made during the process of constructing a slip-bark whistle:

1) Trying to tap and slip the bark without first making the test of removing the collar of bark.

2) Trying to make the mouth end of the whistle at the lower end of the section of bark to be slipped. This procedure always fails because the diameter of the wood at the lower end will be greater than that at the upper end. Although the bark will slip sideways, the large end of the wooden section near the collar cannot be slipped out of the small-diametered cylinder of bark without splitting the bark from one end to the other.

3) Not cutting out enough wood slivers to make a large enough air space in the middle of the whistle.

4) Not making clean cuts, but fuzzy irregular ones which prevent clarity of tone. Use a sharp knife and small blade.

5) Making the handle too small, leaving no handle when trying to twist the bark to make it slip. The handle should be as long as the width of your palm.

6) Not tapping long enough to completely cover every spot on the bark to be slipped.

Variations of Basic Whistle

Having successfully made your first slip-bark whistle, make several others with different lengths of air columns and experiment with their pitch.

Tie together two or three of these whistles with different pitch and blow simultaneously for a multitone horn effect. The whistles should be lashed or tied parallel at the handles with (1) strips of bark peeled from spring-green hemlock shoots or branches, one inch in diameter or less, (2) bark of leatherwood, (3) inner bark of basswood or elm, or (4) Indian cordage made from these or other cordage materials. Of course, one could use ordinary string or cord from the store, but this is not nearly as interesting or as much fun as using Indian cordage (see Chapter 2 for instructions on making cordage).

Two-Tone Whistle

A two-tone whistle can be made easily by boring a smooth round hole about three-thirty-seconds of an inch in diameter through the top surface of the bark at a point about three-sixteenths of an inch from the start of the long slanting cut illustrated in Step E of Figure 1-3. If a small straight wire were pushed through the hole, it would touch the slanting cut about three-sixteenths of an inch down towards the mouth end from the start of the cut. Placing an index or other finger over the hole and lifting it off periodically while blowing a long steady blast of air into the whistle results in a whistle of two different alternating tones. The higher tone is produced when the finger is lifted from the hole.

The handles of single whistles can, of course, be flattened on one or two sides with a knife and names written thereon. Holes can also be drilled in handles so that cordage or other whistle cord materials can be inserted, looped, and carried around the neck (see Fig. 1-3, Step F).

Slide-Trombone Whistle

Having successfully made a basic slip-bark whistle, the construction of the slide-trombone type is easy. Principles relative to the selection of wood are the same. It is well, however, to use a somewhat longer section of very straight wood.

Follow the instructions for making the basic slip-bark whistle until you slip the hollow bark cylinder off the stick. Then place the smooth white naked mouth end of wood plus one or two inches of adjacent wood on the edge of a flat cutting board or bench, top side up (as indicated by the place where the small shield of wood under the bark window was removed).

Place the knifeblade exactly in the first cut used to make the window, bear down hard, and roll the stick around, at the same time cutting entirely through the wood. The little plug which has been cut off is liable to fly off suddenly at the moment it is severed. Anticipate this by placing an inch or so of the open end of a paper bag just under the part you are cutting to catch this little wooden plug for the mouth end of the whistle as it flys up and off to the right.

Carefully noting the top and bottom of this small wooden plug (by means of the slanting cut of the mouth end on the underside), cut off from the whole length of the topside a sliver of wood approximately one-sixteenth of an inch thick. This will provide a blow-way or air channel to the window. Then carefully replace the plug in the mouth or upper end of the cylinder of bark just exactly as it was before it was slipped.

Lubricate the white, smooth, wood area of the lower part of the whistle thoroughly with saliva. Carefully insert the lubricated area, top side up, about one-half its length into the lower half of the bark cylinder. The trombone whistle is now complete.

Try blowing the whistle. It should make a clear whistle of a certain pitch. Slide the lower plug or plunger end higher into the bark cylinder, thus shortening the air space, and the pitch of the whistle becomes higher. Pull it down farther away from the window, lengthening the air column, and the pitch becomes lower (see Fig. 1-4).

While whistling, keep one hand down on the handle of the whistle and the other hand always on the lower part of the bark cylinder that encircles the sliding piece of wood. This prevents damage to the bark. If both hands (holding the different parts of whistle) can be in steady contact with each other while the trombone whistle is being operated, the results will be better. Try out simple tunes. If your ear is good you will be surprised how soon you can guess how far to slide the stick up or down to produce the desired pitch. Sliding the stick up and down while continuously blowing will produce a siren effect.

MORE PERMANENT WHISTLES

Any tubular piece of material—be it glass, piping, bamboo, or bottle with a closed bottom and an open top not to exceed half an inch in inside diameter, and not deeper than a Coca Cola bottle—will make an excellent whistle if one presses it close to the lower lip and blows forcefully across the top of the opening and slightly downward as well. Try this with a short piece (two to six inches) of copper or glass tubing by placing a thumb over the bottom to prevent air from escaping.

An excellent whistle of this type is a section of bamboo cut so a natural joint blocks the bottom, the upper part being open. The distance from the bottom or closed joint to the top should be about three inches.

A more permanent whistle can be made by using a section of bamboo as above but imitating the structure of the slip-bark whistle at the upper or mouth end. Cut out the window with a coping saw and then, with a sharp knife and sandpaper, carve a cork plug, which will leave an adequate blow-way or channel, to fit snugly in the mouth end. The cork's upper surface (bottom of blow-way) should be flat and pushed into the mouth end of the whistle from 1/16 to 1/8 inch beyond the beginning of the window (whichever distance yields the loudest and clearest tone) in order to provide the shelf over which the air is blown down into the large cylindrical chamber of the whistle. The cork can be glued in the right place or forced in so tightly it stays. Do not have it too tight as in forcing the cork into position you may split the sides of the bamboo.

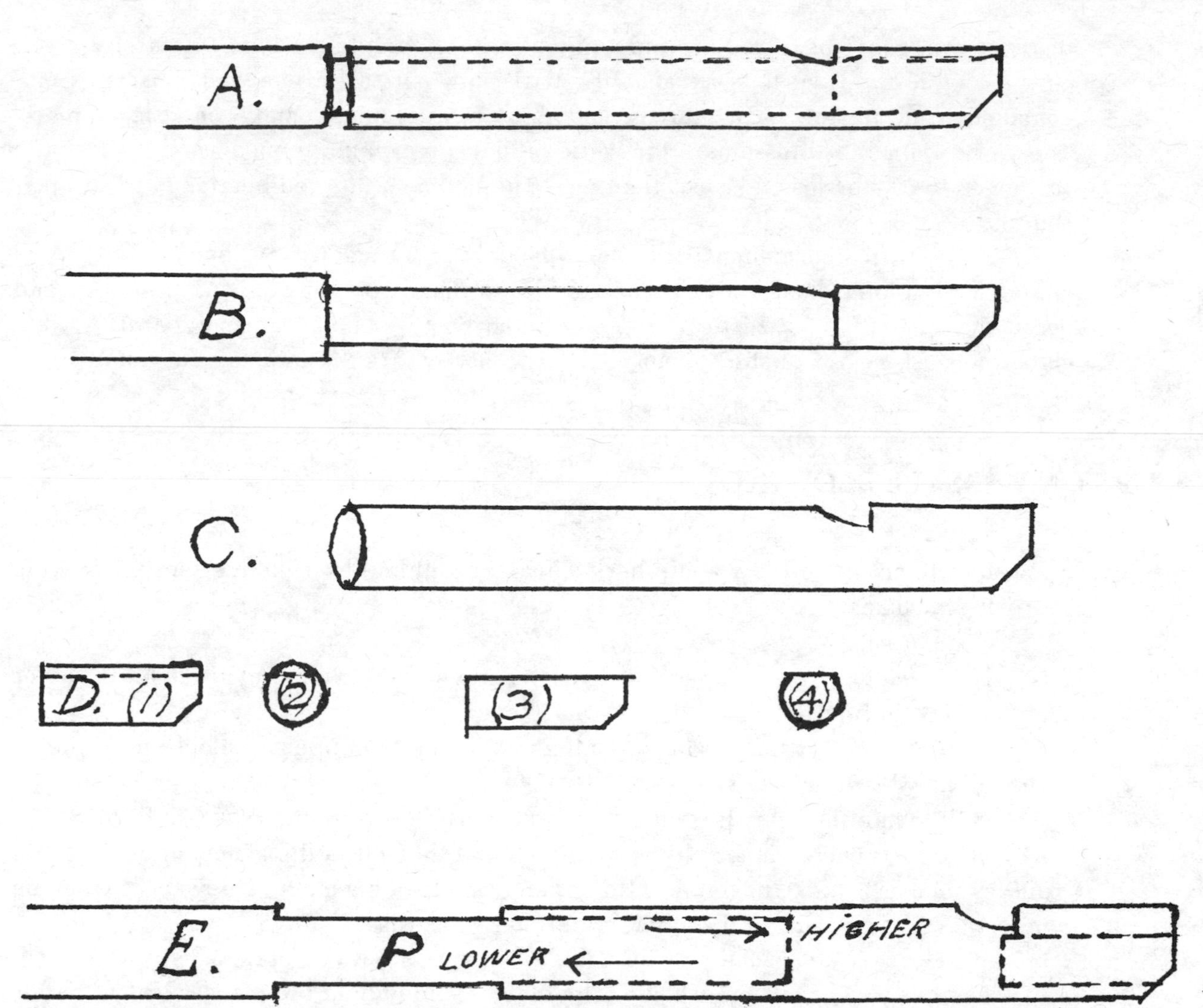

Fig. 1-4. Stages in making a slide-trombone whistle. ***A.*** **Collar of bark removed for slip test. Cut for window completed. Dotted horizontal lines show where slip takes place between bark and wood. Vertical dotted line indicates where plug is to be cut off after stick has been pounded and bark cylinder removed.** ***B.*** **Smooth white wooden plunger after bark cylinder is removed.** ***C.*** **Bark cylinder removed.** ***D.*** **(1) Side view of embryo mouth plug. Dotted horizontal line shows where sliver of wood will be removed to make blow-way. (2) Cross-section of (1). (3) Side view of completed plug. (4) Cross-section of (3).** ***E.*** **Completed whistle. The plunger** ***(P)***, **when moved, changes pitch.**

Similar type permanent whistles can be made from sections of the common elder or sumac (staghorn, or smooth sumac) with its pith punched or drilled out. Close the lower end tightly with a wooden plug or cork and glue it. The upper or mouth end must have the window and be fitted with properly shaped cork as described above in the directions for making a permanent bamboo whistle.

If you use elder (either *Sambucus canadensis*—black-berried and white-pithed—

or *Sambucus racemosa*—red-berried and tan-pithed), whittle the bark off carefully and cover it with adhesive tape because the bark and roots are somewhat poisonous and constantly putting the bark into the mouth to whistle might make one sick. This is noteworthy since the blossoms of the white-pithed common elder make good waffles and its purple-black berries make excellent pies. The berries of the red-berried elder are poisonous.

A relatively permanent multitone whistle can be made from bamboo, elder, or sumac, with a long, close-fitting plunger or dowel that can be pushed and pulled up and down the tube of the whistle to vary its pitch or tone. Lubricants of paraffin wax, glycerine, cork grease, or slide oil may help. The last two are available at music stores.

TIPS ON WHISTLE BLOWING

In attempting to blow a slip-bark whistle, small children inadvertently make the following mistakes:

1) Placing the tip of the tongue over the air channel when they try to blow, rather than blowing through the channel.

2) Putting the whistle so far into the mouth that the upper lip blocks the window on top of the whistle.

3) Placing the whistle in the mouth properly but pressing down so hard on the bark above the air channel with the upper lip that they close the air channel. To avoid troubles such as 2 and 3, have the child put the whistle in his mouth sideways, so that the window faces to one side or the other, rather than upwards.

4) Holding the whistle at the middle over the hollowed bark. This practice will soon damage or wear out the whistle. The blower should hold the whistle by its handle, which is the lower end, below the test collar, where wood and bark are still intact.

CARE AND REPAIR OF WHISTLES

Youngsters are frequently disappointed that their whistles, especially the slip-bark type, are not longer-lasting. If a slip-bark whistle fails to work after a few minutes, the reason is generally that its owner has been too rough with the whistle and damaged the hollow bark cylinder, or the bark has slipped from the original whistling position. In the latter case it can be immediately repaired by carefully sliding the bark back to the position it was in when you first gave it to the child to whistle.

If, however, the whistle fails to whistle freely after two days, it is generally because in that time the bark has dried out and contracted enough to close the opening of the air channel. To prevent this closing of the blow-way, wedge a small piece of toothpick in the channel from the mouth end; this frequently allows enough air to blow around the toothpick to fix the whistle.

If the bark is too dry and too contracted to respond to the toothpick treatment, surgery is necessary. Use the smallest, sharpest blade of your pocketknife and, starting at the mouth end of the whistle and inserting the small blade under the bark in the blow-way, cut very thin slices from the top of the wood in such a way as to enlarge the air channel from the mouth end to the window of the whistle. Carefully blow these pieces of wood out or pick out with tweezers. Once this is done and the air channel is sufficiently enlarged, the whistle is fixed and will last a long time if well treated.

Generally a slip-bark whistle made of a basswood sucker shoot, once properly made and with a large blow-way, lasts indefinitely because the inner and outer bark together are so thick that in drying they do not contract enough to completely close the air channel. However, with basswood, choose a shoot at least seven-eighths to one inch in diameter, or in twisting to remove bark the wood will twist and break.

SQUASH LEAF HORNS

Queer, raucous, and outlandish noises are fun to make at appropriate times and places; although, because "a little goes a long way," it should not be overdone.

Some fascinating noises can be made from horns or squawkers fashioned from stalks of the mature leaves of any species of squash or pumpkin (see the illustration of two species in Fig. 1-5). Squash and pumpkin leaves can easily be obtained from nearby farmers, but it is more fun to plant your own squash or pumpkins in your back yard or camp garden each year. Readers living in the South, especially Florida, can make better and more durable horns from the leaves of mature papaya plants.

In selecting the leaves, cut those with the longest stalks, since they will make the lowest or deepest tones; if you want a higher pitch, you can always cut off more of the stalk at the bottom end.

The first step is to cut the broad leafblade off perpendicularly to the stalk, but not so close to the stalk that the cut penetrates any of the hollow part (see Fig. 1-6). If it should do this, one would have simply a hollow tube; whereas what you want is some solid material 1/8 to 3/16 inch wide to block the tube at its upper end.

The second step is to make a vertical closed cut down from the small end or top part of the stalk at its exact middle for a distance of 3/4 to 1 inch, which will divide this part of the stalk into two equal parts. This will generally leave a wedge-shaped opening about 1/16 to 3/32 inch wide at its outer or upper end (see Fig. 1-6). The horn is now ready to use except for scraping a few short bristles off the outside and upper third of the stalk's surface with the back of your knife, if they are felt to be objectionable.

Place the parted or split end of the stalk into the mouth about 1-1/2 inches so that the two split parts are free to vibrate and make music when you blow. The resulting sound can be made to resemble very closely the bawling of a calf or the mooing of a cow. The

Fig. 1-5. Squash leaves for making squawkers and horns.

author has frequently gotten cows to answer the moo of his horn and to approach him from across the barnyard. For best mooing results, stalks should be cut in lengths 16 inches or more. For bawling calves, stems about 10 or 12 inches are best. Tone or pitch is determined mainly by the lengths of the stalks, although increasing and decreasing the pressure of the blowing will change the tone some (the greater the pressure the higher the pitch). To further vary the sound, try cutting a few holes in the side of the stem and fingering them like a shepherd's pipe.

If when you first try to blow one of these horns it does not operate and the two parts close tightly with a noticeable click or snap, the chances are that the parts are a bit too stiff. Move them around a very little or make the dividing cut 1/16 to 1/8 inch deeper and then try again with careful blows. If the adjustments made are proper, you will soon be rewarded by the hoped-for deep, rich, sonorous tone.

When giving a party for people of any age (five to eighty), you can conduct a "barnyard symphony" with fun for all by giving each guest squash leaf horns of varying length.

With a medium-sized leaf stalk of a squash, try making a horn with the following finger holes. Make the first thumbhole on the bottom surface of the horn three inches above the lower end of the stem. Make another thumbhole also on the bottom of the stem

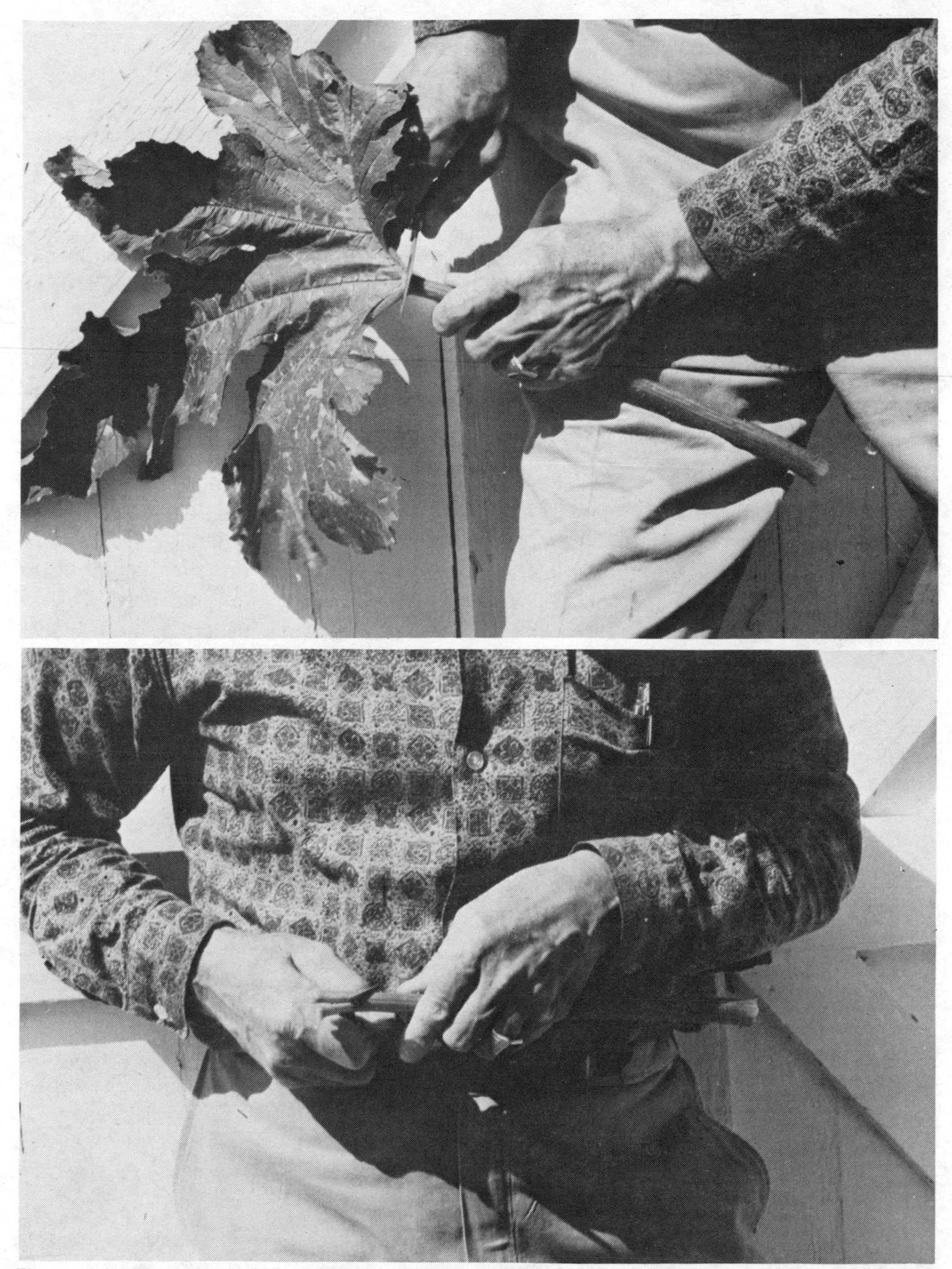

Fig. 1-6. Steps in cutting a squash stalk. *Top:* **Cutting off the leafblade.** *Bottom:* **Cutting stalk straight down the middle for about one inch from the top end.**

but six inches above the lower end. Then on the top surface of the stem make a finger hole halfway between the two holes on the opposite surface. Place the right thumb (lefthanded readers should reverse these instructions) on the upper thumbhole to close it, the ring finger (or little finger if it feels better) of the right hand on the finger hole on the top surface to close it, and the left thumb on the lower thumbhole on the bottom surface to close it. With all three holes closed a blow on the horn should produce a tone of the same pitch it did before the three holes were made. Calling this note *do*, lifting the left thumb from its hole but keeping the upper two holes covered should yield the note *re* when the horn is blown. Raising in addition the finger from the top hole should give the note *me*, and lifting all fingers from their holes ought to produce the note *fa*. At least the above is possible if one has good imagination, and it is a lot of fun to boot. Try it out.

DANDELION STEM HORNS

Select a long dandelion stem, preferably one growing in tall uncut grass. Many such stems are as long as twelve to sixteen inches. Using the top or small upper end, with knife or fingernail cut a slit in the middle a quarter-inch deep. Put this slit end into your mouth and blow. Hopefully, a tone of intriguing timbre will result, quite similar to that of the squash leaf horn but lacking its volume and resonance. The dandelion stem horn, with the little quarter-inch flaps vibrating together, operates on the same principle as the squash leaf horn. Like the latter, it may not blow the first time but need slight adjustment, possibly flattening the two flaps toward each other by pinching them together with the thumb and index finger or perhaps very slightly deepening the cut. To make horns of different pitch, use stems of differing length. To make a multitone horn, cut a few finger holes on the side of the stem. The use of the dandelion stem horn was first introduced to the author by Dr. George Jones, Professor Emeritus of Botany and Ecology at Oberlin College.

GRASS LEAF SQUAWKER

This kind of squawker is familiar to most boys and girls. Where the grass is long and tall, select a long blade of grass from 3/8 to 1/2 inch wide. Hold it vertically between the tightly appressed vertical thumbs of both hands. Now raise it to the mouth and blow hard through the vertical cracks between the thumbs and around the blade of grass. The resulting noise is a variety of squeaky squawks most satisfying to the ears of those first achieving it. Incidentally, it makes a good crow caller.

THE HIDDEN SQUAWKER

This squawker can be made from most any leaf of any tree or shrub approximately 1 inch long and 1/4 to 1/2 inch or more wide. One can also use a freshly plucked elm seed. However, for the best results, use the leaf of a dandelion.

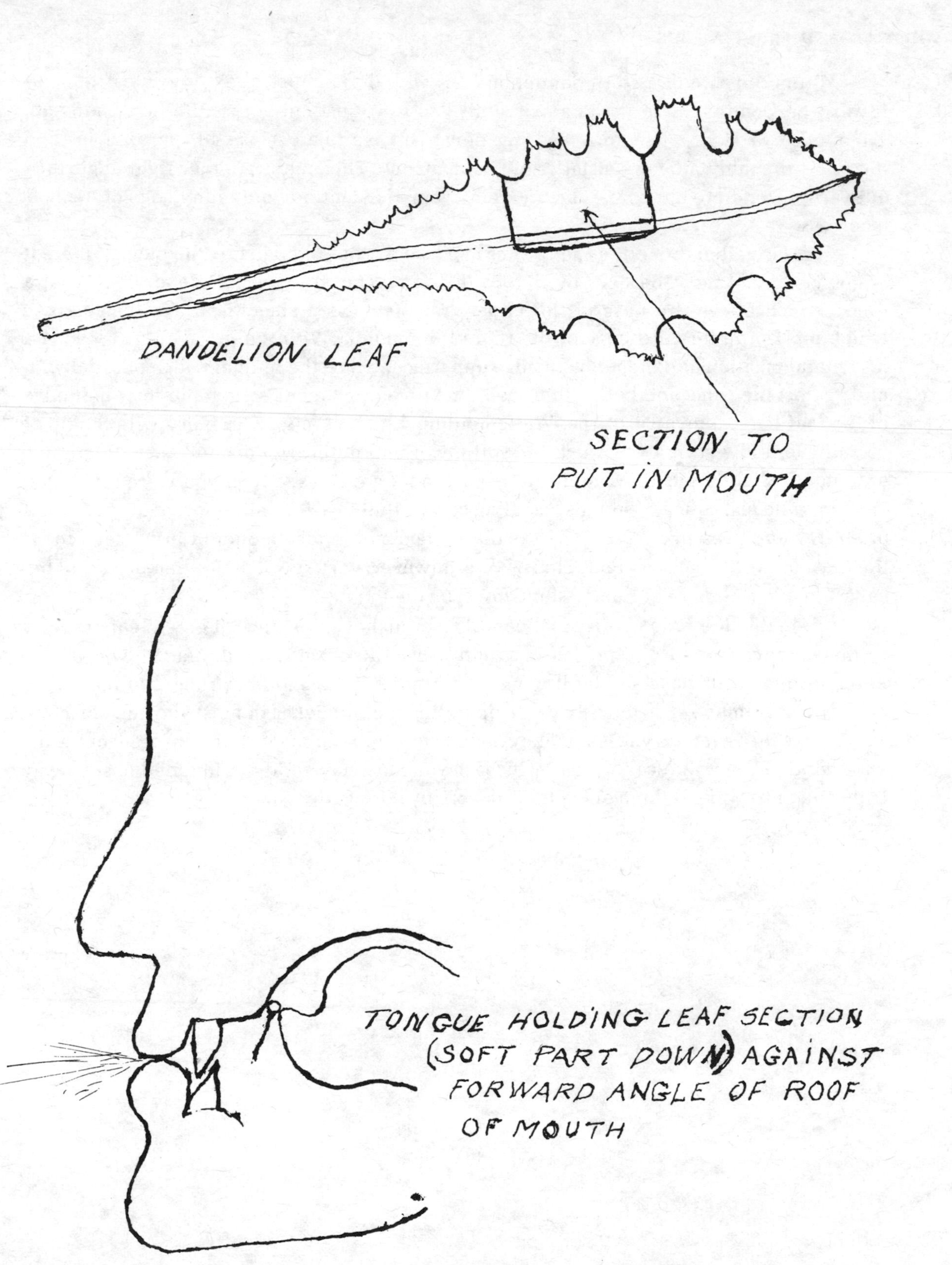

Fig. 1-7. The hidden squawker.

From the side of a fresh dandelion leaf, with thumb and index finger tear the leaf inward perpendicular to its long axis until you have just cut across the large midvein. Then make a right-angle turn, tearing down the leafblade close to, parallel to, and including the midvein, for a distance of about an inch. Then make another right-angle turn outward. From here cut across the midvein again and continue out to the edge of the leaf (see Fig. 1-7).

This is called the hidden squawker because it is operated inside the mouth where it is not visible; it must be held by the tip of the tongue in a special place. Just about a quarter-inch above the base of the upper front teeth is a smooth obtuse-angled ridge which marks the forward edge of the roof of the mouth. With the piece of torn leaf in a horizontal position and the midvein edge uppermost, place the midvein edge parallel with and against the ridge and hold it there with the tip of the tongue so that the soft outer edge of the leaf hangs downward free. While holding the leaf securely in place with the tip of the tongue, blow strongly through the soft lower and outer part of the leaf with the lips and mouth slightly parted. The mouth is positioned much as though you were saying tss, tss. The raucous, squeaky sounds resulting can be quite varied but it does take quite a bit of energy and pressure built up by the diaphragm and a fair amount of practice to focus the blast of air through the leaf. This trick is, however, very rewarding when mastered because people cannot see or understand how you do it.

Probably the prank which is the most fun is to have the piece of green leaf properly in place, move in with the person or group you want to amaze and, placing your handkerchief over your nose so that it dangles in front of your mouth, pretend to blow your nose several times very violently while operating the squawker in most alarming fashion. This keeps the listeners guessing. They may be too polite to say so but they are wondering what kind of a terrible cold or other disease you must have and are inclined to shy away from you until you put them out of their misery by letting them in on the secret.

chapter 2

The Outdoor Cordage Workshop: Cordage From Raw Material to Finished Product

PREDATING THE BOW AND ARROW, THE SPEARTHROWER, THE spear, and the boomerang, in the survival equipment of primitive man, was a substance he could use to tie materials into bundles, to make snares for small game, and to lash poles together for crude temporary shelters. This was the forerunner of cordage. The caveman used various vines and strips of bark first. Later when the sharp edges of broken stones proved their ability to cut animal skin and flesh, strips of skin and sinews were used for lashing and tying.

Later man discovered that plant fibers from palm leaves and the inner bark of certain trees and shrubs, became stronger and more enduring if woven or twisted into a long thread, string, cord, or rope. This was the beginning of cordage.

Thousands of years ago the Egyptians were making cordage from rawhide thongs and such fibrous plants as flax, hemp, and papyrus. They used it to make rigging for sailing vessels, fish nets, bird nets, and bolas. The bola was a cord six feet or more in length which was weighted at each end. It was grasped near the middle of the cord, whirled around the head a few times and thrown toward a game animal. The cord would wrap itself tightly around the legs and trip the animal, stopping it because of the weights. Boys and girls today can have great fun making their own bolas and throwing them at ski poles or other sticks stuck in the ground as targets.

The North American Indians used many different materials for making cordage depending on whatever they could find in their territory that would suit their purpose. The Southwest Indians pounded the leaves of the yucca plant until the fiber was partly broken away from the pulp. Then they would wash and comb it, and repeat the process until the fibers were clean and ready for spinning. Other North American Indians used the inner bark of a shrub called Indian hemp for cordage. It was *Apocynum cannabinum*, a species of dogbane. (*Apocynum androsaemilfolium*, its close cousin, is shown in Fig. 2-3.) Still other plants employed by the Indians to make cordage were leatherwood, red elm, and basswood. Animal materials were also used. The Iroquois made their finest burden straps from braided and woven moose hair, and the Omaha Indians made saddle ropes of buffalo hair.

Youngsters today enjoy making cordage and the many useful and attractive items that can be made from it. Among these items are coasters for cold drinks, hot plate holders, hats, and baskets. Directions for making them will be found later in this chapter.

WHERE TO FIND NATURE'S OWN CORDAGE MATERIAL

Making cordage the way the American Indians did is a fascinating pastime. The first step, of course, is finding nature's own cordage material. The reader should not regard the sources suggested below as all-inclusive. Not all good natural cordage material has been discovered yet and the reader should have the fun of finding new ones, without, of course, endangering scarce species of trees and plants.

Late Spring and Early Summer Sources

Some plant materials for making cordage are best procured in the early summer and others are only available in the fall. The former will be considered first.

Basswood or Linden (Tilea americana)

American Indians favored the inner bark of the basswood tree for making cordage, because it felt so soft to the hands. Basswood specimens are to be found quite generally throughout the eastern and midwestern states as far west as eastern Texas. They are also found north from Georgia as far as Manitoba, Canada.

Basswood is easily recognized by the following characteristics: the leaves are alternate, and, on a mature tree, about five inches long and nearly as broad. On young shoots the leaves may be two or three times as big. They are heart-shaped and have incurved serrate edges. Generally, the parts of the leaf on either side of the central vein are not quite symmetrical, one side being noticeably bigger than the other. The blossoms,

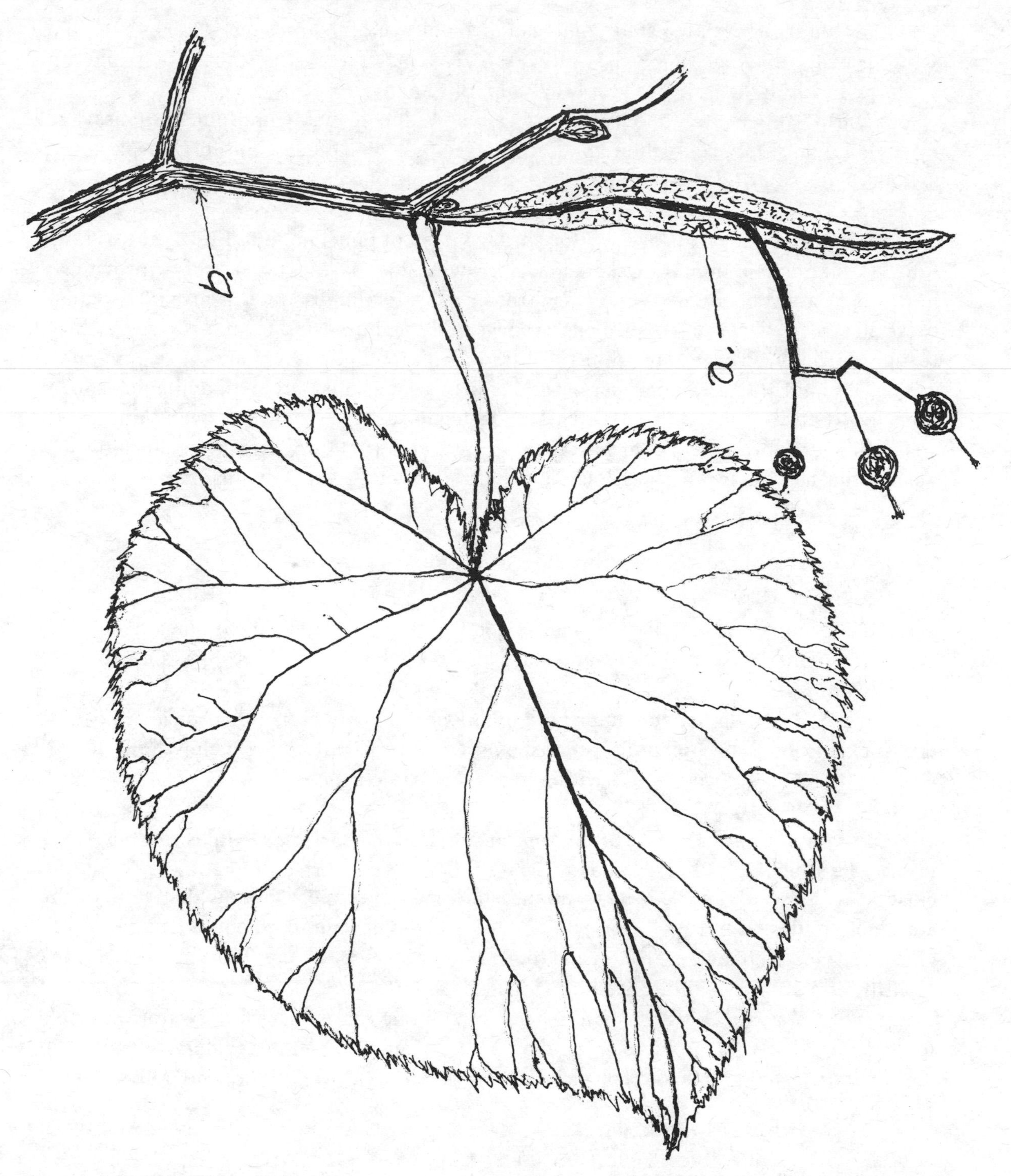

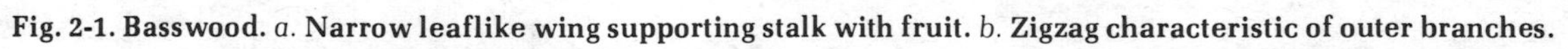
Fig. 2-1. Basswood. *a.* **Narrow leaflike wing supporting stalk with fruit.** *b.* **Zigzag characteristic of outer branches.**

and later the fruit, are on a stalk coming out from the middle of a special narrow leaflike wing growing between the twigs and the leaf stems (see Fig. 2-1). The blossoms are fragrant and with the help of bees yield a superior honey.

During the winter and early spring before the leaves come out, the basswood exhibits large, shiny, reddish brown buds. These buds make excellent food for deer and rabbits. They can find them on the numerous "sucker" shoots sprouting out from the base of the tree.

When seeking out basswood for cordage it is not uncommon to find a ring of large four- to six-inch diameter sucker shoots growing out of the bottom of a previously harvested basswood stump measuring three or more feet in diameter. Naturally, some of these shoots (possibly one or two each year) should be harvested for inner bark cordage, leaving one to three of the straightest shoots to develop into fine lumber.

The light white wood of basswood is fairly strong, close-grained, and much sought after for woodcarving with a pocketknife. The shoots, after the bark has been skinned off, shoud be saved, protected from mildew, seasoned, and used for woodcarving, turning on a wood lathe, and other purposes. Basswood bark strips make excellent lashing.

Elms

The inner bark of all elms makes good Indian cordage. The Indians also made canoes from the bark of red elm, and slabs of this bark were used as sidings for some of their dwellings.

If you desire to use the inner bark of one of the many elms for cordage or lashing, use sucker shoots, or the initial long shoots which are without branches (only leaves which can be easily brushed off with a hand) and can easily be made right up into fresh cordage.

Both the American elm *(Ulmus americana)* and the cork elm *(Ulmus racemosa)* are large trees reaching 100 feet in height. The trunk of the American elm, however, divides close to the ground, giving it its characteristic vaselike shape, whereas the trunk of the cork elm divides higher up. The trunk of the English elm (*Ulmus campestris*) does not divide. It is a large shade tree somewhat like a sugar or a Norway maple, although the trunk is a little straighter and taller. It was introduced from Europe.

In all elms the blossoms appear before the leaves, and the thin, waferlike fruits mature just following the blossoms and about the same time as the developing leaves. All elms have alternate buds and leaves which are generally oval, serrate, and pointed at the tip.

Tulip Tree

The inner bark of the tulip tree (*Liriodendron Tulipifera*), also called tulip poplar, makes cordage which is whiter and silkier than that from basswood but which has less tensile strength. The tulip tree is abundant in the southern states and southern midwestern states, but in the northern states it should not be used for cordage since it is so scarce.

Walnut and Butternut

The black walnut (*Juglans nigra*), and the butternut, or white walnut (*Juglans cinerea*), also yield cordage, but should be used for this purpose only where they are sufficiently abundant. The inner bark of the black walnut makes cordage with a beautiful dark brown color. The author first discovered this one fall on a trip to the Hawk Mountain Sanctuary in Pennsylvania to see the hawk migration. The author's party was camping out and, while exploring near the campsite, he ran across a dead decaying tree about five inches in diameter. The upper crown and most of the limbs had fallen off. The outer bark had fallen away in patches, exposing part of the almost black inner bark, some of which had deteriorated and rotted to the point where it was very easy to pull off and separate ribbonlike strips of beautiful brown inner bark three to four feet long. In about half an hour the author had twisted and hand-laid a brown cord about twelve feet long from which he later made a beautiful and serviceable bow handle for an Osage orange bow he had just completed. By a fortunate coincidence nature had just completed the rotting process for the author in its longtime work of making humus and topsoil.

Red Mulberry

The red mulberry (*Morus rubra*) will yield cordage. It is prevalent in many of the southern states. The Indians made a cloth from its fiber. The author has experimented with quarter-inch to half-inch strips of red mulberry bark in the early summer as a bark sinew for tying and splicing, and found it quite satisfactory.

The leaves of the red mulberry could easily be confused with the leaves of the basswood except for two things: the base of the basswood leaf is cut in more, making it more heart-shaped, whereas careful scrutiny of many of the mulberry leaves will reveal one side of the leaf cut in or indented, making two lobes of the leaf (a large one and a small one), and sometimes two small lobes and one central large one. This variation in leaves is characteristic of the mulberries and also of the sassafras tree (*Sassafras albidum*).

Hemlocks

Bark stripped off young hemlocks one to two inches in diameter can be used to make lashing. Such bark strips from three-eighths inch to one-half inch in width also make good weavers for baskets. However, hemlock bark should be used for these purposes only where hemlocks are very abundant and crowded and need to be thinned out.

Hickories

The inner bark of pignut, bitternut, and other hickories makes good lashing. The bark of most species of young hickories is excellent for making small containers and barkcraft in general.

A special use of young, half-inch diameter shoots and branches of shagbark hickory (*Carya ovata*) is for tying, using the bark and the wood together as a withe. To use such a withe, one takes the shoot in both hands with palms up and bends and twists the shoot in all directions. This should be done at every point on the shoot or branch until it becomes pliable. One can actually tie knots in it. The author was first introduced to the use of the hickory withes in the fall of 1939 while hunting wild boar with bow and arrow in the Cherokee National Forest in Tennessee. The wild boar had been shot, it was a long way back to the car, and no one had cord or rope to tie the legs of the boar to a stout pole so it could be carried more easily. The guide disappeared for a moment and returned with two small green branches of young shagbark hickory which he twisted and turned back and forth to make them pliable. With these the guide tied the boar's feet to the pole securely; and with the boar between us, each of us, with an end of the pole on his shoulder, sloshed down the bed of a creek to a waiting car too many miles away.

Late Summer and Fall Sources

Materials available in late summer and fall are mostly various shrubs and weeds; their inner bark fibers are not sufficiently mature or tough until this season of the year.

Common Milkweed

Inner bark fibers of the common milkweed (*Asclepias syriaca*) make one of the very strongest cords or ropes. The author has made bowstrings of this material and has shot one of these in a thirty-pound bow periodically (not constantly or for a long period of time), and he is sure that in the fall, if survival were at stake, one could make a bow and arrows from native woods with a pocketknife (see Chapter 9 for directions on making a bow) and a bowstring from milkweed fibers (using the perfection loop for upper loop of bowstring as shown in Fig. 9-8) for securing wild game.

Milkweed should be collected only when its seedpods are completely filled out. In collecting milkweed for cordage there is no danger of imperiling the propagation of the plant since one needs such a small amount. If you are collecting milkweed leaves, buds, and pods for food, however, be sure to leave many of the buds and pods in clumps where you can gather harvests in future years.

Swamp Milkweed

Another plant which yields cordage with tensile strength as great as the common milkweed and possibly stronger is swamp milkweed (*Asclepias incarnata*). This can be easily distinguished from the common milkweed not only because it is found only in swamps but because the seedpods stick straight up and are much smaller and narrower than those of the common milkweed, whose pod points slant out and down (see Fig. 2-2). There are many varieties or species of milkweed and the author suspects that most of them will yield good cordage using the same two methods as described for common and swamp milkweed later in this chapter.

The Dogbanes

Two other cordage plants when maturely podded are the two common species of dogbane: (1) Indian hemp (*Apocynum cannabinum*) and (2) spreading dogbane (*Apocynum androsaemilfolium*) (see Fig. 2-3). The first of these will be found in fair

Fig. 2-2. Milkweed. *Left:* **Common milkweed** (*Asclepias syriaca*), **with larger pods.** *Right:* **Swamp milkweed** (*Asclepias incarnata*), **with smaller, narrower, and pointed pods placed closer to the top of the plant.**—*Photo courtesy Spaulding Studio, Cortland, N.Y.*

Fig. 2-3. Spreading dogbane *(Apocynum androsaemilfolium)*. **The inner bark of dogbanes makes cordage exceeded in strength only by that made from swamp milkweed and common milkweed.**

abundance on the gravelly shorelines of many ponds and lakes. In some places the plant is less than a foot to over eight feet high. Those plants with the longest stalks make the best cordage. The spreading dogbane may be found in dry thickets and open woods and sometimes on the plateaus of high hills.

The milkweed and the dogbanes harvested in the fall (when mature with seedpods) can be cured by keeping them dry and free from mildew, and can be made into fine cordage months and even years later by using the pounding method described later in this chapter. In fact, some of the author's best cordage from dogbane was made up from specimens that had been forgotten about and drying in his cellar for fifteen years.

Stinging Nettle

One should use the pounding method as described below under Preparation of Cordage Materials for dried or cured materials from the stinging nettle (*Urtica Dioica*). The stalk and undersurface of the leaves of this plant are covered with bristling, stinging hairs. Leather gloves should be used in procuring and handling it. The Latin name *Urtica* comes from *urere*, to burn. The annoying stinging rash called hives is known medically as "Urticaria," a word which comes from the same root. Historically the fiber from stinging nettle has been used to make not only cordage but also a linen-type cloth.

Leatherwood

The bark of leatherwood (*Dirca palustris*), also called leatherbark, wicopy, and wickup, can be used as an emergency thong material or cordage. It was used in this manner by Indians and pioneers. Leatherbark is a better name for it than leatherwood since it is the bark, not the wood, that has the strength. Because the bark contains certain properties very irritating to the skin of some people, it is advisable to wear gloves and handle it carefully.

Velvetleaf

Another emergency thong material is the bark of velvetleaf or butter print (*Abutilon theophrasti*). The reason for the name butter print is that the top of the dried seedpod was often used by housewives to make an attractive symmetrical print on small pads of butter for service at meals.

Cattails

An emergency fishline or other type cordage can be made up immediately by cutting cattail plants, either the broad leaf or the narrow leaf species (*Typha latifolia* or *Typha angustifolia*), near their base under water, then tearing off narrow thin white vertical strips from the white lower outer edges of the bottom six to twelve inches of the leaves, where they closely enfold the inner leaves.

Spanish Bayonet

Spanish bayonet (*Yucca filamentosa*) or Adam's needle is another plant yielding good cordage. This plant, native from South Carolina to Mississippi and Florida, is successfully planted and grown in most of the United States. Another tropical plant, found in Florida, is sisal (*Agave sisalana*), a species of cactus. Its leaves have much stronger fibers.

Other Sources of Cordage

The pounding method, described later in this chapter, will make cordage from the leaves of many different palm trees when they are dry. The same method will make very fine cordage from the dry sinew of cows, deer, elk, moose, and many other animals. The longer hair from moose, mules, horses, buffalo, and some other animals can be made into cordage as is. Hairs from the tail of a horse were the first leaders used in fly-casting and can still be used in this way.

PREPARATION OF CORDAGE MATERIALS

The directions for following the soak and boil methods which appear below were written with basswood in mind since the inner bark of the basswood tree makes the best Indian-style cordage, but the instructions also apply to the inner bark of the following trees: all elms, tulip tree, black walnut, and butternut. The methods described may vary in slight detail from those used by the Indians but are substantially the same.

The Soak Method

Look for a clump of several basswood trees growing close together so that thinning out some will give the others a better chance to grow into good lumber. Two or three trees or sucker shoots four to six inches in diameter should yield enough fibers and cordage material for most camps to make the cord and baskets campers would like to make the first summer; then the nature-crafts or other counselor can better judge how much basswood fiber will be needed the following summer.

After the shoots are cut down, they should be cut into lengths of at least six feet, for it is desirable to have fibers this long. Next the campers should collect all the branches that have been trimmed off the trees and arrange them in piles with butts in one direction and small branches in the other. Take one of the branches that has a butt end about the diameter of a man's thumb, cut into the bark on opposite sides of the butt, and peel the bark all the way off the branch in two pieces. Using the two bark strips as thongs or lashings, pass one end of one piece of bark around all the butt ends of the branches of one pile

Fig. 2-4. Chippewa Indian kitchen.

and tie a timber hitch (see Fig. 9-8), pulling it tight. A camper can now either drag the bundle of branches behind him or carry it over his shoulder. Other piles of branches should likewise be tied. The six-foot poles should be shouldered by other campers, carried back to camp, and deposited close to the crafts shop or area.

The group of campers should have the experience of stripping bark off the branches that have been brought in and then using the bark thongs right on the spot in lashing sticks together. If planning and time permit, let campers with these bark thongs tied end to end to lengthen as needed, lash the framework of a crude shelter together, and construct a Chippewa kitchen with a flat work-table area by lashing straight 3/8-inch to 1/2-inch diameter sticks parallel and close together (see Figs. 2-4 and 2-5).

Stripping the Bark

The basswood poles or logs should now be laid on the ground and blocked with split chunks of wood or chips to keep them from turning. Starting at the upper end with a large

Fig. 2-5. Table surface of Chippewa kitchen, showing method of lashing parallel sticks together. Lashing materials are hemlock bark in right-front area, fresh basswood bark in front-left section, and basswood bark made into cordage at far side of table surface.

pocketknife or sheath knife, make a straight, continuous cut longitudinally down the whole length of each basswood log, cutting through both outer and inner bark to the sapwood beneath. Make other similar longitudinal cuts approximately one and a half inches apart on all sides of the log, turning it on the ground each time if necessary to be in the best position to make the cut. From one end pull off each long strip of bark. This bark will come off so easily (you may need to loosen it at the end with a knife to get it started) and smoothly it is good fun and every member of the group should be given an opportunity to strip off at least one piece (see Fig. 2-6).

Soaking the Bark

If possible, place the strips in a long frame or box of galvanized chicken wire seven feet long, a foot wide and a foot deep, and with or without a cover. Submerge this container with the bark strips in water, either under a dock or on a side or end of a dock where it will not be disturbed by aquatic activities. Suspend it by rope or wire so that it is completely submerged but sufficiently above the bottom of the lake not to become muddy and discolored following storms. If you cannot secure or construct a long container for holding the bark under water during the soaking process, bundle the strips of bark neatly

Fig. 2-6. Stripping bark from basswood log.

together and suspend them under or beside the dock in the water at the proper distance from the lake or river bottom with cord, rope, or bark sinew.

During the period of soaking, a disintegration or actual rotting of materials lying between each annular growth layer of tough inner bark fiber takes place. If one should raise a bark strip out of the water prematurely and smell it, a disagreeable odor will be noted. However, the lake, pond, or stream in which the bark soaks usually has sufficient circulation of currents so that this smell is at a minimum. Furthermore, four or more weeks of soaking, plus the scraping away of excess materials and a rinse, followed by separating and drying annular growth ribbons, will leave the cordage with a clean fresh smell. The author once tried the soak method with basswood bark in a fifty-gallon drum of water. The resulting stout stench made him regret it. Always use a system of soaking with changing, circulating water.

Preparing the Inner Bark Sinews

After the inner bark sinew has soaked for a period of four weeks, it should be very soft and slippery. Find a smooth flat place on the end of the dock to work. If there is not such a place make one by placing a smooth flat board on the end of the dock. Also have in readiness a six- to eight-inch section of a two-by-two or two-by-four piece of wood. Remove one strip of bark sinew from the container or bundle that has been under water. Note that it has a very smooth surface (where it originally contacted the sapwood of the basswood) and a rough outer bark surface. Place the smooth side down on the board on the end of the dock. With one hand pick up the short stick of wood with four sharp right-angled corners and place it on top of the bark and perpendicular to the long axis at the middle of the strip. Holding this stick down tightly against the bark and the board below, grasp the bark with the other hand just below the short piece of wood, and by pulling the far half of the bark through between the two surfaces of wood, scrape from its top surface all loose outer bark plus a lot of yellowish white, slippery, slimy waste material. Push this waste material forward off the dock into the lake or stream. Next reverse the position of the bark strip so that the cleaned half is now held in the pulling hand and the other top half of the bark is cleaned off. Swish the bark strip once or twice in the lake for a final rinse, and it is now ready to be separated into thin growth rings or ribbons of inner bark.

Separating Growth Rings

Just as every tree has growth rings of wood, it also has annular growth ribbons of inner bark. It is fascinating fun to separate these thin strips of bark; so, when you have a group with you, each person should have an opportunity to separate some of these growth strips. Frequently they will adhere together, but if you hold them tightly between thumb and finger and move your thumb up and your finger down, the bark ribbons will slip and show where they can be separated. As the individual annual growth layers are secured, lay them carefully across the lower branches of nearby trees and shrubs for drying, a process which takes only twenty to thirty minutes sinch they are so thin. When dry, they will be beautiful white silky ribbons. Carefully separate them as to quality, lay them parallel, and loosely tie them in the middle. Roughly three qualities of inner bark ribbons should be distinguished: (1) those with the largest elongated perforations which were originally closest to the outer bark, (2) those that are silkiest and smoothest with practically no visible perforations (closest to the smooth white sapwood of the tree), and (3) the strips with small, short visible perforations which were bark layers between bark ribbons (1) and (2).

The Boil Method

If cordage material is needed within a day's time the boil method is satisfactory, but only a limited amount can be made at one time—namely, the amount that can be prepared in the kettle to be used. Instead of using inner bark strips 1 1/2 inches wide, use strips about 1/2 inch wide or less, and only 8 to 10 of these. To an 8-quart kettle add a quart or more of hardwood ashes (ashes from maple, beech, birch, or oak) that have been kept dry under cover and not vitiated by rain. Then put the bark in and fill the kettle with water. Bring the contents to a boil and turn the heat down so that it just boils without running over. Keep it stewing in this manner four or more hours until the annular growth ribbons of inner bark can be easily separated. The lye in the hardwood ashes cuts or disintegrates the resins and other waste materials between the tough fiber layers, the disposal of which in the soaking method requires so much time.

The major disadvantages of the boiling method are that one can make up so little cordage at a time and that the cordage, instead of being white or light straw-colored, will be a dark brownish gray.

Fresh-Stripped Method

In an emergency when you need cordage in a hurry all of the trees, weeds, and shrubs listed previously under Late Spring and Early Summer Sources and Later Summer and Fall Sources can be utilized. For example, using basswood as representing the first group, one can use the inner bark of very small sucker shoots from 1/2 to 3/4 inch in diameter, the inner bark of smaller branches such as were trimmed off the trees, or some of the large 6-foot-by-1 1/2-inch strips of bark sinew that have not been soaked. In all these cases try to shred or pull apart the inner bark into very small-diametered pieces, getting them as long as possible. Frequently after the removal of a long six-foot piece of bark from a basswood pole or log, a very long slender piece of inner bark sinew adheres to the wood, making it immediately ready to twist and hand-lay into cordage. Probably it is easiest to get this fresh nonsoaked or nonboiled basswood cordage from the small sucker shoots. Cut each shoot off at the bottom. It will have few if any branches. Peel the bark off. Then with thumb and index finger peel the inner bark off the outer bark in the smallest-diametered but longest possible strips.

This fresh-stripped method can be carried out with similar and equal ease with all the elms, the tulip tree, black walnut, butternut and several other trees. While green or fresh, the inner bark of these trees makes good usable cordage for fishing lines, servings, wrappings, and lashings, but when it gets dry it becomes brittle and is more likely to break than is the soaked or boiled inner bark cordage, unless dressed with bowyer's wax or fly-tying wax to keep it pliable.

Additional Procedures Required in Some Plants

The fresh-stripped method when used with mature (podded) common or swamp milkweed and dogbane seems to produce cordage almost equally as strong as that made by the pounding method. This method when applied to the above species, however, involves some additional procedures due to the unique structures of the plants.

First cut some healthy mature stalks of milkweed about four feet tall. Pluck or pull off all the leaves and pods on the stalk. (You can expect to get your hands sticky from the exuding white milky sap, but it washes off easily.) With a knife cut longitudinally through the stalk the entire length of the main part from end to end. Once the cut is started, one is frequently able to split the stalk with his fingers. Split these half-stalks once again so that you now have four or more long pieces of the stalk, each consisting of green bark on the outside and white woody material on the inside. By taking one of these pieces and breaking the woody part by bending it outward (toward the bark) in several places, you can easily separate the entire bark strip (outer and inner surfaces) from the broken pieces of the woody stalk. Next comes the process of separating the outer and inner barks. Actually, what is desired is to secure the pearly white silken fibers imbedded in the inner bark. Hold the milkweed bark strip with outer bark uppermost. Bend the bark at about the middle so that the inner surfaces of the bark come together. With thumb and index finger pinch the bent place tightly, causing the outer bark to break (which it will do if really fresh) at this point. Place the index finger of either hand underneath the inner bark under the break in the outer bark. Place the thumb and index finger of the other hand on a broken edge of either the lefthand or righthand section of the outer bark. Holding the index fingers of both hands tightly together (inner bark between them), carefully pull the outer bark away from the inner bark, which will turn out to be eight to ten parallel white silken fibers. Because the fibers are much stronger than the outer bark, pull the white fibers downward as well as apart. Also, pull out only about an inch of the fibers at a time and then regrasp them up close to where the separation is taking place. The outer bark will break off frequently since it is weakest. After you have removed the outer bark from one-half of the strip, turn the strip end for end and remove the outer bark from the remaining half. One is rarely able to get continuous fibers the entire length of the bark but save all white silk fibers which are six inches or longer. Sometimes the fibers are secured but have a light green substance sticking to them. This can carefully be removed with thumbnail and index fingernail. Time is saved and efficiency increased by first processing and laying to one side the amount of silk fibers estimated as needed for the cord desired. It also helps to make three piles of parallel fibers: short ones (six to eight inches), the longest ones, and the ones in between. They are then ready for the hand-laying and twisting process to be described later in this chapter.

The same fresh stripped procedures just described for securing the fibers of milkweed may also be used in securing inner bark fibers from the two dogbanes (*Apocynum cannabinum* and *Apocynum androsaemilfolium*). In the case of leatherwood (*Dirca palustris*) and velvet leaf or butter print (*Abutilon theophrasti*), it is not necessary to separate the outer and inner bark. Just strip off the bark including the inner bark and use as is.

Incidentally, the fresh-stripped method was used in making a milkweed fiber bowstring which was and is still used in a thirty-pound Osage orange bow. The loop for this bowstring was made by tying a perfection loop knot (see Fig. 9-8) in one end.

These fresh-stripped milkweed fiber cords have a beautiful very light green sheen the first week or two and gradually change to a very attractive white or ivory color.

The Pounding Method

For practically all the cordage materials which are collected in the late summer and fall, and which have been cured or dried sufficiently (two or more months), the pounding system will also work very well.

Use a clean well-seasoned chunk of hardwood (sugar maple or American beech) one and one-half to two feet long and one or more feet in diameter for a pounding block. This chunk should have been sawed squarely with ends perpendicular to the long axis so that it will stand straight when placed on one end. A large wooden mallet, baseball bat, or discarded bowling pin with at least one smooth side completes the equipment needed. However, a smooth-topped iron or steel surface, like the flat top of an iron vise, and a hammer will also work well if care is taken not to injure the fibers by striking the material with an angled edge of the hammer.

The pounding method should be used on most all the cordage materials collected in the late summer and fall which have been cured and dried long enough (about three months or more).

Assuming one has a bundle of well-cured dogbane plants 3 1/2 to 4 feet long ready to pound, trim off all small branches near the top and the slender seedpods (3 to 4 inches long and about 3/16 inch in diameter when closed). Grasp one end of the dogbane stalk with the left hand (lefthanded people should use the right hand), place the stalk across the middle of the pounding block, and start pounding the stalk at the lefthand end close to the left hand. Continue pounding the stalk as you turn or twist the stalk so that all sides of it are hit. Then pull a few inches more of the stalk across the block and pound it as it is twirled and twisted. Continue pulling, twisting, and pounding the stalk until the other end is reached. Then reverse the ends of the stalk and pound the area previously held in the left hand. This procedure has broken most of the woody part of the stalk into small, sharp wooden slivers which are loosely adhering to the silky fibers needed for cordage.

Next put on some good old leather gloves, or very strong tightly woven canvas gloves, and pull the pounded stalk back and forth between the lightly closed gloved hands to clean off all the slivers from the silken fibers. Then lay the cleaned long fibers (possibly 2 1/2 to 3 feet long) together in one loose pile; lay medium-length fibers in a loose parallel pile, and have another pile of short fibers, but none shorter than 7 or 8 inches.

Of course, if one is using fibers from coconut husks, which have very short fibers to begin with, one would be lucky to have any as long as 7 or 8 inches, and fibers as short as 4 inches might have to be used. In working with coconut fibers, combs and brushes will be found useful in cleaning the fibers after sufficient pounding has been done, to loosen up the material. In starting the pounding of coconut fibers, use only small amounts. Tear little bundles 7 to 10 inches long and about 1/2 inch in diameter off from the husks.

The pounding method usually must be used with all palm leaves and the yucca plant. It must also be used on all hard, dry strips of sinew from deer, moose, elk, or cattle. With the above sinews a flat-topped piece of iron or steel and an iron or steel hammer should be used to get the material shredded and into fibers from which cordage can be made.

MAKING AMERINDIAN CORDAGE

After securing and preparing the fibers of a particular tree or plant, the next step is making the cordage. The American Indians preferred the inner bark of basswood for general cordage purposes not only because it was of medium strength and could be used in so many different ways, but because it felt so smooth and comfortable on the bare hands as they worked with it. It is recommended that one start with basswood. The various steps to be taken follow.

Selection of Fibers

Select a few of the longest strips of inner bark fibers. Remember that the greater the number of fibers the greater will be the diameter of the cord or rope. By selecting two annular growth ribbons of fibers 1/8 inch wide one could make up a string or cord that would average about .043 inch in diameter and make a good fish net. By adding a few more strands one could make a top-string or a string to make a sling, and by adding enough additional fibers a rope 1/4 inch or more in diameter. Let us, for example, select enough fibers to make a cord the diameter of which would be appropriate for making a sling of the type David used on Goliath. For this the total width of annular growth ribbons should be one inch. These measurements should be made at approximately the middle of each strip. Each of the ends of a strip should be considerably narrower than the parts of the strip between, so that in replacing or adding new strips the result will be gradual and smooth rather than bulky. If either end of a selected strip is blunt, one can with the thumbs and index fingers of both hands tear off short pieces of bark at the blunt end until it tapers somewhat.

Arranging the Strips of Fibers

Pick up the parallel longish fiber strips so that at neither end do the strips come flush together but rather so that the end of each strip overlaps the end of another strip by one to three inches. Next with thumb and index finger of the left hand (lefthanded readers should reverse "left" and "right" in these directions) grasp the bunch of fiber strips together at a point three inches to one side of the middle so that if the fibers were bent 180 degrees at that point the ends of the two halves would not equally come together but again would overlap and make for future strength and smoothness of the cord.

Starting the Twisting and Hand-Laying Process

Still holding the fibers tightly with the thumb and index finger of the left hand, grasp the bunch of fibers with the right thumb and index finger at a place about one inch to the right of the lefthand fingers, and with the right index finger and thumb twist the fibers in a clockwise direction (the thumb moving upward on top of the fiber and the index finger moving downward underneath the fiber). At the same time twist the thumb and index fingers of the left hand in the opposite direction (the thumb moving downward on top of the fibers and the index finger moving upwards). Then, without lessening the pressure of the twist in either hand, move the two hands closer together. This causes the middle of the twisted fiber (between the two hands) to bend back on itself 180 degrees and form a kink in which the twisted fiber held in the right thumb and index finger lies behind or on the far side underneath the twisted fiber held in the left fingers. Next, without letting fibers untwist, grasp the end of the kink securely with the thumb and index finger of the left hand. One can now observe that there are two strands of fiber strips facing out to the right coming from the kink. The upper strand comes out from the kink just underneath the lower of the two strands. Still holding the kink securely in the thumb and index finger of the left hand, grasp the upper strand with thumb and index finger of the right hand just 1/4 inch or a bit less from the two lefthand fingers and make one tight twist with the two right fingers in a clockwise direction (thumb going upward and the pointer finger going downward with the fiber roll tightly between); then lay this roll of

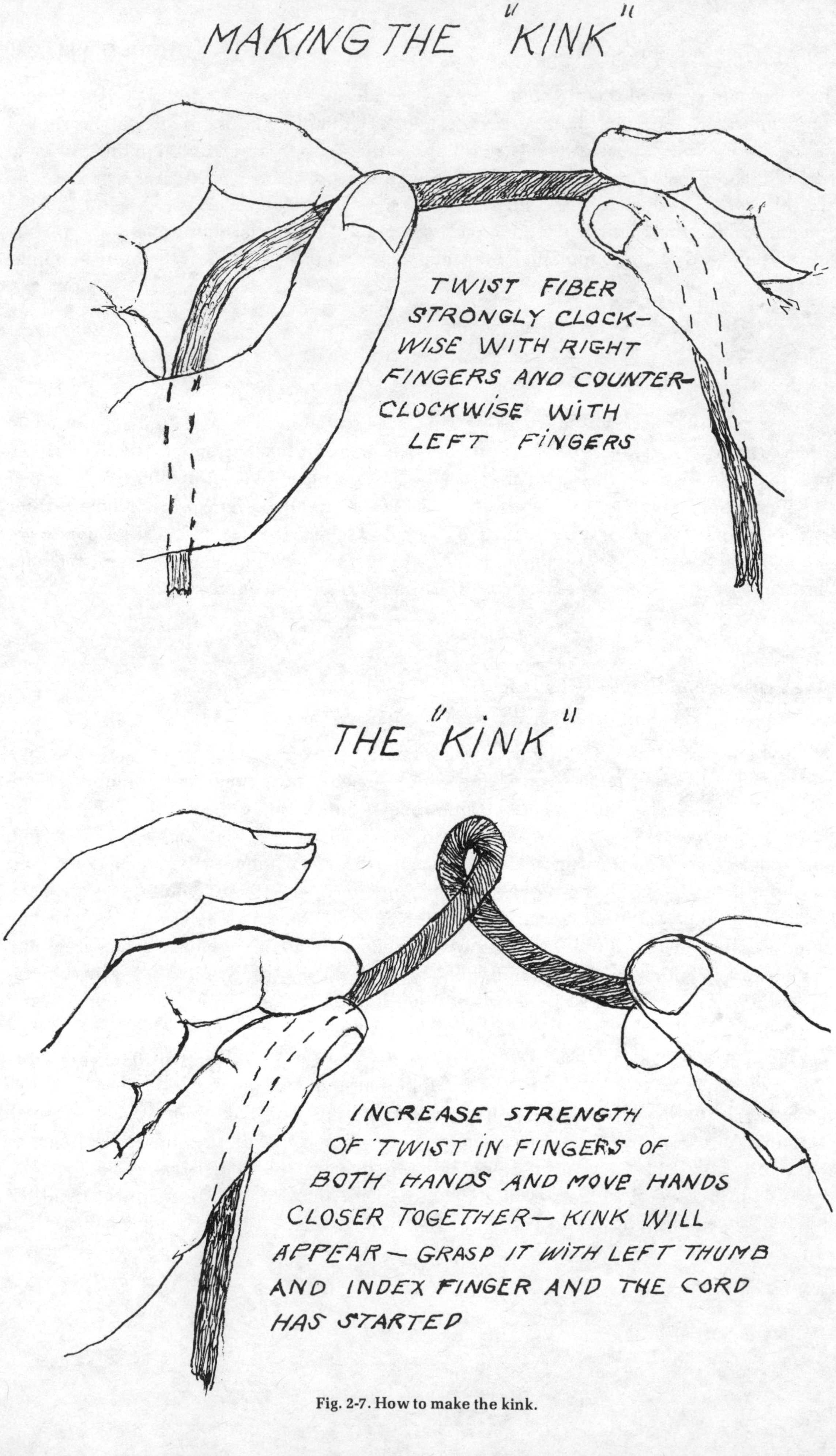

MAKING THE "KINK"

TWIST FIBER STRONGLY CLOCKWISE WITH RIGHT FINGERS AND COUNTER-CLOCKWISE WITH LEFT FINGERS

THE "KINK"

INCREASE STRENGTH OF TWIST IN FINGERS OF BOTH HANDS AND MOVE HANDS CLOSER TOGETHER—KINK WILL APPEAR—GRASP IT WITH LEFT THUMB AND INDEX FINGER AND THE CORD HAS STARTED

Fig. 2-7. How to make the kink.

twisted fiber on top of the lower strand of fibers close up to the kink and slide it snugly under the edge of the left thumb. At the same time this process is made a little easier if the tips of both index fingers are dipped under the other strand to raise it so that it then becomes the upper strand, which again is grasped by the two righthand fingers (1/4 inch or less from where the left thumb and index fingers are now holding the previously twisted roll of fibers) and again given one vigorous twist or tighter roll up and over in a clockwise direction, right thumb moving upward and the index finger moving downward with the roll of fibers between. Again, as before, this tightly twisted roll of fibers is placed down on top of the other roll of fibers and slid snugly underneath the edge of the left thumb and the two index fingers dip down and raise the other strand to be again grasped by the right fingers not more than a quarter of an inch from where the left two fingers hold the developing cord in place. This process continues indefinitely. It is important that when making the twist with the right thumb and index finger, the grasp be made at a distance of 1/8 to 1/4 inch only from the two fingers of the left hand. If this distance is more than 1/4 inch, it will take more than one tight twist, which will take longer, and the cord will not be so even and consistent.

Maintaining a Consistent Diameter

Ordinarily the first eight to ten inches of a newly started piece of cordage will maintain an even and consistent diameter. After this distance, however, the diameter will gradually become smaller since the bark strips in the two strands get narrower as they approach the tapered ends. Furthermore, because of the arrangement of fibers at the start, one of the two strands will always be shorter than the other, and as one progresses one should continually add additional bark fibers to the short strand, thus keeping it thick enough so that when added or twisted in with the other strand it maintains the consistent diameter of the resulting cord. An additional point to watch (as one notices that the short strand is getting smaller in diameter) is that the shortest of the bark strips in the shortest strand is possibly only about two inches long. At this point one should stop the hand-laying and twisting process and search for a new strip among the bunch of long fibers. Holding the short strand securely in the thumb and fingers of the left hand and with the two-inch remnant uppermost, put the left or near end of the replacement strip parallel to and on top of the remnant strip, overlapping it at the place where the width of the base of the remnant strip and the width of the tapered part of the new strip are the same. Holding the new strip down in place with the left index finger, twist the new strip into the upper strand and carry on as before. Whenever you approach within an inch or two of the end of a particular bark strip in a strand, replace the strip with a new one as described above. Wherever this is done the tapered end of the replacing strips will tag out from the main cord one or more inches. After one has made the cord as long as needed for its particular purpose, these tag-ends can be neatly snipped off close to the cord with a sharp knife or scissors.

In addition to watching for the short ends of individual bark strips and replacing them, one must be looking to see whether either of the two strands is noticeably thinner than the other. If so, back up or untwist two or three turns and add to the thinner strand replacements to bring it up to the desired thickness. Throughout the process of hand-laying and twisting cordage, it helps to have the kink end or the complete part running through and underneath the palm of the left hand and slightly gripped by the left little and ring finger so there is definite and consistent tension always from inside the left hand to the point where the upper strand is gripped by the left thumb and index finger. This procedure together with the *one* vigorous twist (made possible by grasping the upper strand each time at a distance of less than 1/4 inch from the grip of the left thumb and index finger) of the two fingers of the right hand will make for neatness and consistency in the resulting cord.

Ending the Cord

You can end the cord when you have the amount and size needed for your purpose in a number of different ways.

If making a simple cord to wrap around a package or bundle, when the cord is sufficiently long, cut the two strands off at the end of the last twist, and tie a simple overhand knot (see Fig. 9-9) which will prevent the cord from unravelling.

If making a top-string, make a small wooden disc about 1 inch in diameter and 1/8 inch thick and put a small hole about 1/8 inch in diameter (or whatever the diameter of the top-string is) in the center of the disc. Run the closed end (kinked end) of the string through the hole in the disc all the way except for the last three to six inches of the open end, where one or two overhand knots should be tied to secure the disc from coming off at that end. One could substitute a good-sized button for the disc, running the cord through one of the two or more holes of the button.

If making a lanyard, or bola tie, you can close the open ends with an end splice. It is possible to make an end splice with a two-strand cord although it is more usual to use the end splice with a three-strand cord or rope. If you prefer the latter, just unravel the two-strand cord for eight to ten inches, arrange the bark strips into three strands of equal diameter (each strand being slightly thinner in diameter than either of the two former strands), and then, using the same process of twisting each strand in a clockwise direction and hand-laying it properly and in the right consecutive order, finish with a three-strand cord which lends itself better to making the end splice.

To make a rope or whip of the "crack the whip" type, select basswood bark ribbons with a larger diameter to start with. Also, since each of the two strands is so much thicker, it is more tiring to give sufficient twist to each strand with thumb and index finger of the right hand; so lay the strand to be twisted each time across your right thigh and rub your whole right hand downwards on them from fingertips to heel of hand one time or as many as are needed. This method was often used by the Indians. For making the whip maintain the original rope diameter for two or three feet and then gradually allow the two strands to diminish in diameter by not adding so many replacement strips, and tapering it down as long, as short, or as narrow as desired. One or two simple overhand knots tied an inch or two from the end completes the whip.

USES OF DEBARKED BASSWOOD POLES

The smooth white debarked poles of basswood sucker shoots should be placed under cover where they can season without mildew, and yet not be too dry. An unheated garage where the air has about the same humidity as the outdoors is often the best place. The basswood poles can easily be sawed into miniature boards for making small boxes, shuttles for making nets, and many other items. Short chunks of the wood can be used for wood carvings of various sizes. Some of the chunks a foot long can be split or sawed into sizes that can be carved into excellent salad spoons and forks. Some of the wood can be used in teaching beginners how to do wood-turning on a lathe. The wood is soft enough so that beginners do not get into trouble with it while using the lathe, and yet it sands down to a beautiful polish. The debarked branches are excellent for smaller whittling projects, and the smaller branches and pieces of outer bark make good kindling for the fireplace.

See Figure 2-8 for an illustration of different pieces of cordage made from several different plants.

THINGS TO MAKE WITH CORDAGE

Finding, gathering, and processing nature's own cordage materials and then making the cordage does take a long time and involves a lot of work, but the many useful and beautiful items which can be made from such cordage make all the effort worthwhile. Take coasters for an example. Figure 2-9 shows an eye-catching coaster, on which to place tumblers of cold drinks, made entirely from the inner bark of basswood. Figure 2-10 shows how to make such a coaster. First make the switch, a bunch of bark ribbons of different widths about three to four feet long. Trim off one end of the switch straight with scissors so all pieces of bark end at the same place (flush). Thread a blunt-pointed tapestry needle with a sewing ribbon of bark about 1/4 inch wide and five to six feet long (see Step A in Fig. 2-10). Lay the last seven or eight inches of the end of the sewing ribbon in parallel with the switch fibers. About 2-1/2 inches from the trimmed end start binding the switch to the end in a neat compact roll 3/16 inch in diameter (see Step B in Fig. 2-10). Come back over the roll two or three wraps, stick the needle through under the third and fourth wraps from the end, and pull the sewing ribbon through in a modified half-hitch. Bend the wrapped part on itself into a small circle. Make two or more wraps over the side of the circle with the sewing ribbon to hold the circle roughly (see Step C in Fig. 2-10). Make four or five new wraps on the switch to the left and attach this to the outside of the small circle

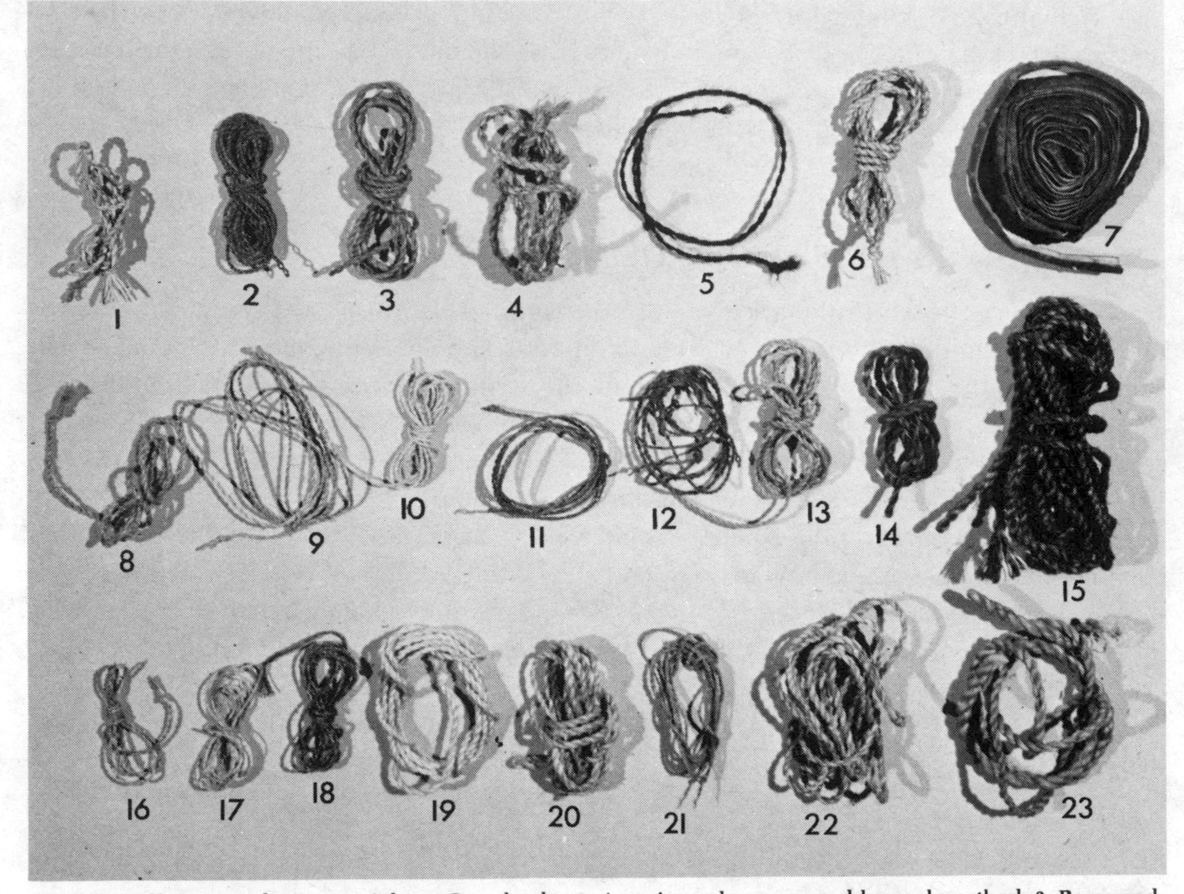

Fig. 2-8. Different cordage materials. 1. Corn husks. 2. American elm, prepared by soak method. 3. Basswood, stripped and made up fresh. 4. Stinging nettle, prepared by partial soak method. 5. Buffalo hair, hand-laid when natural and dry. 6. Fibers from palm leaf. 7. Inner and outer bark of hemlock. Use for lashing after soaking for 3 hours. 8. Stinging nettle, prepared by partial soak method. 9. Spreading dogbane, prepared by pounding method. 10. Swamp milkweed. 11. American elm, prepared by fresh-stripped method. 12. Black walnut, prepared by soak or boil method. 13. American elm, prepared by fresh-stripped method. 14. Inner bark of balsa, prepared by soak method. 15. Black walnut, prepared by soak or boil method. 16. Swamp milkweed. 17. White fiber at base of cat-tail leaves. 18. Basswood, prepared by fresh-stripped method. 19. Common milkweed, prepared by fresh-stripped method. 20. Tulip tree, prepared by soak method. 21. American elm, prepared by fresh-stripped method. 22. Small cord made from basswood. 23. Large and tapering cord for whip, made from basswood.

by sticking the needle up through the center of the circle. Continue this (four wraps around and up through the center) until a new ring has been coiled around the small circle, making a larger one (see Step D in Fig. 2-10). Continue this process until the coaster is complete (3-1/4 inch or more in diameter) but bring the needle up through the nearest spot at the base of the adjacent ring below, not through the center of the small circle. The coaster is finished except for cutting off the switch and adding several wraps to tie it down permanently. In order to make a hot plate holder, simply continue the process used in making the coaster until the mat becomes large enough. If you want to make a hat or a basket, use the same process but make the vertical sides by anchoring the next coil on top of the previous adjacent coil instead of outside it on the side.

When the wrapping and stitching ribbon is used up or so short it cannot be used any more, wrap it once or twice more around the switch and then slide it in with the switch to finish up its days as a part of the switch. Select another good stitching ribbon of bark and thread it. Lay three or four inches of the far end of the wrapping ribbon in with the switch, and with the left thumb and index finger (lefthanded readers should use the right thumb and index finger) hold it tight against the spot of the previous stitch and round off the coil with about four or five wraps and then around the coil underneath and continue as usual. To keep the switch consistent in thickness take one or more strands of bark, square off one end with scissors and lay this end flush against the end of the previous wrap. Then stitch and start wrapping the four or five wraps and stitch and you are in business again. Incidentally, anything that can be made out of or with raffia can be made with the inner bark of basswood, only much better since basswood is so much stronger.

Basswood makes excellent caps. Figure 2-9 shows a cap made entirely of basswood inner bark using the same system described above for making coasters. Note the different stitch used halfway up the vertical sides of the hat. This stitch left openings for better ventilation. Note also that the visor of the cap is darker in shade. This is because the visor was made from basswood bark that had been boiled in water plus hardwood ashes rich in

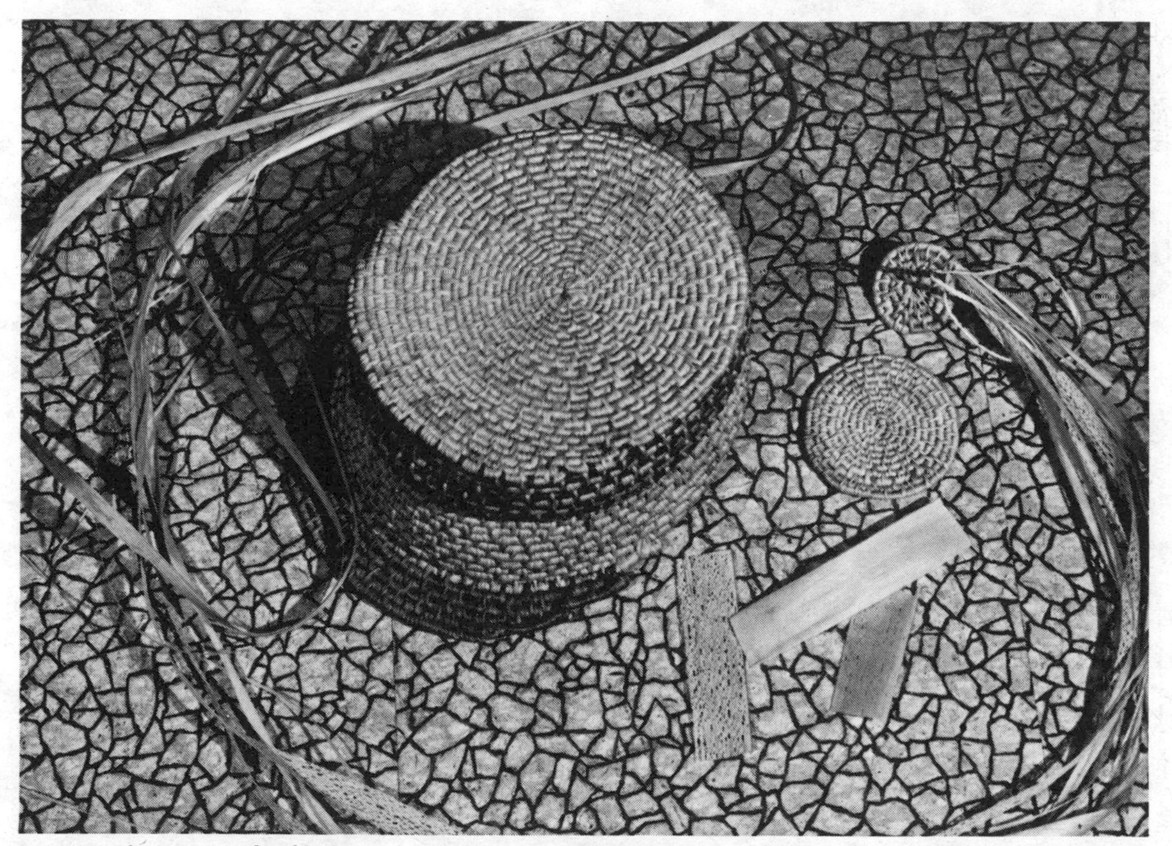

Fig. 2-9. *Left:* **A cap made of basswood inner bark.** *Right:* **A completed coaster 3 inches in diameter and one half-made showing switch.**—*Photo courtesy Spaulding Studio, Cortland, N.Y.*

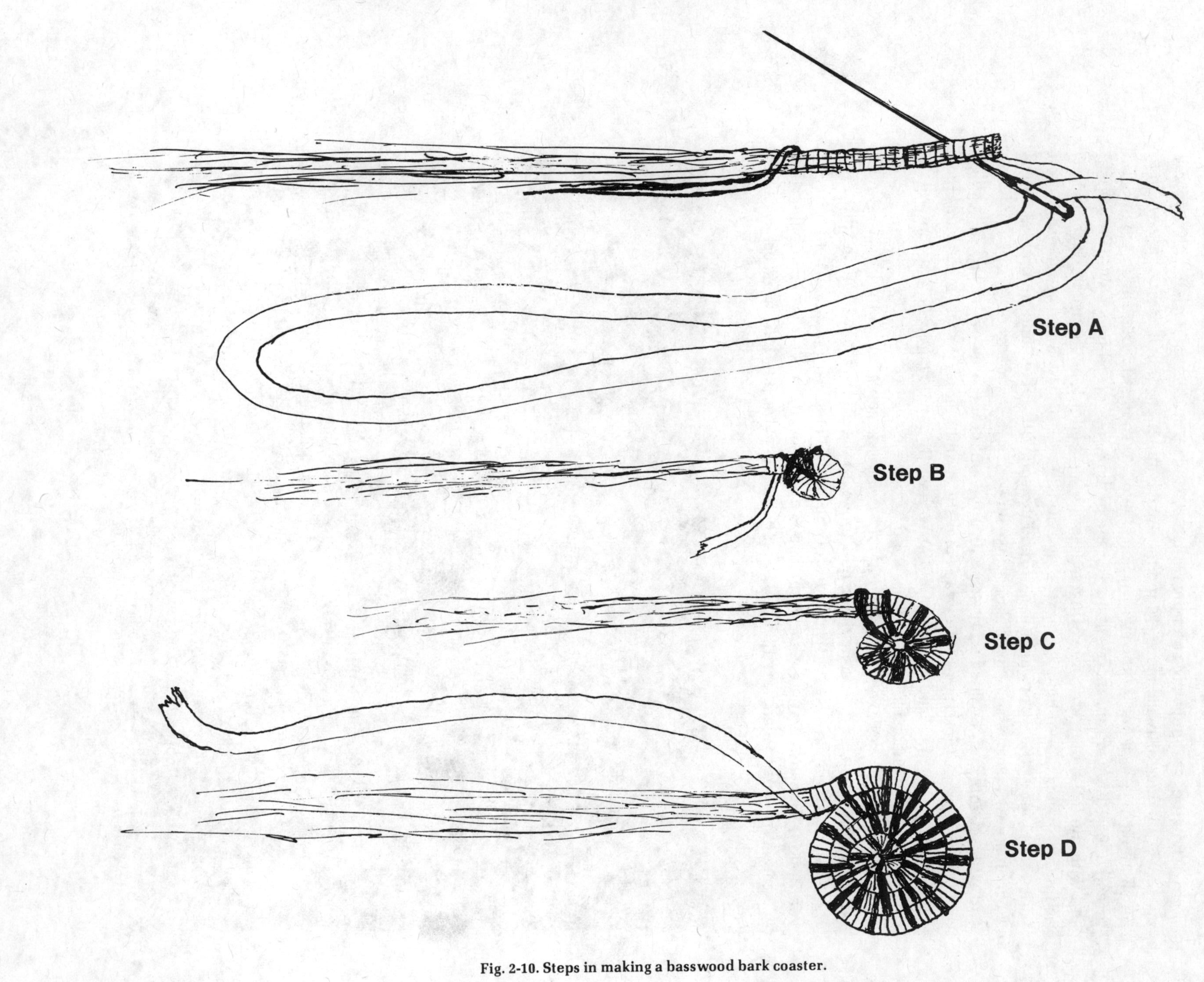

Fig. 2-10. Steps in making a basswood bark coaster.

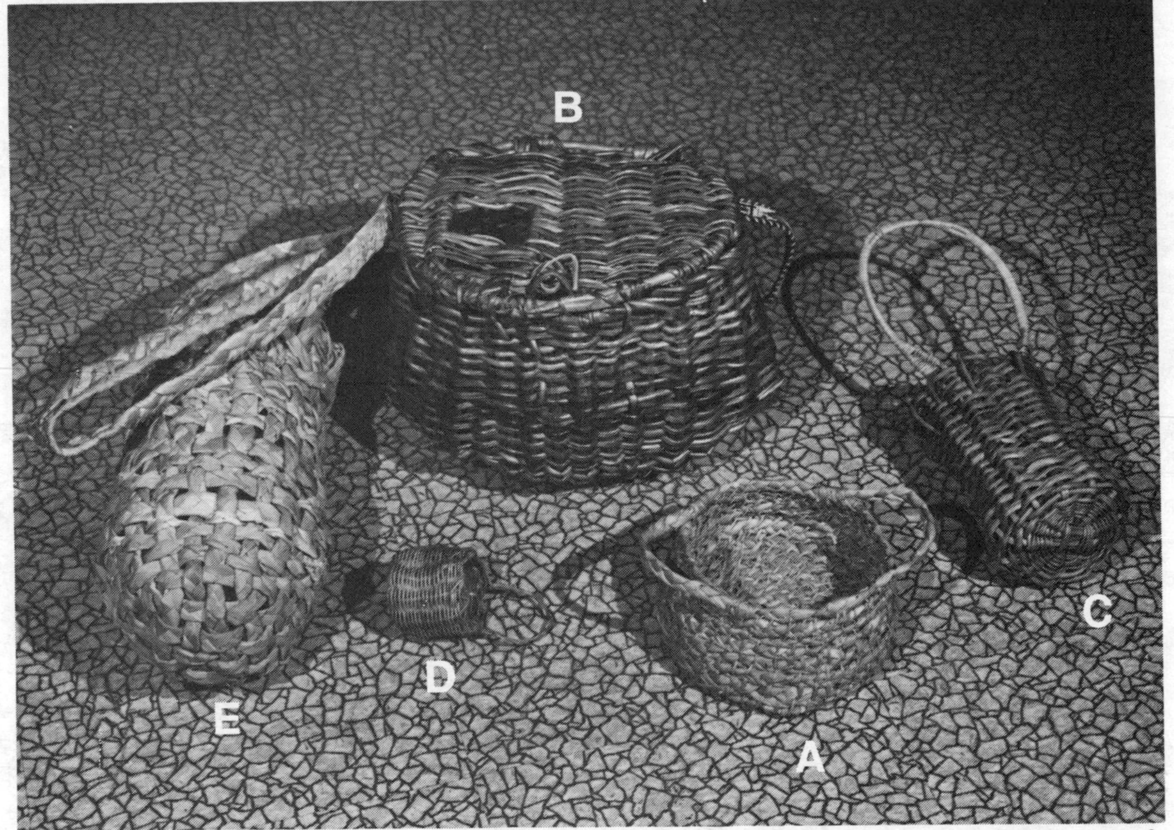

Fig. 2-11. *A.* **Two-handled basket made from leaves of narrow-leaved cattail.** *B.* **Fishing creel made from roots of red spruce.** *C.* **Wall basket for flowers made from red spruce roots.** *D.* **Miniature wall basket with warp from hemlock roots and weavers of honeysuckle vines.** *E.* **Shoulder basket made from broad-leaved cattail leaves.—** *Photo courtesy Spaulding Studio, Cortland, N.Y.*

lye for three or more hours in order to separate the annular ribbons of bark. The dark color was stain from the ashes.

Useful and attractive baskets of all shapes and sizes can be made from the cordage materials already discussed in this chapter as well as from various leaves, roots, and vines. Figure 2-11(*A*) shows a basket made from the leaves of the narrow-leafed cattail (*Typha angustifolia*). To make such a basket, cure the leaves by laying them out on the grass side by side in the sun for a few hours and then turning them over on the other side for a similar period. After curing, braid the leaves into a long coarse ribbon. Then, starting at the beginning end of the ribbon, coil it flat side down and sew the inner edges of the coils together with basswood inner bark fibers. When the mat of coils gets large enough for the bottom of the basket, start the vertical sides by anchoring the next coil on top of the previous adjacent coil and proceed at an angle of ninety degrees. Continue sewing the inner edges of the rush ribbons as before with basswood bark.

In country where spruce, hemlock, and yellow birch are abundant, beautiful baskets can be made from their roots. The principles of careful selection of trees from which to harvest roots and thinning out trees that are too close together to allow any to grow into salable timber should be followed. However, if you are in a camp where wood is selectively cut for fuel, dig the roots from the stump of a relatively fresh-cut tree. The roots should be quite usable if the felling occured not over a year ago. You will have just as much fun and will not injure a growing tree. If you note a farmer cutting a birch, spruce, or hemlock tree you could ask him if he would allow you to dig up some of the roots. Many times farmers follow up the tree felling by pulling out the stump of the tree by the roots. Sometimes a tornado or storm will furnish a good supply of roots by uprooting trees.

Indians in the northwestern United States and Alaska made baskets from the roots of Sitka spruce. The author has experimented with many species of spruce and finds all of their roots suitable for basketry, particularly those of the red and white spruce.

Figure 2-11(*B*) shows a fishing creel made by the author in the Adirondacks following a severe blow-down that uprooted thousands of large mature trees, particularly red spruce. The suitable exposed roots (up to 3/8 inch in diameter) were traced out into the humus and carefully pulled from the soil. The roots were then washed in the lake and the bark rubbed off by friction against other trees, stumps, and edges of boards and rocks. The roots were then kept damp and pliable in shallow water with rocks placed on them to keep them from drifting away. In this creel roots for the warp or base and uprights generally consisted of the larger roots up to 1/4 inch in diameter. The weft or weavers were smooth uniform roots rarely larger than 1/8 inch in diameter. Since these were scarce, roots 3/8 inch to 1/4 inch in diameter were carefully split, first into halves and then into quarters. These quarters made good weavers, although not as smooth and beautiful as the whole roots.

With practice, a root 1/4 inch in diameter can be split evenly from the large end to the other. The trick is to keep the split always through the middle of the root. Start the split at the large end through the middle with a knifeblade. Then grasp the half roots one in each hand with palms up. Keep the thumbs up in the split and the other four fingers of each hand underneath their respective root halves. As long as the root keeps splitting right in the middle, everything is fine, but if one half-root is noted to be getting thicker than the other, the fingers on that side must bend that half of the splitting root downward at a more acute angle than is done on the narrow side. Almost immediately the split evens out.

Incidentally, the roots of most spruce and hemlock trees have cross-sections oval in shape, and a debarked root resembles a double wire without the insulation. The first splitting (into halves) suggests a separation of the two wires.

Note the split root weavers used in the top of the basket; some are half-roots and some are quarter-roots. Notice also that in the back or hinged surface of the top of the creel there are some extremely small roots. These are terminal roots of the yellow birch tree. They are so flexible they can easily be used to wrap very closely and neatly and can also be used as thread for sewing.

Figure 2-11(*C*) is a wall basket with a tumbler inside to hold water for flowers. It can be hung on the wall on a picture hook or small nail. It also was made from red spruce roots following the Adirondack blow-down.

A miniature wall basket for flowers in which the warp structure is made from hemlock roots and the weavers are lengths of honeysuckle vines is shown in Figure 2-11(*D*). The latter are very plentiful in Pennsylvania and states south of it. The bark of honeysuckle is easily removed following a few minutes of soaking in boiling water. Where hemlocks are plentiful, as they are in parts of New York State and Pennsylvania, one often finds clusters of young hemlocks about 1 1/2 inches in diameter growing so close together that they need thinning out. The bark of some of these young trees can be stripped off in the spring, cut or torn into strips 1/4 inch wide, and used as weavers in basketry. The warp material might be spruce or hemlock roots, young branches of yellow birch, or larger shoots of purple willow. These strips of hemlock bark are also excellent material for lashing in making Chippewa Indian kitchens (see Figure 2-4), willow shoot beds, and other useful items. Excess hemlock bark strips should be rolled up into circular compact

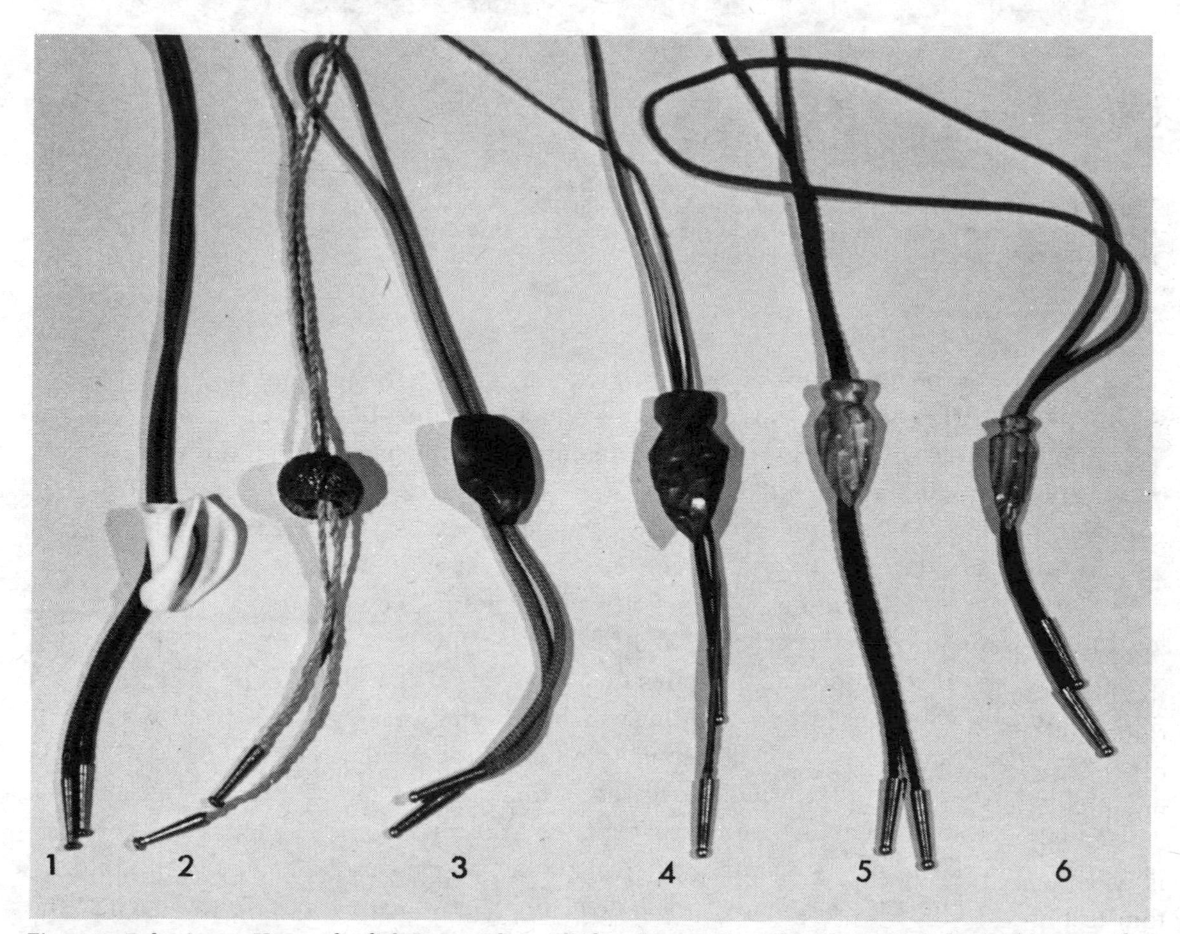

Fig. 2-12. Bola ties. 1. Heart of a fighting conch. 2. Black walnut with cordage from inner bark of basswood. 3. Jewel made from heartwood of Osage orange. 4, 5, and 6. Indian arrowheads carved from sumac.—*Photo courtesy Spaulding Studio, Cortland, N.Y.*

Fig. 2-13. Staghorn sumac *(Rhus typhina)*. **Its wood is one of the most beautiful to carve and polish. The grain stands out in colors of green, yellow, and sometimes orange. It is called staghorn as the velvety fuzz on its branches resembles the velvet on the buck deer's antlers in early fall.**

rolls. These can be stored for many years without losing strength and flexibility, if one first soaks the dried circular rolls of bark in water a few hours before their use.

Figure 2-11(*E*) illustrates an experimental multipurpose shoulder basket made from cured broad-leafed cattail leaves braided into a continuous ribbon and plaited checkerboard style. The shoulder strap was made by sewing together the inside edges of two braided cattail rush ribbons with grade A basswood inner bark.

Making beautiful and unusual bola ties from nature's own cordage and fine woods and shells is not only very satisfying but offers many opportunities for the development of creativity. Figure 2-12 shows six bola ties that were lots of fun to make. Bola tie number 1 was made with what was left of a fighting conch from the west coast of Florida. Most of its outside surface had been eroded by sand, wind, and waves but it was still beautiful. Bola tie number 2 was made from a black walnut which an animal had gnawed into on both sides to get the meat, leaving two symmetrical holes through which a loop of cord of basswood inner bark was easily inserted with just enough pressure to keep it from slipping.

The third bola tie was made from a piece of heartwood of Osage orange carved into a beautiful design by Mr. George Gibbons, Director of Outdoor Education at Florence State Teachers College, Florence, Alabama. Osage orange heartwood turns a deeper, more beautiful brown every year. Its grain is lovely, and when sanded, steel-wooled, and burnished with another piece of Osage it becomes a jewel to cherish.

The last three bola ties were carved into arrowhead shapes by the author from dead and seasoned sumac wood. The color of the wood is a greenish gold and takes a beautiful polish. Frequently the pith of the sumac can be pushed out; the canal thus made is generally just the right size for the cord part of the tie to slip through with the proper tightness. If not, the width of the canal can easily be adjusted. Fish, frogs, turtles, birds, and many other shapes can be carved from this wood, and from seasoned basswood as well. Of course creating bola ties and ladies' pins oneself and giving them away to appreciative friends provides the greatest pleasure and satisfaction.

chapter 3

The Joy of Throwing: Tips on Hurling Stones and Javelins

THROWING IS ONE OF THE BASIC NATURAL ACTIVITIES OF MAN. It followed striking and the use of a club in man's struggle for survival. By throwing projectiles man found he could keep his enemies at bay, drive them away, and possibly destroy them.

Most boys of any age get great enjoyment from throwing stones, sticks, and spears for both distance and accuracy. The trunk of a tree thirty yards away, a floating stick in a pond, or a hornet's nest near the top of a black locust tree make attractive targets.

Many youngsters today develop their throwing ability by participating in sports. However, to compete in pitching with Vida Blue, in passing with Joe Namath or Johnny Unitas, or to participate in the Olympic games requires practice. The essential ability to throw must be developed by throwing things in childhood and youth.

For a righthander to throw a stone or javelin for distance he must have his left side facing the direction of throw with left leg forward, right leg back, and body bent sidewards and backwards away from the direction of throw (lefthanders reverse this position). With the projectile held in the fingers, shoulder and arm extended way back and low on the right side, and weight mostly on the right leg, he is in position to make the throw.

The throw is made by a complex sequence and overlapping use of muscles starting with the larger ones of trunk and legs shifting the weight in the throwing direction, and smoothly adding muscles moving forward: first the right shoulder girdle and then the muscles that bring the upper arm forward. As the upper arm comes forward the elbow begins to flex in order to stretch the elbow extensors prior to their use. As soon as the forearm has passed the shoulder the extensor muscles of the arm contract with increasing strength and speed, and the throw is finished with a final push by the flexor muscles of wrist and fingers.

To get maximum distance, no matter with what speed one starts the throw, he must keep increasing the speed so that by the end of the sequence the acceleration of speed when using the wrist and finger flexors is infinitely greater than at any other time. Immediately following the throw a natural follow-through may occur in which the legs may reverse their position and the right arm and hand will swing forward and downward in the direction of throw. Possibly the hand might touch the ground or come close to it.

SKIPPING STONES

Skipping stones on a pond or lake when the water is calm is a most fascinating sport if you can do it. Here's how!

Select several flat stones preferably about 1-1/2 to 3 inches in diameter and 1/4 to 1/2 inch thick. Hold the stone between the first two fingers and thumb of your throwing hand. With the hand in relaxed position, thumb up and the little finger down, place the lower surface of the stone on top of the curved long finger. Place the thumb on the top side of the stone. These two fingers hold the stone securely and are responsible for keeping it in proper position in a line parallel to the surface of the water. Curve the index finger around the back edge of the stone. This will impart the final power to the throw as well as a clockwise spin to the stone.

If right-handed, stand with your left foot as close to the water's edge as possible and the right foot back (if lefthanded, reverse this position). Also, take a somewhat crouched position to help in keeping the throw close to the water. On the throw the weight shifts from the rear to the forward foot. The object is to present the surface of the stone parallel to the surface of the water, with the forward edge of the stone raised at an angle of about three degrees from the surface of the water, just enough for a very slight planing effect to keep the stone riding on the water. The force behind the stone should be completely forward along the surface of the water, and none of it downward or upward. If downward force is added, the stone after hitting the surface will bounce high off the water, go a considerable distance, and then drop into the water with few or no skips. If upward force is given, the stone will not hit the surface before it sails and curves into positions not parallel to the surface of the water. When it does hit the water, it sinks without any skip.

A perfectly flat skipping stone with rounded edges, properly presented to the water's surface, will skip and slide over the surface with many short skips that are practically uncountable.

After practice in skipping well-formed flat stones, you will find you can make any stone skip which is not too big or heavy and that has one flat side with no concavities.

If you have a relatively flat stone with one side slightly convex and the other side somewhat concave, present the convex surface to the water to make it skip. Having the concave side hit the water will reduce or eliminate the skips, as the stone is likely to plane down into the water rather than on top of it. Skipping stones is challenging and satisfying and will keep one happily busy alone or competing with others. Try it. You'll like it.

THROWING HOMEMADE SPEARS OR JAVELINS

Many boys love to throw spears for distance and accuracy. In the South the projectiles used may be tall straight reeds, the stalk of a cattail, or a bamboo or cane shoot. In the North a straight young shoot of sugar maple from a clump that needs thinning will make a good spear. Put a point on the heavy end and throw with that end forward. For accuracy, grasp the spear at the balance point with the spear resting on the palm, held up, and thumb and index finger grasping the projectile to give it forward impetus. However, if distance rather than accuracy is desired, try placing the index finger of the throwing hand over the back end of the spear. In most cases it is probably best to use the grip first described. This is the grip used by college athletes throwing the javelin for distance.

If a boy or girl hopes to participate in the javelin throwing event later on in college, amateur athletic competition, or the Olympics, there are certain basic points of form which should be mastered in practice with homemade spears or javelins. First of all, the throw must be a straight overhead one with no side motion in which the rear end of the spear swings off to the right or left. Imagine that you have a six-inch diameter wire ring suspended in front of you about four or five yards away at a height of 6 feet in the direction of your throw, and another ring suspended at the same height seven or eight feet beyond the first ring and in the same direction with both rings parallel to each other but perpendicular to your line of throw. Now see if you can throw the spear so straight that it passes cleanly through both rings without any part of the spear touching the inside edge of either ring. To do this one's throw must really be a straight, true overhead one.

Practice short hard throws for accuracy with small targets (such as a leaf, acorn, or small stick) on the ground at distances of about five to ten yards away. After each throw, note carefully what the rear end of the spear does after the point has hit the ground or target. Does it swing to left or right? If so, it was not thrown straight, but was given a curve. Did it swing back upward? Then it was not thrown quite straight but was given too much downward motion. Did the rear end remain in the line of sight between the eye of the thrower and the point of the spear, with possibly only a slight quiver? Then the spear was thrown correctly—straight—and that is the way you must practice it. A fun way of practicing with two or three people is to play what the author calls "roving spear." Take turns choosing and throwing at different objects at different distances as you rove through a meadow, open woods, or pasture. If two play, the person coming closer to the target scores one point; if the target is hit, the thrower gets three points. With three playing the one hitting closest scores two points, the next closest one point, and again anyone hitting the target scores three points. In general the muscular action involved in throwing the spear or javelin is similar to that described in throwing a stone for distance.

Although the above points of form for throwing the spear or javelin are fairly standard, the form of the final heave at takeoff and reverse (or windup in baseball language) is subject to individual differences of javelin throwers. Some carry the javelin in front of and above the shoulder with arm flexed during the running approach to the takeoff board and when within about ten or fifteen feet from it give a forward inward hop on the rear foot while bending the body back and extending the arm back to stretch all the throwing muscles before the final heave. Others in making the running approach carry the javelin with the arm extended backward and the shoulder and arm rotated inward directly over the javelin. At the time of the hop they rotate the shoulder and arm outward, bringing the javelin on top of the shoulder, arm, and palm of the hand with all throwing muscles on a stretch before the final heave. Both of these methods of takeoff can and should be practiced by the young thrower to see which style he likes best and finds to be most effective. He can, of course, also experiment with other methods of approach. Since throwing a spear with a spearthrower has much in common with throwing the javelin, the spearthrower will be discussed in the next chapter.

chapter **4**

All About Spearthrowers: Primitive Prototypes and Modern Versions

THE SPEARTHROWER IS A VERY ANCIENT DEVICE FOR THROWING a spear which adds greatly to the speed and distance of the projectile's flight and its penetration. It lengthens the arm of the person throwing a spear by the length of the spearthrower. Very likely, it was invented by a small man with short arms who needed more arm-length to compete in spear throwing with larger men.

The average length of a spearthrower is about two feet. On one end is the handle; on the other end is a short spur which fits into a shallow socket or concavity on the rear end of the spear to be thrown.

Spearthrower handles are of several types: those with a single hole for the index finger, those with two holes for the long finger as well as the index finger, and other types without finger holes.

Spearthrowers date back to prehistoric times and have been used in many parts of the world. In America they were known to Eskimos in Alaska. They were also used by pre-cliff dwellers, or Basket Makers, in the Southwest, inhabitants of the Florida keys, people of the Peruvian coast, the Aztec, Toltec, and Tarascan Indians in Mexico, and the Kuikuru Indians of central Brazil.

The Aztecs called the spearthrower the atlatl, and probably this term is more widely known in America than any other. The author feels the term should be preserved

Fig. 4-1. *Top:* **An aborigine from the Warburton Ranges of West Australia demonstrating use of the spearthrower. Note his starting position.** *Bottom:* **Spear is about to leave spearthrower. Note severe strain in rear of spear. Wood chosen for spears must have this flexibility.**—*Photos courtesy American Museum of Natural History.*

and used by Americans. It will therefore be used in the text occasionally in place of spearthrower.

Today, the Nunivak Eskimos of western Alaska use the spearthrower for hunting birds and small seal, the Tarascan Indians on the shores of Lake Pátzcuaro in Mexico use it for hunting ducks, coots and large birds, while the Kuikuru Indians and some other tribes in central Brazil use it as one of the main events for their intertribal tournaments. In Australia, although most of the aborigines now use rifles for hunting, a significant number of the nomadic aborigine tribes of the western desert area still use spearthrowers for hunting kangaroos and other game and sometimes even for settling personal disputes.

One advantage of the spearthrower over the bow and arrow is that only one arm is used. This leaves the other arm available to hold a shield for protection in combat, or to raise a very long spear to its proper height and to keep one's balance in a small boat when hunting birds.

The *mira nakata,* one name used by two or more tribes of aboriginal Australians for atlatl, is perhaps better suited for its purpose than any other known spearthrower. Its back is convex, and its upper side is deeply concave (see Fig. 4-2). This concavity allows the spear to lie perfectly free between the hook and the hand. It is about two feet two inches long, three and a half inches wide at its broadest part, and narrowly tapering towards the handle. At the handle end a piece of flint that serves as a chisel is attached with a lump of spinifex cement, which also prevents the hand from slipping when the spear is thrown. The hook at the other end, which contacts the concave rear end of the spear, consists of a short, pointed kangaroo's claw, wild dog's tooth, or spine of hardwood firmly affixed with sinew and homemade cement from spinifex shrubs.

Throughout the spearthrowing world the method of grasping the handle along with the spear in the same hand is universal. However, as in intercollegiate and Olympic javelin throwing, there are certain individual differences in stance and windup during the throw. Some individuals like to use the free hand or wrist to steady the spear during the throw, while others use only the one hand holding the spear. Some use a fully upright stance during the throw, even rising on tiptoe. Some of those using the upright stance shift their weight back on the rear foot and raise the front foot off the ground, rocking back to gain forward momentum for the throw. Others prefer a slight crouch to initiate their throw. Still others like to take a few short running steps before throwing.

For making a spearthrower simply for the fun of hurling spears for distance and competition in accuracy, the author recommends the type used by the Kuikuru Indians as a model, since it is much simpler and easier to make than those used by the aborigines of Australia.

KUIKURU INDIAN SPEARTHROWERS

Through the kindness of Dr. Robert L. Carneiro, head of the Department of Anthropology at the American Museum of Natural History in New York City, the author was able

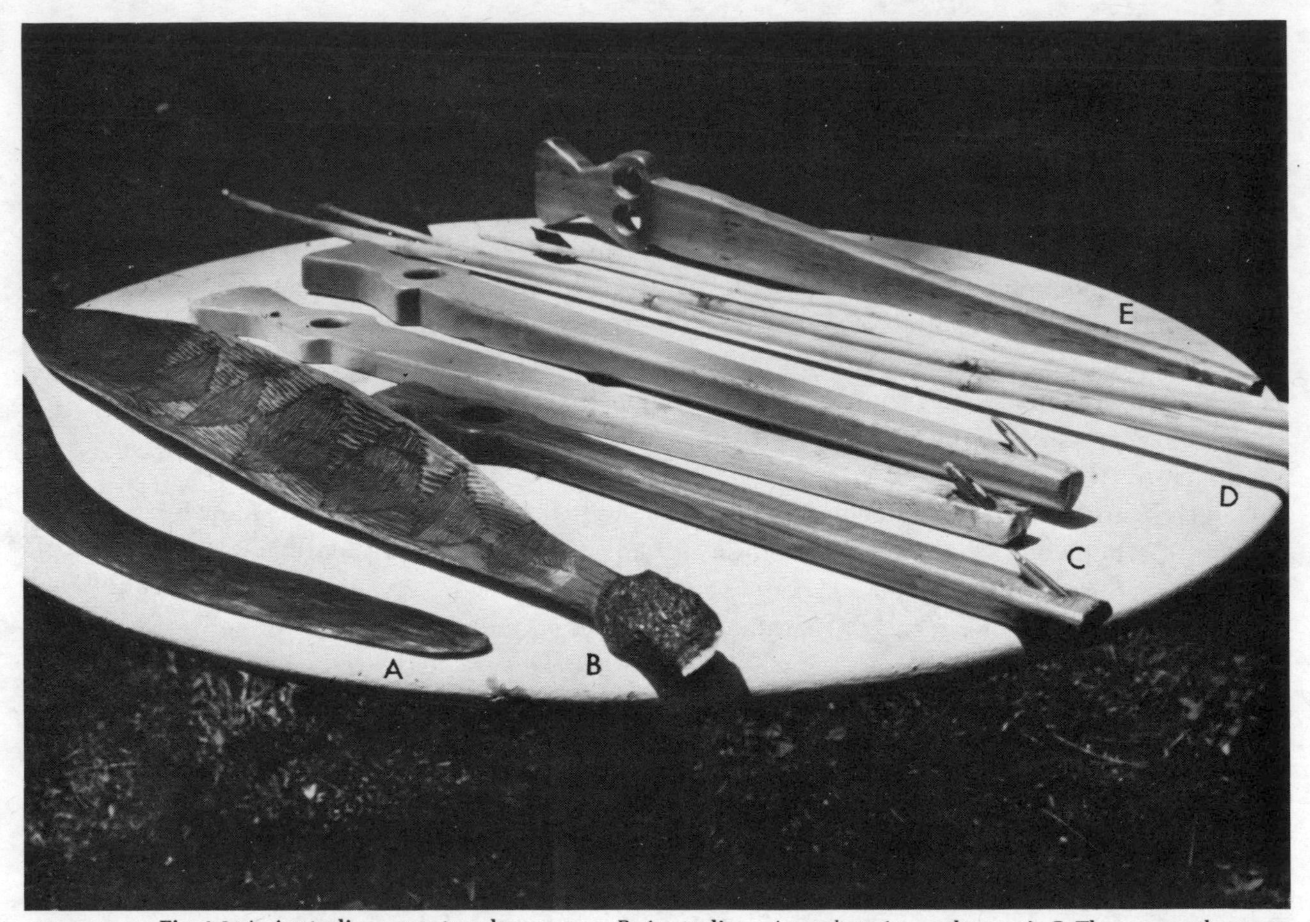

Fig. 4-2. *A.* **Australian nonreturn boomerang.** *B.* **Australian** *mira nakata* **(spearthrower).** *C.* **Three spearthrowers of the Kuikuru Indian type, showing index finger hole at far end and hooks at right ends.** *D.* **Three spears.** *E.* **Spearthrower with two finger holes.**

to secure photographs of a spearthrower in the museum's collection which was made and used by the Kuikuru Indian tribes located near the head of the Xingu River in central Brazil. Views of this specimen are shown in Fig. 4-4. Following the specifications for the spearthrower in the museum, the author has made many copies of slightly different sizes, and has had a great deal of fun throwing various homemade spears with lengths anywhere from two to five times that of the spearthrower.

Spears should be straight and properly balanced with weight forward. The author prefers to fletch the rear end of his spears with three feather vanes as the spears tend to fly straighter this way, although very few tribes did this, and it is not necessary.

For spears one can use any green shoot of wood that is straight, long enough, and not too heavy. The author has found that shoots from privet hedge and sugar maple make satisfactory spears. To straighten out minor bends, heat the bent places one at a time over a flame, or in the coals of an open fire (as the aborigines of Australia did, and as American Indians straightened arrow shafts), and then bend the curves in the opposite direction till they stay straight. The heads of the spears should not be pointed but blunt or rounded to prevent injury. However, there should be no danger in spearthrowing games or contests for all contestants should stand behind the throwing line until all have thrown and all distances been marked. After this, spears may be retrieved. The author recommends that the front end of the spear be served with strong fishline for an inch or more and that the served area be smeared with good glue or cement. This tends to prevent the spear from splitting unduly. Better still, fit the end of the spear into an empty cartridge casing of appropriate diameter.

A single length of bamboo five and one-half to six feet long will probably not make a good spear in and of itself because of its very slight variation in weight distribution and its great stiffness. However, the weight distribution can be corrected by fitting two or three feet of a shoot of hard maple or birch into the forward end of the bamboo about four inches, until it is stopped by the first joint. Glue the inner fittings of this joint; then serve this area, one inch of the maple closest to the joint, and one inch over the bamboo area overlapping the maple with very strong fishline, and cover all this serving with glue. The

Fig. 4-3. A senior citizen who with his spearthrower can hurl a spear 100 yards, and is getting fairly accurate at 35 yards.

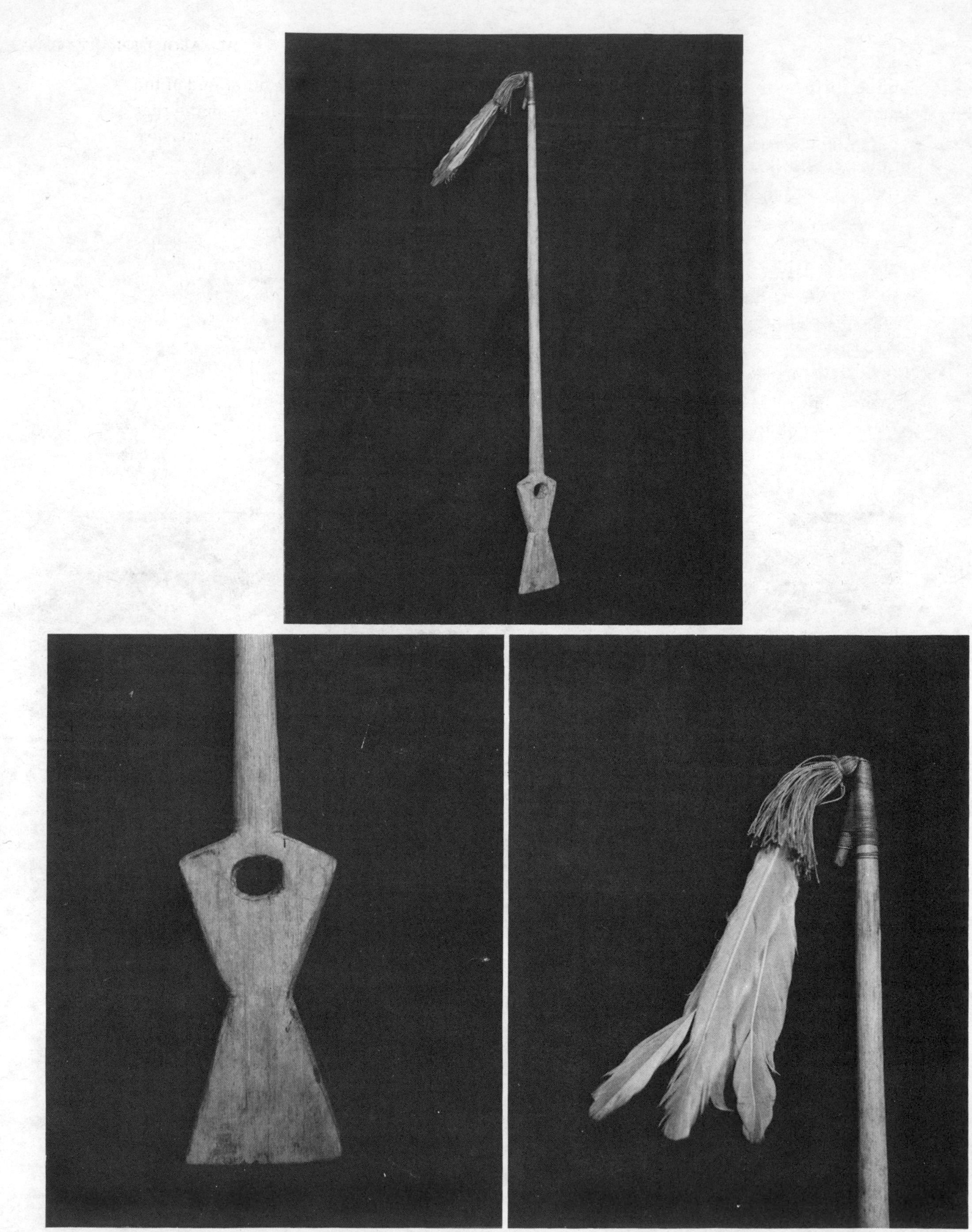

Fig. 4-4. *Top:* **Spearthrower of the Kuikuru Indians.** *Bottom left:* **detail of handle area.** *Bottom right:* **Detail of hook area.**—*Photo courtesy Dr. Robert L. Carneiro.*

undue stiffness in the spear can be remedied by fitting and gluing into the other end of the bamboo (for a distance of 4 to 5 inches before it is arrested by the first joint from the rear end of bamboo) a piece of strong, resilient wood such as hard maple, birch or Osage orange, two or three feet long. This will make a good spear eight to nine feet long, of a type often used by South American Indians.

To make a spearthrower of the Kuikuru Indian design, secure a clear, straight-grained piece of white pine, basswood, or other seasoned wood 26.5 inches long, 3 inches wide, and 1 to 1-1/8 inches thick. These dimensions will allow for proper smoothing, sanding, and finishing of the spearthrower. With yardstick or dark-colored chalk line make a straight line down the whole length of the board at its middle so that each parallel side is 1-1/2 inches from this middle line. Make a similar middle line on the other side of the board. By taking identical measurements out from the middle line on either side of the board one can lay out the spearthrower and make it straight. See this layout with dimensions in Figure 4-5.

GAMES PLAYED WITH SPEARTHROWERS

A very popular childhood game played by the aborigines of Australia is called *malu* (kangaroo). In this game young boys fashion impromptu spears and spearthrowers as they have watched their fathers do. They imitate their fathers' procedures even to lighting small fires to get coals to heat and straighten their toy spears. They also secure some thick bark from a eucalyptus tree growing along the edge of a creek bed. From this they cut a target 10 to 15 inches in diameter, but elliptical rather than perfectly round; so that when it is rolled down the creek bed it hops and jumps like a kangaroo. One boy rolls the disc down the creek bed while the others stationed on one side of the watercourse hurl their spears at the target as it goes by. It is amazing how many times hits are made. Of course, all the boys take turns rolling the *malu*. American boys and girls will also find this game lots of fun. Make a fifteen-inch diameter ring of number 9 wire. Bend it a little to make it slightly egg-shaped rather than perfectly round. Cover the space inside the wire ring by sewing or lacing in white cloth, or pasting in wrapping paper as one would paste it over the string and stick framework of a homemade kite. Then with a group of three to five boys and girls, take turns rolling the wire and fabric *malu* so that the rest of the group can throw their spears (with spearthrowers) at the target from varying distances. Start throwing at the *malu* from about ten yards away, gradually increasing the distance. Do not throw at distances less than ten yards, since this will endanger the roller of the *malu*.

Roving atlatl spear is played with the same rules as the game of roving spear, described under Throwing Homemade Spears or Javelins in the preceding chapter; only it is even more fun.

Atlatl golf is particularly enjoyable if you have a place large enough to play it, such as a large open space in a park. This game employs nine circles six feet in diameter with flags in the center of each circle approximately six feet above the ground to show at a

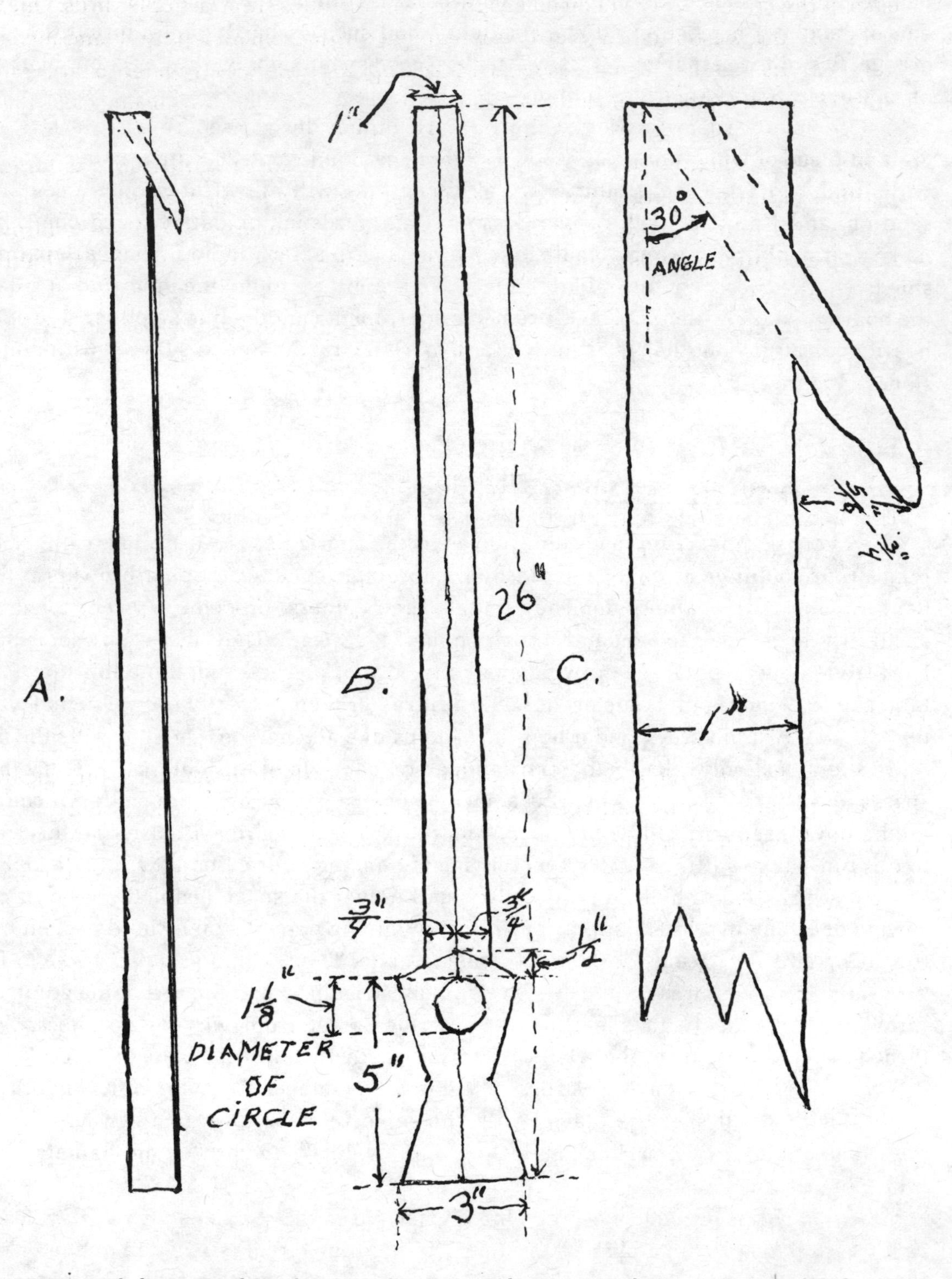

Fig. 4-5. Layout with dimensions for making spearthrower. *A.* **Side view.** *B.* **Back view.** *C.* **Blowup of hook area.**

distance where the circles are. Erect nine tee markers to show the direction to throw for each of the circles. Vary the distances from tees to circles from 50 to 200 yards. One scores as in golf; the least number of throws needed to throw from all tees and land the point of the spear inside all of the circles wins. Make 2 par for distances from tee to target circle of 50 to 75 yards, 3 par for distances of 75 to 150 yards, and 4 par for distances of 150 to 200 yards.

Another activity the readers should try with children and friends is target competition in hitting a target face about four feet in diameter, stapled with wire against a backstop of four to six bales of straw or hay. Try a "kangaroo round": five throws at a distance of fifteen yards from the target, five throws at twenty yards, and five throws at twenty-five yards.

Competing for distance with spears using spearthrowers is great fun for everyone from eight to eighty! Try it.

TIPS ON THROWING SPEARS WITH THE ATLATL

1) Throw the spear straight overhand without any curves or sideways motion. Throw like a baseball fielder to home plate to put a runner out.

2) Keep a tight contact between the hook or pin at the end of the atlatl and the small concavity at the end of the spear. The most common failure among beginners is to pull the pin of the atlatl out from the concave hole on the end of the spear before the throw is made.

3) Do not stop the throwing motion halfway. "Follow through" with the throw all the way.

The author feels that with officially established dimensions for spears and spearthrowers of different groups and with official rules, this sport could become a popular and beneficial interscholastic and intercollegiate athletic event. The use of the spearthrower places far less strain on the wrist and finger flexors than does throwing the javelin in intercollegiate athletics.

chapter 5

Marksmanship Practice with Simple Weapons: The Whip-Dart and Slingshot

MARKSMANSHIP IS NOT ONLY A BASIC SURVIVAL SKILL, IT IS A lot of fun to practice. Fortunately, target practice does not require a rifle, an air gun, or any other expensive, factory-made equipment. Any youngster can make the aiming devices described and illustrated in this chapter from such easily available materials as sticks, strings, rubber bands, wooden shingles, and small pieces of leather.

THE WHIP-DART

This is a fascinating device for shooting a light stick for amazing distances and for accuracy as well. The author chooses to call it the whip-dart, since the name best describes what it does and how it works. It shoots an arrow made of a shingle with a bow made of a stick. The bow has the string attached only to one end, and on the end of the string there is a loop. The loop fits snugly into a small acute-angled notch whittled into the side of the arrow at its balance point. The righthanded shooter holds the rear end of the arrow between thumb and index finger of the left hand and holds the free end of the bow in the right hand (lefthanded shooters should reverse the directions given here). The string joins the arrow with the bow where the loop fits into the notch on the far side of the

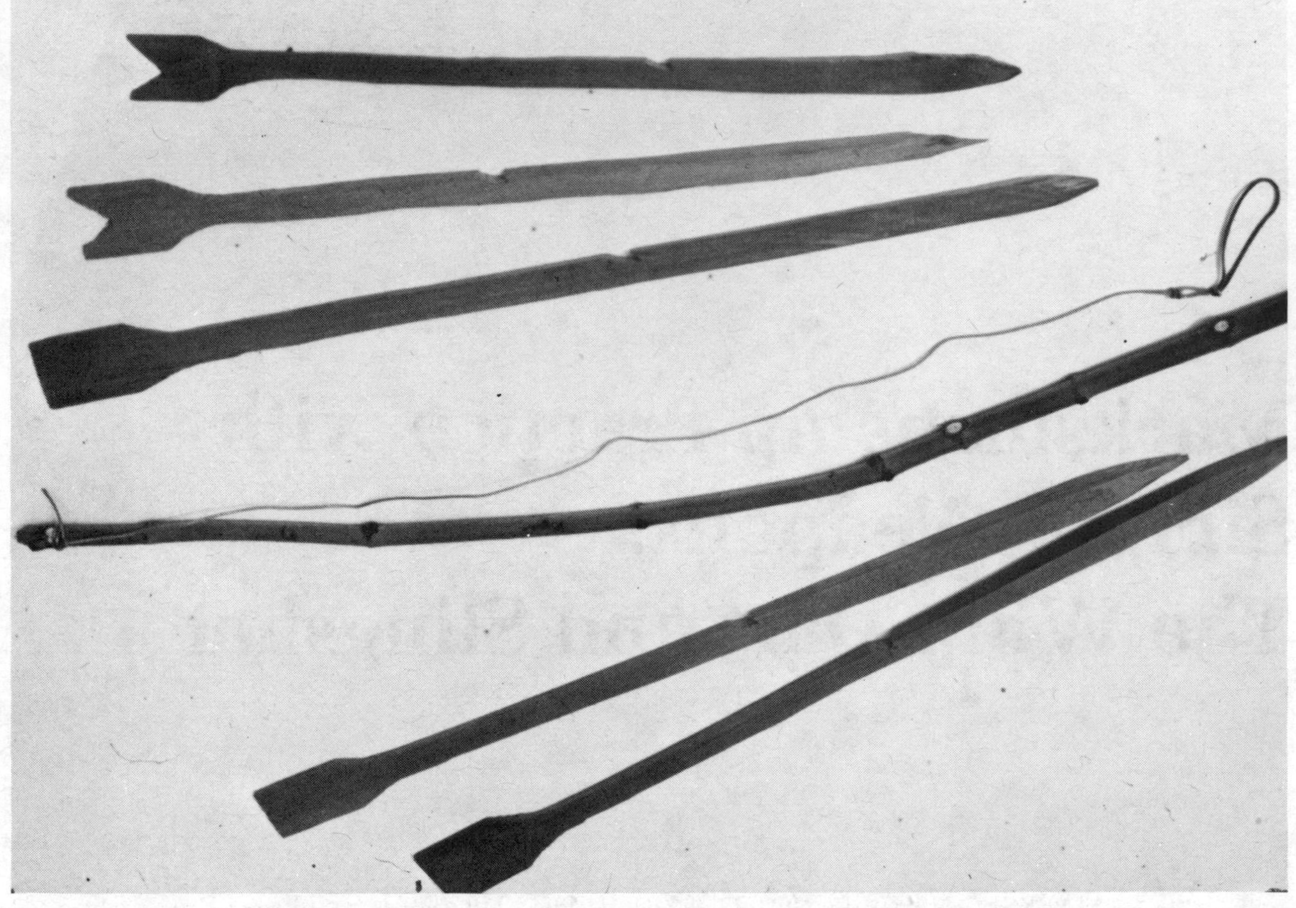

Fig. 5-1. Whip-darts and whip. The notches made at the balance points of the darts engage the rubber band at the end of the whip.

arrow. The string must be kept taut and the lower seven or eight inches of it kept in line with and touching the inside forward end of the arrow so that the knot will not slip out of the arrow's notch. The arrow is now ready to shoot.

The right hand with bow (or whip) leads in the direction of aim. Just before whipping the arrow or dart forward, move both hands back away from the direction the dart will be going, to put the swinging or whipping muscles on a stretch and give the dart more room in which to gather momentum. Then whip or swing the arms, hands, bow, and dart forward as fast as possible; the dart frees itself smoothly from the knot or loop in the string after moving forward about three feet and shoots out a very long distance if the whipping or swinging motion of the arms is sideward and upward or from below upward. For accuracy it is best to stand with whip arm side facing the target and whip the dart from behind the left side of the head straight over the top of the head forward in the direction of the target, although more distance can be achieved by sideward and backward plus immediate sideward forward swings (see Fig. 5-2).

Fig. 5-2. Whip-dart shooting positions. *Top:* **Position for achieving greatest accuracy.** *Bottom:* **Position for shooting greatest distance.**

The bow or whip can be made from most any straight or slightly curved stick about three feet long, preferably with a little spring or cast to it. It should be about 5/8 inch wide at the large handle end and about 3/8 inch wide where the string is attached. The string should be about two feet long, not including the loop. In place of the loop one might tie a rubber band about 1/8 inch wide to the end of the string and place the end of the band in the notch on the dart. See which you like best. (The notch on the dart holds up best with use of a rubber band.)

To make the darts, secure an ordinary shingle with very straight grain. Shingles vary somewhat in length from about sixteen to twenty inches, but any of these lengths will do. With a shingle of straight grain that is four inches wide one can make four darts.

Split the 4-inch-wide shingle into four narrow ones each about 1 inch wide. Take one of these and draw a straight line down the middle of the long axis and parallel to its long edges. This will help one keep the dart straight in the construction process. Shingles have a natural taper with the upper end about 1/8 inch thick and the bottom or butt end about 3/8 inch thick.

About 1-3/4 inches from the upper and thinner end draw a transverse line across the shingle. About 1 inch below the above line draw another one parallel to it. On this last line place a dot 1/4 inch out from the long midcenter line on both sides of it. About 8 to 10 inches down towards the butt end of the narrow shingle place two similar dots each 1/4 inch out from the long midline. Connect the dots by a long line parallel to the midline way down to the butt end of the shingle. You now have laid out the shaft of the dart, two sides of which are 1/2 inch wide, and the other two sides are the natural taper of the shingle.

Leave the right or upper end of the shingle the width that it is (about 1 inch), and from both ends of the first transverse or cross line (1-3/4 inches below the edge of shingle), mark symmetrical, concave lines down to the second cross line (1 inch from the first one), intersecting it at the beginning of the sidelines 1/4 inch out from the midline.

Now cut the dart out with a sharp knife or coping saw, sharpen the tip end so that the point begins to taper 3/4 inch from the tip, sand edges or corners off, cut in the notch with sharp knife or coping saw at the balance point, and get ready to shoot.

The top end can be left flat or one can round it off or put a V in it to give the impression of an Indian arrow. In cutting out the dart with a sharp pocketknife cut only a small amount of wood at a time, carefully observing the direction of the grain. If you can see that a particular cut is going to follow the grain and cut across the shaft of the arrow, stop the cutting stroke immediately, turn the shingle end for end, and cut from the other direction.

In learning to shoot the whip-dart, and even after one has learned, it is best to use it in a very large field, and those watching the shooting or waiting their turn should stand behind and a bit to the side of the shooter. Never try to see how high you can shoot the dart as it will go out of sight for many people and might come down on them.

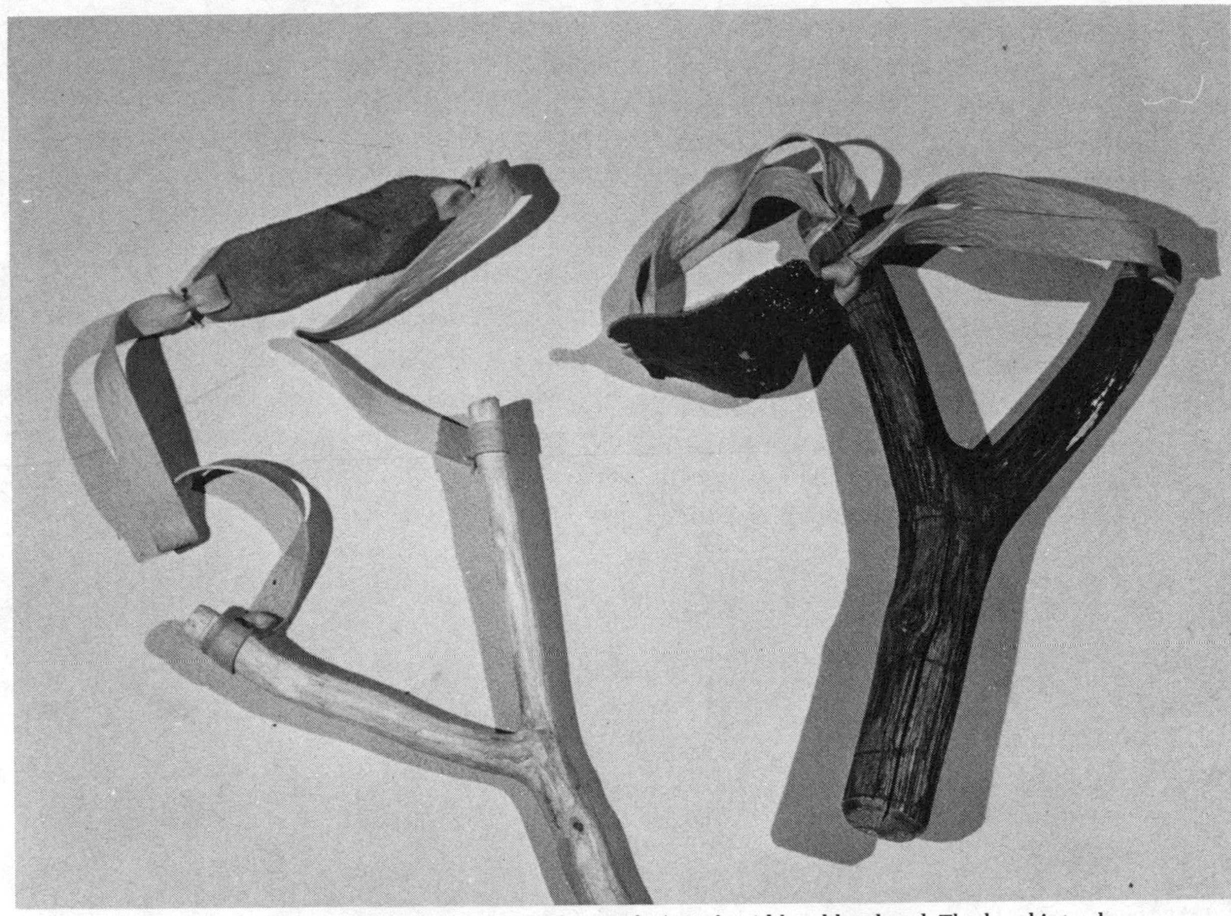

Fig. 5-3. Two slingshots. *Left:* **Slingshot with single thickness of 3/4-inch width rubber band. The band is too long since it has to be drawn very far back to get any speed behind the missile.** *Right:* **Slingshot with double thickness of 3/4-inch width rubber band, half the length of the band to the left. This slingshot is very difficult to pull all the way back to the chin when the holding arm is straight. It will shoot a tremendous distance.**—*Photo courtesy Spaulding Studio, Cortland, N.Y.*

SLINGSHOTS

The most valued birthday gift the author remembers receiving as a boy was a beautiful homemade slingshot given to him by a cousin. In the author's boyhood slingshots used to be standard equipment for boys. They carried them in their hip pockets where they could get to them in short order for competition in shooting for distance or at inanimate targets such as stumps, sticks, trees, or pine cones from various challenging distances. Especially enticing targets would be a stick floating in the water, or colored balloons staked on the ground or on an archery target with string and stick.

In the fall when acorns from red oaks (which have the largest acorns) are plentiful, it is a good idea to collect several cansful and have them ready to shoot in slingshots when your friends of any age arrive and need entertainment. Figure 5-3 shows how to make slingshots from crotched sticks, rubber bands 3/4 inch wide, and small pieces of leather, 4 inches long and about 1-1/2 inches wide, to hold the stones, or pellets.

The most accurate person with a slingshot that the author ever knew or heard of was "Slingshot Charley." This man for many years traveled sometimes with vaudeville shows and sometimes on his own giving special shows at sportsmen's clubs and conferences. He was a great showman unbelievable in his skill with the slingshot. During the summertime he lived at his camp on the east shore of Reelfoot Lake in Tennessee, where he rented boats to fishermen. I always rented boats from Slingshot Charley's camp, hoping to see him do some shooting. One time when I was with him and a friend in a rowboat I asked him to demonstrate for me and my pal. He said he was sorry but he had no pellets to shoot with. Seeing our disappointment, he reached over the gunwale of the boat, plucked a seedpod of a lotus lily, and extracted a round seed about the size of a small marble. He placed the seed in his slingshot and let fly at a bird flying by. He hit it and greatly startled it. However, the seed was too light to hurt the bird and it flew on at an increased speed.

chapter 6

Throwing Stones With Power: Use of the Sling

MOST PEOPLE HAVE HEARD OR READ THE STORY OF HOW DAVID slew Goliath with a smooth round stone which he hurled from his sling. Relatively few people, however, know what such a sling really looks like, and most confuse it with the slingshot. Nothing outside of gunpowder can throw a stone as hard, fast, and far as a sling of this type. The sling is made from two pieces of three-foot length string about the thickness of chalk line, a little larger in diameter than top string, and a soft but strong piece of leather five inches long and about two inches wide from which to make the cradle, hammock, or seat to hold the stone. One end of each piece of string is tied to the two ends of the leather cradle through small slits about 1/2 inch from these ends. The leather cradle will now be approximately in the middle of the two strings. Make a perfection loop (see Fig. 9-8) in the end of one string that will fit the end of the right index finger (lefthanded people should reverse these instructions). The other string is kept free as is. The sling is now complete except for measuring it for size. To do this put the right index finger through the loop so its inside outer end contacts the inside surface of the end (distal) joint. Place the end of the free string between the right thumb and right index finger against the loop. Place the left thumb on the middle of the leather cradle so that the pad of the thumb faces downward against the inside of the cradle. Now stretch both strings evenly by moving the end of the free string up or down in the light grasp of the right fingers until the leather hangs evenly in the middle with its ends flush. An overhand knot (see Fig. 9-9) in the end of the free string which can be felt at the point of pinch with right index finger and thumb helps to prevent the string from slipping down out of position. Place bottom of leather cradle on the floor or ground a couple of inches to the right of the right foot. Standing erect with arms relaxed at the sides and gripping the ends of the sling properly, the middle of the cradle should be just barely touching the ground when the strings are taut from the weight of the stone. If you have slack in the two strings, shorten them. In swinging and slinging the stone in the sling, you should have plenty of open space both in front and behind; if you have an audience, they should be clearly to the side and well away from and out of the plane of the swing.

To sling the stone face about 80 degrees to the right of the direction of throw (if lefthanded, face to the left of the direction of throw). Start the throw by swinging forward and upward (in direction of throw) and downward in complete circles, slowly at first, and then increasing the speed up to the last forward upward swing, when you release the free string, which in turn releases the stone. If the free string is released too late, the stone will go too high or even backwards, either of which is bad. If the string is released too soon, the stone will hit the ground ahead of you or go only a short distance. Do not try to sling the stone too hard or fast at first but get the feel of it. Through practice, strive to release the stone so it is thrown at a 35- to 45-degree angle with the ground. A 45-degreee angle will give the most distance. A pleasant and generally safe place to practice the use of the sling is on the shore of a lake, bay, or ocean.

The Incas and some other Peruvian peoples used slings for war, hunting, and sport. Their slings were more rugged, heavier, and made from wool.

A friend of the author, Mr. Antonio Cusihuaman from Peru, a direct descendant of the Incas, gave him a demonstration of how they used the sling for accuracy rather than for distance, and coached him in doing it. To make the transition from the underhand upward sweeping throw to the Peruvian method, start the sling swing as previously described, and while starting it in the vertical plane (forward, upward, backward, and downward), gradually raise the plane of the swing during four or five swings to one about eighty degrees from ground level. Then, swinging in this plane, accelerate the speed in the last three or four swings and release the stone on the sideward-forward swing, concentrating on the target to be hit. One should actually have the same kinesthetic feelings in shoulder, arms, and wrist that a baseball pitcher would have in throwing a straight sideward overhand baseball, and the accelerated prethrow swings constitute the windup. The final act of slinging the stone gives one the same feeling one has when throwing a stone to hit a tree stump or other target. Since this throwing coordination has most likely been well established during childhood and youth, and since accuracy improves with practice, employing the windup technique in throwing a sling may greatly increase one's accuracy. Try it out yourself. Of course, after getting the feel of this throwing release, one can omit the preliminary vertical swings suggested above for those just learning to use a sling and start right in using the Inca method. The author now finds it easier to believe

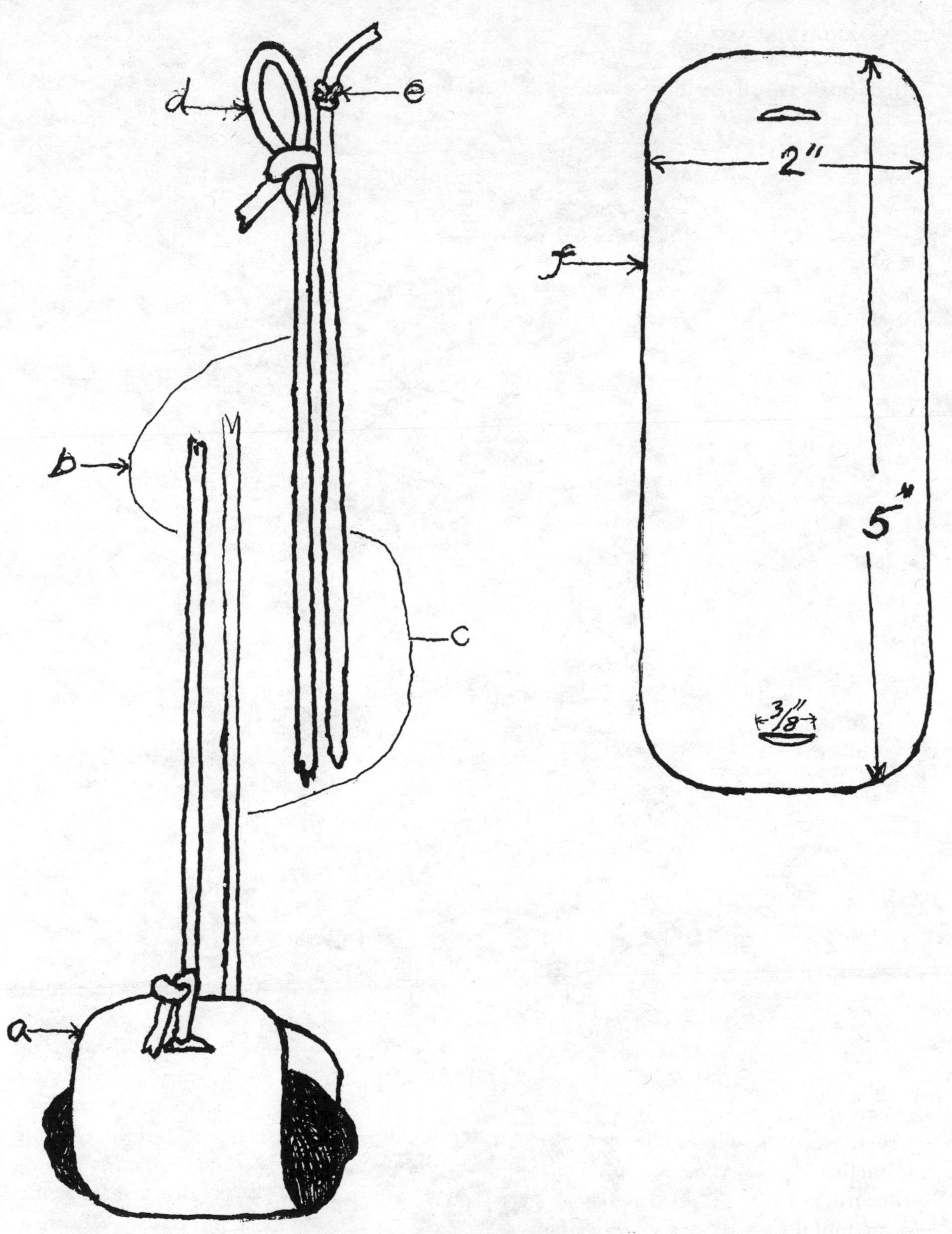

Fig. 6-1. The sling. *a.* Cradle. *b.* Loop string, 31 inches long from tie to end of loop. *c.* Free string, 30-3/4 inches long from tie to knot near end. *d.* Perfection loop. *e.* Knot for holding free string. *f.* Cradle detail.

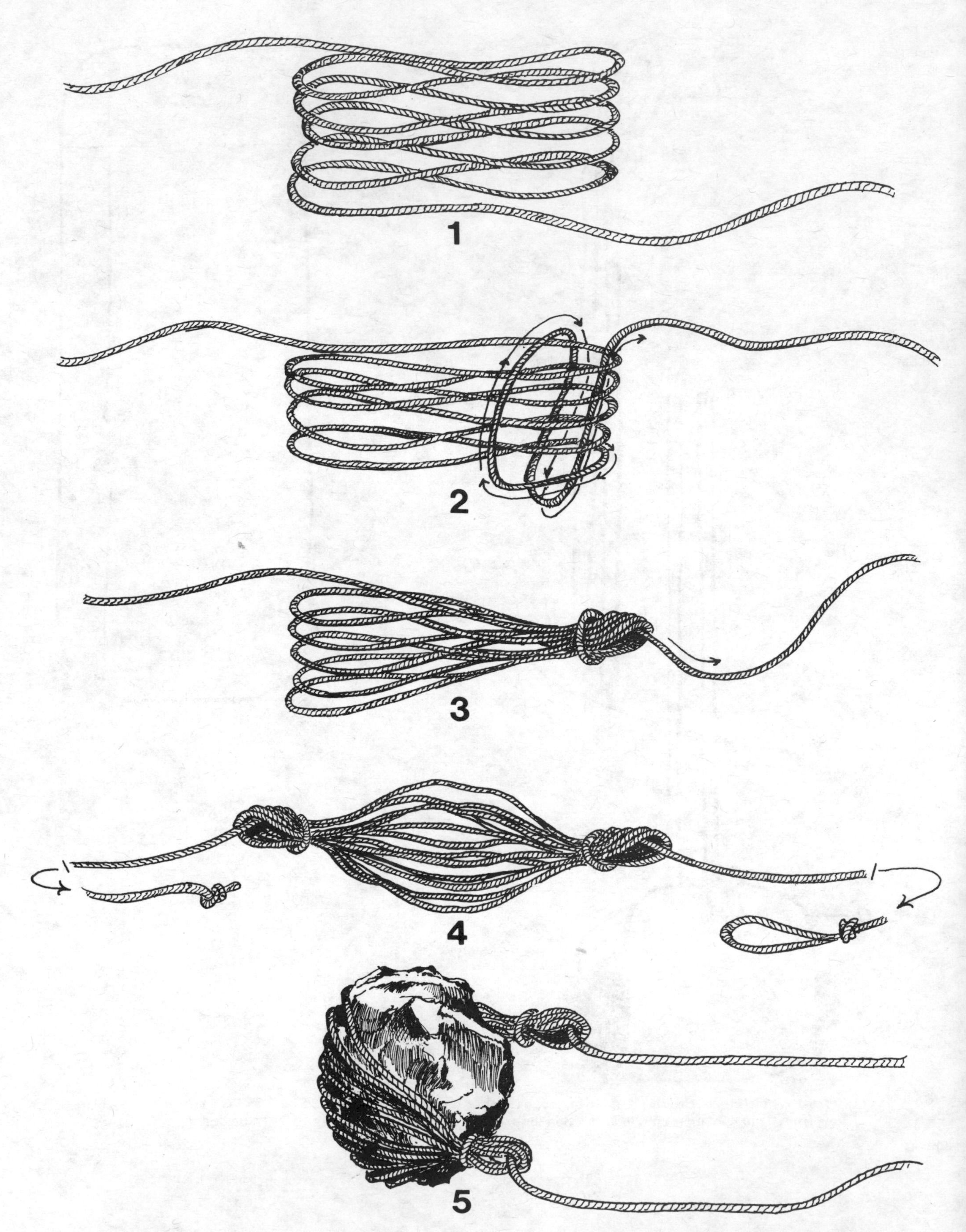

Fig. 6-2. Steps in making and loading sling made from continuous piece of cordage.—*Drawing courtesy Robert Eckard.*

that David actually did sling "a smooth round stone" that hit Goliath in the middle of his forehead.

If one doesn't have suitable leather from which to make the cradle and needs to use a sling, he can quickly make one from a continuous piece of Amerindian cordage twelve feet long (see Fig. 6-2). Better make one out of a 12-foot piece of chalk line or heavy fishline first to get the method, especially if no cordage about 3/16 inch in diameter is available.

To make this sling out of a single piece of cord, lay the cord out on the floor. At a point about 40 inches from one end of the cord bend the cord straight back on itself (180 degrees) for six inches, and then back on itself again for six inches, and keep looping the string back on itself every six inches until you have eleven lengths of cord each six inches long, a total of ten loops (five on each side), and the rest of the string (other end of it) facing in the opposite direction from the starting end of the string. It now looks as though you were going to make a sheepshank knot and shorten the cord by sixty inches. You do start just as you would a sheepshank knot by taking the free end of the cord on one side and wrapping it once around the five adjacent loops 1/4 inch from their ends, but instead of just slipping the end once under itself, tie an overhand knot around the five loops and pull this knot and the loops tight together so that only about 1/4 inch of the loops is left outside. Now to be sure that these loops never pull out, place the end of the string through all five of the loops and pull tight. With the other free end of the string repeat the entire procedure, collecting the five loops on that side together tight. The cradle or hammock of the sling is now finished. Adjust the lengths of the two ends of string for the person using the sling as described in the instructions for making the first sling. In adjusting the stone in the hammock take care to see that its individual strings are spread around the stone properly so that it does not slip out or through (see Fig. 6-2).

chapter 7

The Blowpipe: Adapting a Primitive Skill for Fun and Games

BLOWGUNS, SOMETIMES CALLED BLOWPIPES, ARE TUBES through which a projectile may be impelled by the force of breath. They were employed with poison-tipped darts by people in eastern Sumatra, parts of Borneo, the Malay Archipelago, and the Philippines. The blowgun was a weapon used in fighting and in securing game; its effectiveness depended largely on the user's stalking ability. The Cherokee and Seminole Indians of North America also used the blowgun for small game, but did not tip their arrows with poison. Because one can use some indigenous woods with less difficulty in construction of blowguns, this chapter will tell how to make and use blowguns of the Cherokee and Seminole patterns.

The blowgun of the Cherokee and Seminole Indians was most generally made from straight pieces of bamboo or cane, which are indigenous and available in most of the southeastern states from the Carolinas southward. To make such a blowgun use a straight length of bamboo or cane four to eight feet in length, with inside diameter at the small end measuring from 1/3 of an inch to 5/8 inch. The end with the larger diameter is always the mouth or blowing end.

Burn out the solid cross-sections or diaphragms at the joints of the bamboo by inserting a red-hot metal rod throughout the length of the tube. Then smooth the inside of the bamboo tube by running a long, strong, narrow piece of seasoned oak, hickory, or other tough wood up and down and back and forth inside the tube. Glue or tack an abrasive material onto the far end of the wooden rod, for six to ten inches or so. Friction against this abrasive will grind down the rough ridges on the inside opposite the joints even with the inside edge of the bamboo tube between the joints. Here is how to prepare this abrasive material:

1) Secure a piece of flat tin approximately six by 15 inches. (Frequently a number 10 tin can, with both top and bottom cut out and a vertical cut in the side from top to bottom flattened out will make a satisfactory rectangular piece of tin.)

2) Place the piece of tin down flat on a waste piece of board of soft wood (poplar, tulip tree, or basswood).

3) With a punch or medium-sized nail and using a hammer, pound shallow holes through the tin very close together so that its underside is very rough like a nutmeg grater.

4) With tin-snips cut one or more long narrow strips of this roughened tin about 1/2 to 3/4 inch wide.

5) Tack one end of a strip of tin to the far end of the long slender smoothing stick, and wrap or wind it with the rough side out in spiral fashion tightly and neatly (so that the sides of the strip touch each other) back up the slender rod for six inches or as far as it will go. Then tack this end of the tin strip tightly to the wooden rod. The smoothing stick is now complete, and can be rubbed up and down inside the bamboo tube until the inside ridges at the joints of the bamboo are worn off flush with the long sections between them so they will not slow up the speed of the darts and lessen their distance and velocity.

A satisfactory and perhaps more modern substitute for the above-described Cherokee smoothing stick would be a rat-tailed file 1/3 to 3/8 inch in diameter, welded or brazed on the end of an iron rod 1/4 to 1/3 inch in diameter. Another useful tool would be a narrow, strong wooden rod with half-inch strips of sandpaper or emery cloth, spirally wrapped for six inches or so and tacked on one end.

A long slim hardwood rod with no abrasives can be used to give additional smoothness and burnish to the inside of the tube.

In northern states where bamboo is not available it is possible to find common elder shoots big enough and straight enough to make satisfactory blowguns if one removes the pith. A good tool for removing the pith is an iron rod 4 or 5 feet long about 1/4 inch in diameter on which is brazed at one end a 3/8-inch bit and on the other end a similar piece of iron rod 10 to 12 inches long at right angles to the main rod, making a T, which allows one to turn or twist the rod and little by little drill out the pith.

Another plant that grows in the northern states that will make a fairly good blowgun is wild lettuce (*Lactuca canadensis*), sometimes called horseweed. It is hollow from bottom to top, grows to heights of from five to ten feet and is stiff at maturity in late fall. Select a tall straight plant and cut off a section with the proper inside diameters at top and bottom. The top diameter (far end of the blowgun) should be about 1/3 inch and the bot-

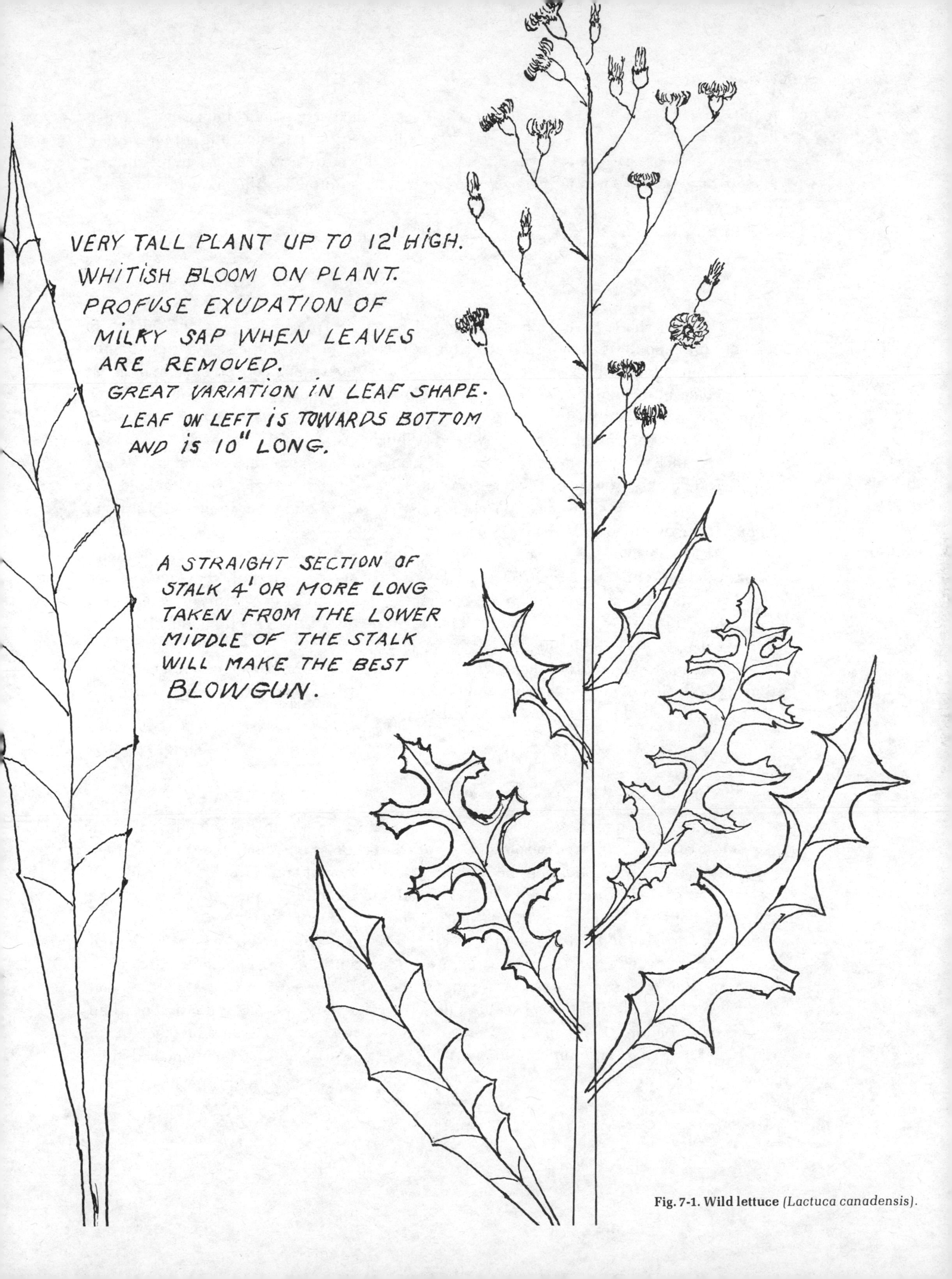

Fig. 7-1. Wild lettuce *(Lactuca canadensis)*.

tom diameter about 1/2 to 5/8 inch. This will usually make a blowgun about 3-1/2 to 4 feet long. This weed, maturing in the late fall, can be used immediately but is better after several weeks of seasoning. Because some of the stalks have curved places in them, they may have to be cut down to two or three feet in length, but will still make blowguns, although short.

DARTS

Darts to shoot in the blowguns should be made from eight to twelve inches in length. In the South they can be made from splints split out from the sections of bamboo between the joints, splints split out and whittled from the leaf stalks of the Sabal palm, or seasoned splints of oak or hard pine. In the North you can use practically any seasoned hardwoods—oak, maple, hickory, birch, ash, black locust, Osage orange—Port Orford cedar, red spruce, white spruce, arrowhead (*Viburnum dentatum*), if it has a thickness of at least 1/8 inch of wood outside the pith, and straight shoots from the privet shrub.

The quickest source of wood for making darts is the hardware store or hobby-crafts store. As a rule such stores carry birch dowels 1/8 inch in diameter and usually straight enough for darts up to 10-12 inches in length.

After splitting out the splints, whittle, round, smooth, and straighten them until their diameter is about 1/8 inch. Sharpen the forward end of each splint and then heat it a bit to give it hardness. Then fletch the rear end of the splint or dart with some very light material which will catch the air behind it and propel it swiftly. This fletching also tends to make the dart fly straight, like the feathered end of an arrow.

The most satisfactory fletching materials which the author has found in the United States are thistledown, and the side and back skin and fur of a rabbit or hare. The process of attaching thistledown will first be described.

Fletching with Thistledown

In the late summer locate healthy patches of the common thistle, sometimes called the bull thistle, with its large purple shaving brush-like blossoms (the Canada thistle is not large enough). In late fall when the blossoms have browned and turned to seedpods but before the thistledown and seeds have emerged, they should be harvested. Use leather gloves and a pair of pruning snips to secure two dozen or more seedpods. With care and good luck one seedpod will fletch one dart. The Cherokee Indians had a good method of keeping these pods in good condition and preventing their opening up and dispersing the down and seeds before they could use them. They split a green stick for about two feet and packed these pods in the split, alternating their placement so that if the first one had the down end to the right and the butt end to the left, the next pod would be placed with down end to the left and butt end to the right. As they were thus alternately placed, they

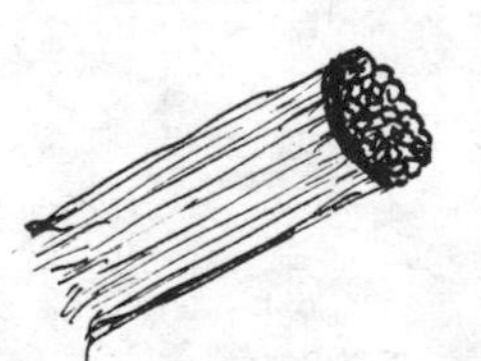

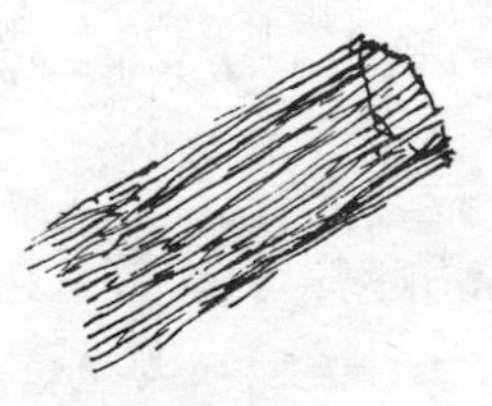

Fig. 7-2. Bull thistle (*Cirsium vulgare*).

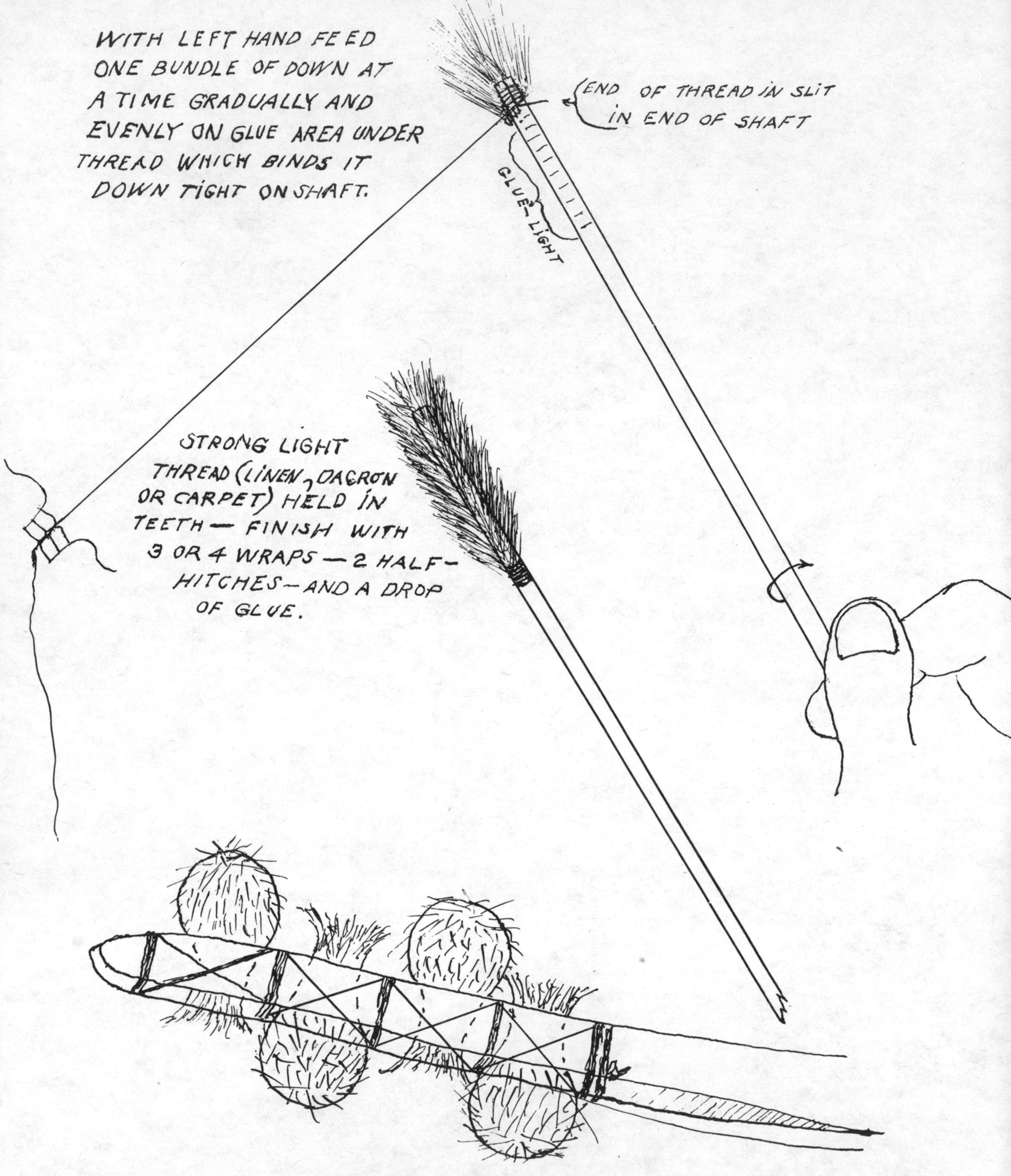

WITH LEFT HAND FEED
ONE BUNDLE OF DOWN AT
A TIME GRADUALLY AND
EVENLY ON GLUE AREA UNDER
THREAD WHICH BINDS IT
DOWN TIGHT ON SHAFT.

END OF THREAD IN SLIT
IN END OF SHAFT

GLUE—LIGHT

STRONG LIGHT
THREAD (LINEN, DACRON
OR CARPET) HELD IN
TEETH — FINISH WITH
3 OR 4 WRAPS — 2 HALF-
HITCHES — AND A DROP
OF GLUE.

THISTLE PODS PICKED IN FALL AND BOUND BETWEEN TWO HALVES
OF A SPLIT GREEN STICK (CHEROKEE INDIAN STYLE) TILL NEXT TIME OF NEED

Fig. 7-3. Making blowgun dart fletched with thistledown.

would be bound tightly in place by two cords being wrapped from the end of the split in the stick up from different directions and circling the two halves of the stick to keep necessary pressure on the pods. The strings were, of course, tightly knotted at the open end of the stick.

When ready to make the dart, take the following steps:

1) With a sharp knife split the rear end of a dart shaft 1/8 inch deep.

2) Place the end of a 3-foot length of dacron or Barbour's Irish linen bowstring thread in the split end of the shaft so that the end of the string hangs out 1/4 inch and tightly wrap the long end of the string around and over the short quarter-inch end of the string a couple of turns to hold it down. Then take two or three more tight turns around the split end of the shaft and finish off with two half-hitches. Seal this off with a drop of Duco or other fast-drying cement. This will, of course, leave the long end of the string (30 inches or so) hanging from the rear end of the dart-to-be.

3) Using a glove or pliers, take the butt end of a seedpod in the left hand (lefthanded readers should reverse "left" and "right" in these directions). With thumb and index fingers of bare right hand, tightly grasp hold of the end of the down at the blossom end and pull it straight out. (If multitudes of seeds still adhere to the base of the lefthand end of the down, rub these seeds off.) Now place the bundle of down carefully (so it doesn't slip into a tangled mess) between the end of the left thumb and the base or bottom of the left index finger.

4) With the right hand pick up the end of the string, place three or four inches of it in the mouth, and bite down on it with the teeth to hold it securely. Then with right hand pick up the shaft of the dart at about the middle so that you are prepared to twist the shaft away from you (clockwise).

5) Hold the string taut between the teeth and the string end of the shaft with the right hand.

6) With left hand (still holding the down tightly, with down ends upward and towards the left and butt ends to the right), push the farthest or uppermost butt ends of the down against the upper surface of the end of the shaft and underneath the string by twisting the shaft with right hand away from you (in clockwise direction), thus binding the butt ends of down tightly to end of shaft. With the left thumb, gradually push uniform amounts of the down butts forward onto the shaft under the tight string while the shaft is being twisted away from you and spiraling the string and the down around the shaft and to the right for an inch or so until the down is used up. Continue to wrap the string along closely to the shaft four or five more turns and finish off with about four half-hitches (see Fig. 7-4). Then, seal down with a few drops of cement. The blowgun dart is now complete except for trimming its down end. To do this: secure a 5- or 6-inch length of bamboo or metal tubing with inside diameter of 5/8 inch. Push the new dart through this tubing until the wooden end of dart has entered about 1/8 inch and 1/4 inch of the down of the down-fletched end sticks out. Holding the shaft and tube tightly together at this point, apply a lighted match to the down sticking out from end of tube. When the down has burned flush

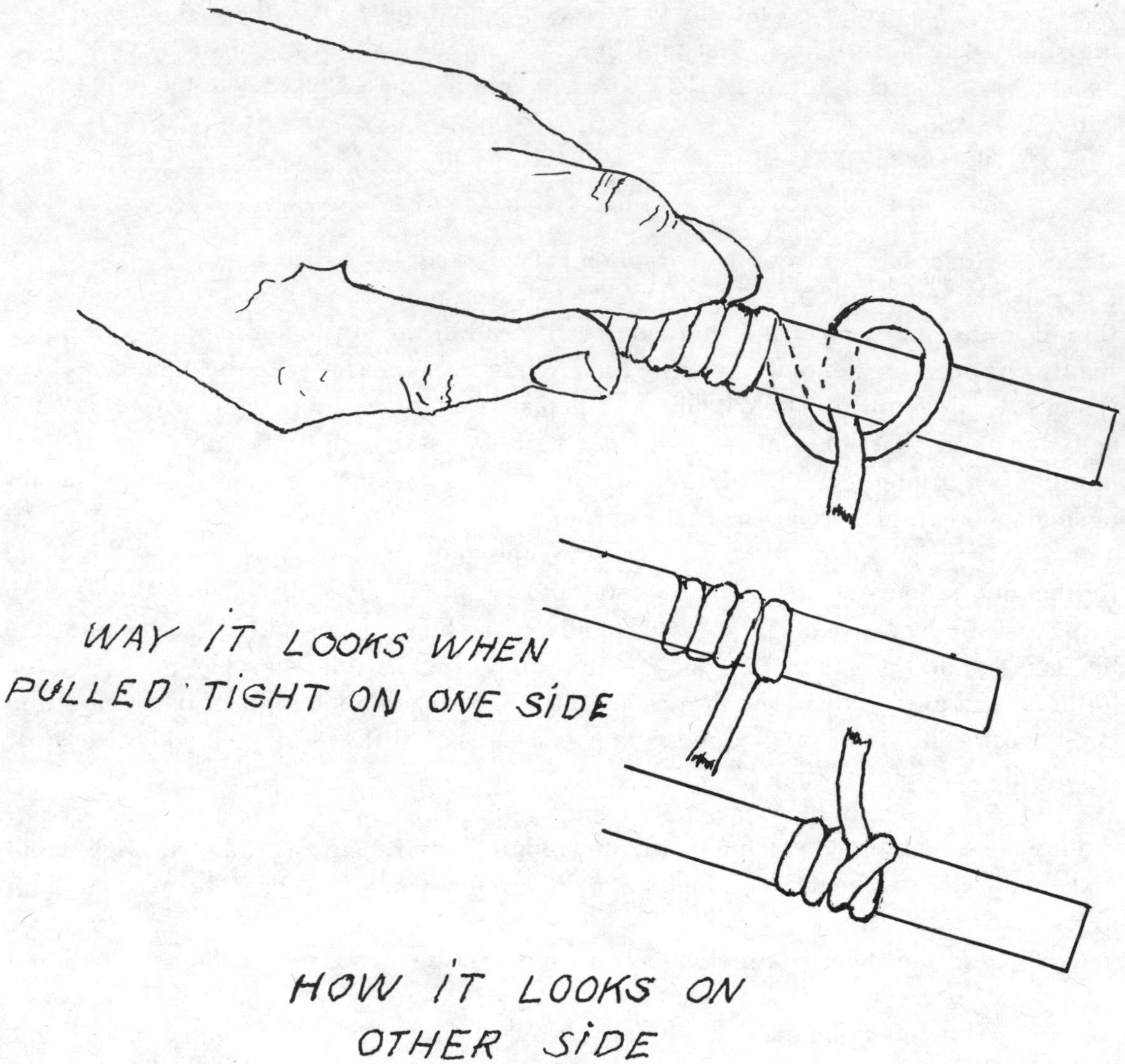

WAY IT LOOKS WHEN PULLED TIGHT ON ONE SIDE

HOW IT LOOKS ON OTHER SIDE

Fig. 7-4. The half-hitch.

to the end of the tube blow out the blaze, take dart out of tube, and with fingers rub off the charred matter from the rest of the down. The dart is now properly trimmed and complete.

Fletching with Rabbit Skin Fur

Clean the rabbit skin and pull all bits of fat off. Then air-tan by tacking the skin on a board or tree outdoors for three or four weeks. The best material for use on the dart comes from the sides of the rabbit or from the middle of the back. Therefore, cut one to three quadrangular pieces of rabbit skin approximately 2 by 2-1/2 inches from the sides and back. When cutting pieces of rabbit skin, do not use scissors but a sharp knife or razor blade. Place the skin on a flat surface fur side down. Carefully support the skin in the area to be cut with the inside of the index and third finger of the left hand held under and against the fur and the left thumb on the top or inside surface of the skin (lefthanded readers should use the right hand for this). With the sharpest edge of the knife cut down between the two fingers and just through the skin, not cutting any of the fur or hairs. It will be noted on close examination of any one of the cut pieces that the fur and guard hairs point backwards from the head end towards the rear of the rabbit. When cutting strips of rabbit skin for fletching the dart, lay the quadrangular piece of skin fur side down and with the skin that was formerly toward the rear of the rabbit facing to the left (this will be the side on which the greatest amount of hair and fur will be protruding). With the piece of skin now in proper position, place the sharp edge of the knife (ready to cut downward) near the upper lefthand corner of the skin just 3/16 inch in from the edge. Now cut down through the skin only and make a thin strip 3/16 inch wide and 2 to 2-1/2 inches long for a spiral wrapping on the rear end of the dart shaft for the fletching.

For this procedure, prepare the dart shaft with string attached the same as used for the thistledown darts. Apply a thin coating of cement (Duco will do) to the last 1-1/4 inch of the string end of the shaft. Holding the shaft in the right hand (lefthanded readers should reverse "left" and "right" in these instructions) and the string in the teeth (as was done in attaching thistledown) and holding (with left hand) the small strip of skin (fur side down and fur sticking out to left), feed skin onto the end of shaft under the tight string. As the right hand twists the shaft away from you, spirally wrap the string tightly down on the skin side of the strip onto the wet cemented area of the shaft. Make a few extra close wraps of the string to the shaft only (since the fur strip has been used up) and finish off with three or four half-hitches (see Figure 7-4) and a drop of cement. This finishes the dart except for trimming the end of the fletching, which is done exactly the same as trimming off the end of a thistledown-fletched dart.

Adjustments may have to be made for best results. The dart should fit the gun. If the dart on use sticks inside the blowgun, some of the fletching should be trimmed off. Also, sometimes the wooden shaft may be too long for best results; if so, shorten it. Or perhaps there is a rough spot on the inside of the blowpipe near one or more joints, in which case smoothing with sandpaper is indicated.

Fletching with Cotton and Nylon

Other satisfactory materials for fletching darts are cotton and nylon. If using cotton, apply a small amount of fast-drying glue to the last 1/4 to 1/2 inch of the rear end of the dart shaft. Pull out a small pinch of cotton that is slightly larger in diameter than the tube (blowpipe). Twirl the cotton on the end of the dart which has the glue on it by twisting or spinning the dart to the right with right thumb and index finger (lefthanders should reverse these directions). With the left thumb and two other fingers, slightly pinch the cotton to mold it while twirling or twisting the shaft of the dart, thus making it small enough to pass through the blowpipe easily. These darts will work very well while they last. One can keep them in working condition by respinning and remolding occasionally.

To fletch darts with nylon cut pieces of 1/4-inch nylon rope into 1-inch pieces. Take each piece and, with an open safety pin, awl, or ice pick, completely unravel it, making soft, fluffy, shiny threads of it. Sort bunches of these threads into parallel bunches and place between left thumb and index finger. Then with the forward end of the dart between right thumb and index finger and a strong thread (the other end of which is fastened securely on rear end of dart) held tightly with the teeth, spin the nylon fibers onto the end of the dart exactly as was described in fletching the thistledown fibers. It also helps to put a bit of fast-drying glue on the rear end of the dart for 1/4 inch as was done in fletching with rabbit fur.

TECHNIQUE OF USING BLOWPIPE

Place the dart into the blow-end of the blowgun with its point foremost. Push fletched end of dart far enough into the pipe so that the rear end of the fletching is 1/4 to 1/2 inch from the blow-end of the pipe. After taking a deep breath, raise the blow-end to the lips, aim the pipe at the target, and blow with a powerful and sudden expulsive blast. Be sure that all air goes into the pipe and none of it escapes outside it during the blast. To get the maximum speed and power back of the dart requires lots of practice.

Place either your right or left hand, tightly cupped and circled, around and slightly overlapping the blow-end of the gun. Place your lips tightly against the thumb and index finger overlapping the blow-end of the pipe so that the lips do not contact the end of the gun. (Obviously, this is a good sanitary practice.) Place the other hand on the gun so that the index finger is on top of the gun, the other three fingers underneath the gun and tightly cupped against the blow-hand, and the thumb on top of the curved joints of the first two fingers of the blow-hand.

This position is similar to that used by the Cherokees. It has the advantage of minimizing the tendency to flinch at the time of the blast. Better control of the pipe can be maintained when both hands are held close together. Also, with the recommended hold, there is less chance for air to escape when the blower shoots the dart. Of course, individual differences are a factor in deciding upon the best grip.

BLOWPIPE GAMES

Games employing darts and blowguns are fun to play and require little or no additional equipment.

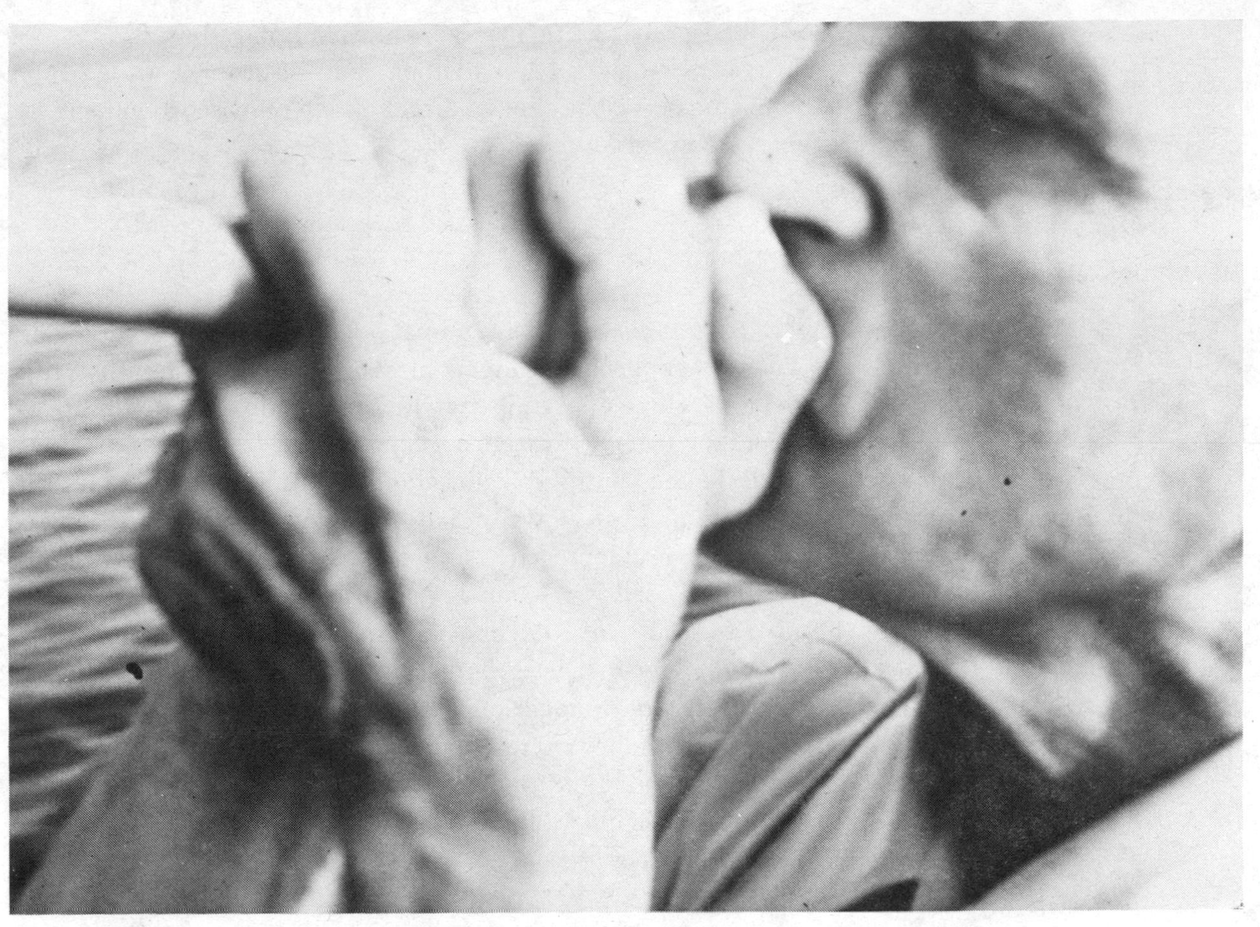

Fig. 7-5. How to hold blowpipe.

Blow Fun

Try shooting darts at a target with bull's eye and concentric rings at a distance of three or four paces if playing indoors and at six or eight paces from the target if competing outdoors.

Balloon Shooting

In this game contestants shoot at blown-up balloons attached to an archery target or bale of straw tied with string and wire staples.

Roving Dart

This game can be played with two to four players strolling in backyard, meadow, or open woods. Each person shoots one (the same) dart only at a particular target such as a brown leaf, a tree stump, or a piece of bark. The distances to each target should vary, and each contestant takes one turn (according to an agreed upon "batting order") choosing the next target. The person shooting his dart closest to the target in one blow scores one point. Any players hitting the target score three points.

Blow-Fun Golf

Bend each of nine wire coat hangers into a circle 10-1/2 to 11 inches in diameter. Spread these wire circles about back and front lawns at distances of five to thirty-five yards from the shooters' positions. Have a starting tee-marker (tee no. 1) with an arrow pointing towards circle no. 1 and the footage to circle no. 1 indicated. Players one at a time blow their dart towards this circle and continue taking shots at it until their dart lands in the circle (keeping track of the number of blows it takes, of course). Just to one side of circle no. 1 is tee no. 2 with direction and footage to circle no. 2. Standing behind tee no. 2, each player in turn blows his dart towards circle no. 2 and continues blow-shots at it until the dart lands inside the circle. As in golf, players must count each blow of the dart throughout the nine circles, and the lowest score or fewest number of dart blows required to hit all targets wins. After his first shot from each tee, each contestant shoots all his succeeding shots at a particular target from behind the place where his last dart landed. The game is really great fun and requires only the simplest and most available materials to set it up. If one does not have spare coat hangers for the circles, baling wire or other wire about the same diameter twisted into a circle works just as well.

Blow-Fun for Distance

Competing in blowing darts for distance is great fun. Have a takeoff mark or line behind which to shoot the darts, and place a pencil, small stick, or flag to mark where darts of the contestants land. Measure the distances of each. See who is the windiest. Keep your own distance record and see how often you can break it. This will strengthen your lungs and your diaphragm while you're having fun.

chapter 8

Sticks That Do Tricks: Putting Boomerangs Through Their Paces

A BOOMERANG IS A CURVED OR SICKLE-SHAPED CLUB THAT returns to the thrower when thrown. It is named after an aboriginal tribe in New South Wales, Australia, its use for hunting being widespread among aborigines throughout Australia. Incidentally, the boomerang does not boom; it whistles.

Weapons with a close resemblance to boomerangs were used in ancient Egypt and are still used in Northeast Africa. They are made of metal and are frequently called throwing knives. Among the Dravidians of South India is found an instrument shaped like a boomerang that can be made to return. It is made of bone and steel. However, whether the so-called boomerangs of Egypt and India have any real historical relationship to the Australian boomerang is uncertain. The Hopi (Moquis) of Arizona used a nonreturn type of throwing stick.

The Australian boomerangs are of two kinds: The return and the nonreturn type. The general form of both these weapons is the same: curved or sickle-shaped, made of hard wood, and weighing up to twelve ounces.

THE AUSTRALIAN RETURN-TYPE BOOMERANG

The return type of Australian boomerang is so modeled that its thickness is about 3/16 to 3/8 inch, its breadth 1-1/2 to 3 inches, and its length 12 to 30 inches. In the Australian return boomerang the two arms are generally curved at an angle of 90 to 130 degrees.

The skews (one for the outer third of each arm) and their direction are essential parts of a return-type boomerang. The boomerang has a relatively flat surface on one side and a beveled, rounded, or convex surface on the other side. Both arms of the boomerang (either singly or together) must be boiled in water twenty to thirty minutes or heated in hot ashes to make them twistable. To get the proper skews, hold the flat surface facing you with the two arms pointing upwards as in a smile. Grasp the end of the left arm of the boomerang with the left hand and the end of the right arm with the right hand. Now twist the left arm clockwise and the right arm counterclockwise. (This can be done more easily with a pipe-wrench in each hand over the ends of the arms, and the middle of the boomerang held tightly in a vise.) Twist the ends about three or four degrees from their original positions and hold them there in the twisted position fifteen or twenty seconds. The ends will now settle back slightly and maintain permanent skews of about two or three degrees (see Fig. 8-1). To some extent the ends *AB* and *DE* are raised above the plane of the weapon at *C*.

Because the Australian boomerangs are made of hardwood (maple, white ash, beech, birch or oak in the United States), they require great strength and energy on the part of the thrower to get proper curves and distance, even with the proper skews. The aboriginal Australians in their daily practice with boomerangs during childhood and youth have developed this necessary strength and coordination. Many of them throw the return-type boomerang so forcefully that it will travel in the air as much as 100 yards before it starts its curve to the left, after which it may rise in the air as much as 50 yards and circle as many as 5 times before returning.

The Australian return-type boomerang must be thrown with the right hand. It is held at one end above and behind the thrower's shoulder with the concave edge to the front. One must swing it forward rapidly with the flatter side underneath. A run of a few steps and a strong wrist movement just before the release of the boomerang add greatly to its impetus and spin. If properly thrown, the boomerang may travel straight for thirty yards or more with nearly vertical rotation; then it inclines to the left, lying over on its flat side, and rises in the air. After describing a circle of fifty yards or more in diameter, it returns to the thrower.

The Australians consider the return-type boomerang more or less of a plaything. It is used by their men as a training device in dodging weapons, and in tournaments to see who can make it weave the greatest number of circles or return nearest to a peg. Hunters spin it above flocks of ducks, parakeets, and pigeons to imitate a hawk and to drive the birds into nets strung from trees.

Many theories as to why the boomerang returns have evolved over the years, but

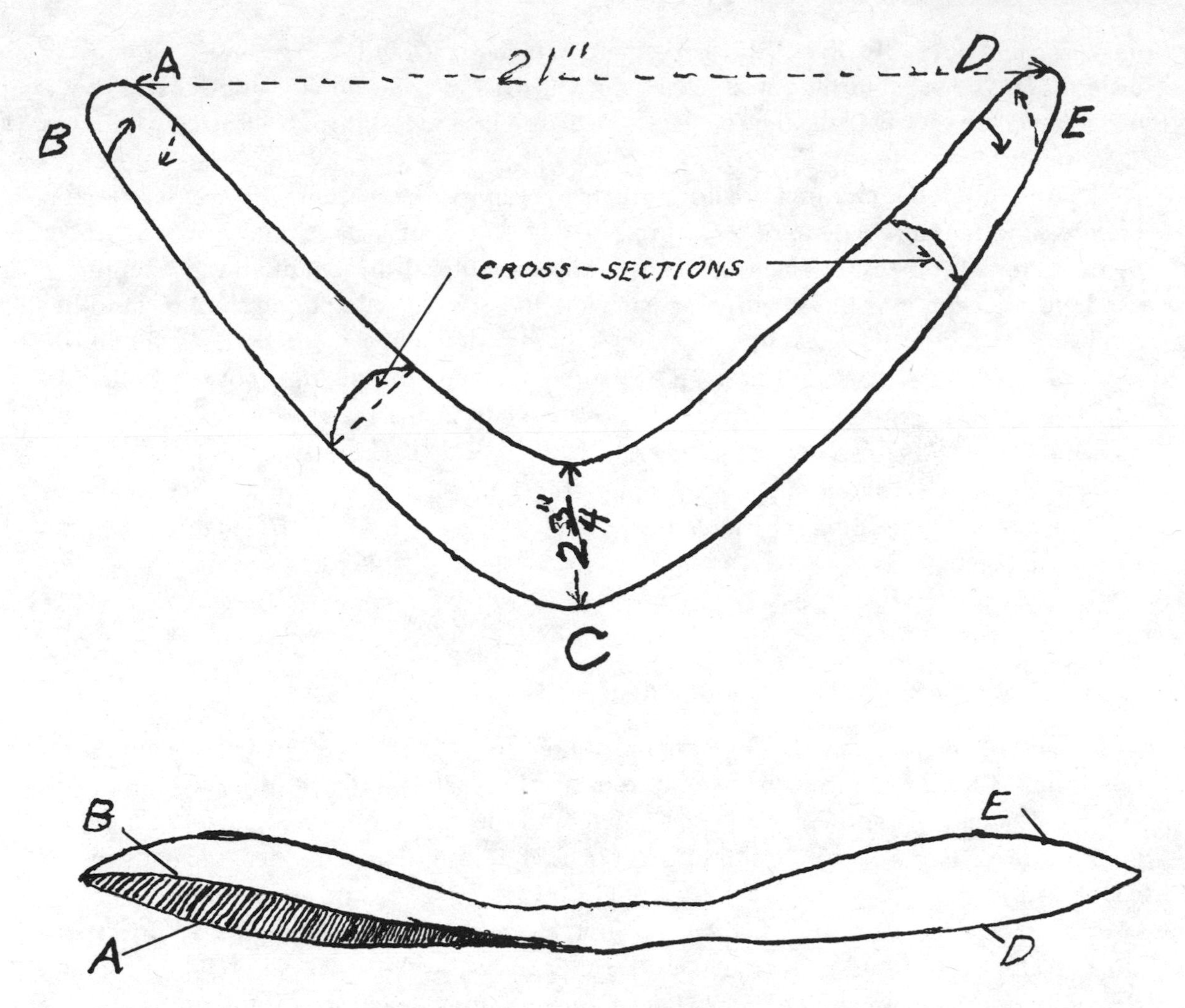

Fig. 8-1. *Top:* **Beveled surface of Australian return-type boomerang before twisting. Arrow shows direction of twist to get proper skew.** *Bottom:* **Side view of boomerang after twisting, showing skews. In left arm, lip** *A* **is low and lip** *B* **is high. In right arm, the far lip,** *E*, **is high and lip** *D* **is low.**

the one generally accepted postulates that this return action is caused by the spinning motion combined with the skew.

THE AUSTRALIAN NONRETURN BOOMERANG

The nonreturn boomerang has a skew in the opposite direction from that of the return type, has a shallow curve in relation to its length of 2 or 3 feet, and weighs up to 1-1/2 pounds, about 3 times the average weight of the return boomerang. This boomerang was a weapon for war, and for hunting kangaroo, emu, and other wild game. The nonreturn boomerang may be made to return in a nearly straight line by throwing it at an angle of 45 degrees, but normally it is thrown like the return type, and will travel an immense distance. It is recorded that an Englishman who was a good bowler at cricket threw a nonreturn boomerang a distance of 180 yards, while his longest throw of a cricket ball was 70 yards.

Australian boomerangs are not suitable for general recreation with groups on playgrounds and recreation centers because of the real danger of serious injury. When thrown by beginners, their return flights are most unpredictable. If thrown at all they should be used only by small groups of three or four, and those not participating should stand behind and to the right of the thrower, and keep an alert watch. Boomerangs should be thrown against the wind and in open space the size of three or four football fields put together. No one should throw with the sun directly in his eyes as he may find it impossible to follow the flight of the boomerang.

For general recreation most people prefer the lighter return-type boomerangs made of two or three sticks crossed in the middle. These are the most fun to throw and the most practical to make.

CROSS-STICK AND PINWHEEL BOOMERANGS

Cross-stick and pinwheel boomerangs are well adapted for individual and group recreation. Challenging return flights are easier to master, and the throws require less energy. Because of their lighter construction, and the relative ease of catching them on their return flights, they are much safer to operate than the heavier Australian boomerangs.

Let's make a cross-stick boomerang first. From a hardware store secure a new yardstick (gratis, since it advertises the store). Cut it in two at the eighteen-inch mark so you have two sticks each eighteen inches long. Keep one side of each stick flat. The other sides of the sticks should be made convex except for two inches at the center of each stick. In other words, the outer eight inches of the ends of each stick should be made convex or beveled. This can be done with a pocketknife or small block plane. Since the grain of the wood is not likely to be straight, be sure to work against the grain on each stroke of the knife or plane. If you work with the grain, the blade will dig the wing (each half of each stick becomes one of the four wings of the boomerang) so far it will spoil it. In making the top surfaces of the wings convex first round off the two ninety-degree angles on the top side of each wing. Take a few more strokes on the top or convex surfaces of the wings to remove any outstanding ridges or obtuse angles, and finally round off the top surfaces with sandpaper. The above procedures should leave the edges of the sides of the bottom or flat surfaces of the four wings very sharp.

Next, find the balance point of each stick. Place the sharp edge of the blade of a knife under the measured middle of one of the sticks. If it balances there, that's fine. Then try it with the other stick. If either stick or both do not balance at the measured middle (which is likely to be the case), but the heavy side teeters downward, place the stick flat on your workbench, take a light stroke with the block plane from the heavy side of the stick, and test again for balance on the knife. If still heavy, shave off a little more and test again. When it seems just about to balance, use sandpaper on the heavy side. Eventually you will get the balance point on the measured middle spot. Then at the balance points glue the two sticks together perpendicular to each other and with the convex or beveled sides up. Or you can wire the sticks together instead of using glue. One additional very important step is to bend each wing slightly upward toward the convex side at a spot two-thirds of the distance from the end of the wing to the center of the boomerang. Since each wing is nine inches long, the spot at which the wing should be bent up is six inches in from the end of the wing. To do this, hold this spot on the beveled surface of the wing directly over a lighted candle flame for a few seconds. Then place thumbs on each side of the hot spot and bend up toward the beveled surface slightly; hold a moment or so, and it will retain this bend permanently. The bend need not be more than 1/4 inch or so from the level. The cross-stick boomerang is now complete except for a paint job of your preference. An overall coat of silver varnish with a few crossing lines of black or red makes attractive designs in the air. When the boomerang is dry, try it out and see how it works.

Stand facing the wind (if not too strong) in a spot where there are no obstacles such as trees, telephone posts, wires, or houses within a radius of thirty yards. In the starting position, hold one end of a wing vertically with the right thumb and the two outer joints of the index finger so that the beveled surfaces of the sticks face inwards towards the right side of the head. The right elbow should be bent with the forearm straight upwards. Keeping the boomerang in the same plane, make a short preparatory backward swing from the elbow and wrist. Then throw the boomerang straight forward with a quick forward movement of the forearm and a forward downward snap of the wrist to get the maximum spinning action of the wings.

This motion should make the boomerang move forward and upward, then sideward to the left in a large circle, returning to a point near the thrower. If it doesn't, vary your throwing position. After many tries one can learn to throw the boomerang so it returns to the sender in a consistent pattern close enough to catch.

Next, make a pinwheel-type boomerang, using three eighteen-inch sticks instead of two. All of the same procedures are taken as were followed in making the cross-stick kind above, except that the sticks cross at sixty-degree rather than ninety-degree angles.

After making light cross-stick and pinwheel boomerangs, assemble larger and heavier ones using longer, slightly broader and thicker sticks. They should be held together with bolts, wing-nuts, and washers. Bolts 3/16 or 1/4 inch thick and 4 inches long will work well if the threaded part of each bolt is long enough. If you are making a cross-stick boomerang with 2 sticks each 1/4 inch thick, the length of the threaded end of the bolt should be 1-1/4 inches long. For making a pinwheel with 3 sticks each 1/4 inch thick, the minimum length of the threaded end of the bolt should be 1-1/2 inches. Such 4-inch bolts can be used for boomerangs with sticks 24, 30, or 36 inches long, with widths from 1-1/2 to 2-1/2 inches and thicknesses from 1/8 to 1/4 inch. The 4-inch bolts hanging down

Fig. 8-2. An assortment of cross-stick and pinwheel boomerangs. The smaller ones are glued together and the two large ones bolted and tightened with wing-nuts.—*Photo courtesy Spaulding Studio, Cortland, N.Y.*

from the centers of the boomerangs make convenient and safe handles for retrieving them after their flights. Whatever the lengths of the sticks used, remember each of the wings must be slightly bent towards the beveled surface at a point two-thirds of the distance from the end of the wing to the center of the boomerang in order to perform properly.

To retrieve a light cross-stick or pinwheel boomerang before it hits the ground, clap the palms of the hands together with one hand on top of the boomerang and the other underneath. If it is a large outdoor bolted type, catch it in the hand by the lower half of the bolt hanging down from the center of the boomerang.

If you are throwing an Australian boomerang, don't try to catch it at the end of its flight, unless you use a large fish net with heavy netting and a handle three or more feet long.

CARDBOARD BOOMERANGS

Great fun can also be had from making and throwing cardboard boomerangs as an indoor sport in a recreation room. Make the boomerangs from cardboard 1/32 inch thick or a bit thicker. Good dimensions for cross-stick and pinwheel kinds would be 9 inches for the lengths of sticks and 1 inch for the widths. The wings would then be 4-1/2 inches long and the slight bend at a point 3 inches from the end of each wing. Heating is not necessary to get the proper bend. It can be done with the hands and fingers.

A small Australian-type return boomerang with 90-degree angle can be made from cardboard 1/32 inch thick. It should be 3/8 inch wide at the ends, 3/4 inch wide at the center, and 4 inches long from end to end. Give it the proper skew on each wing and snap it off the top of the right side of a book with a pencil held vertically. To do this, have 2/3 of the righthand wing hanging over the right edge of book when wings are pointing forward.

Cardboard 3/32 inch thick (or three 1/32-inch-thick pieces of cardboard glued together) will make a fine boomerang of the same shape as the one above but the dimensions should be 3/4 inch wide at the ends, 1-1/4 inch wide at the center, and 8-3/4 to 9 inches long. This can be thrown so it will return. This boomerang should be thrown outdoors unless it is used in a playroom or gymnasium since it is heavy enough to tip something over.

CONTESTS

There are many challenging contests that can be conducted with boomerangs, and you can make up your own. Some ideas follow:

1) An accuracy throwing contest, with cross-stick type. In ten throws while standing in a circle six feet in diameter, how many times can a contestant throw and catch the boomerang on its return without stepping out of the circle? If contestants tie, have them continue an equal number of throws until one misses.

2) Same accuracy throwing contest with a pinwheel-type boomerang.

3) Longest-flying boomerang. Which contestant can keep his boomerang flying for the longest time?

4) Which contestant can make his boomerang travel the greatest distance?

5) Which contestant can make his boomerang fly in the most interesting and unique pattern?

6) Which contestant can construct the most original-looking boomerang that will return and be caught?

7) Catch contest. Which team of two contestants can throw a boomerang back and forth to each other, each one catching the other's throw on its return, the most times without "muffing"?

These contests and others could be packaged for publicity as "The First Annual Boomerang Carnival" and would be excellent special events for community parks and recreation areas, camps, Scout jamborees, etc. Of course, such events require lots of preparation. Naturally, appropriate safety measures should be observed. A schedule of stunts and contests should be made and followed, and only one event should be conducted at a time. Spectators, other than officials, should be kept out of the area to be used by the contestants.

Throwing boomerangs is a lifetime sport. The more you throw them, the more you want more of them to throw and to experiment with; so the more you construct, creating different and more effective designs.

THE TUMBLE STICK

The tumble stick is not a boomerang, but it has one characteristic in common. If properly constructed and thrown, it will come back to you. Constructing the stick so that it will return when thrown and mastering the coordination to make it come back are real challenges. The following instructions will help you to meet these challenges.

The best dimensions for the tumble stick are as follows: length of 24 inches, width of 1-1/2 inches and thickness of 1/8 inch. Choose softwood such as white pine, cedar (red

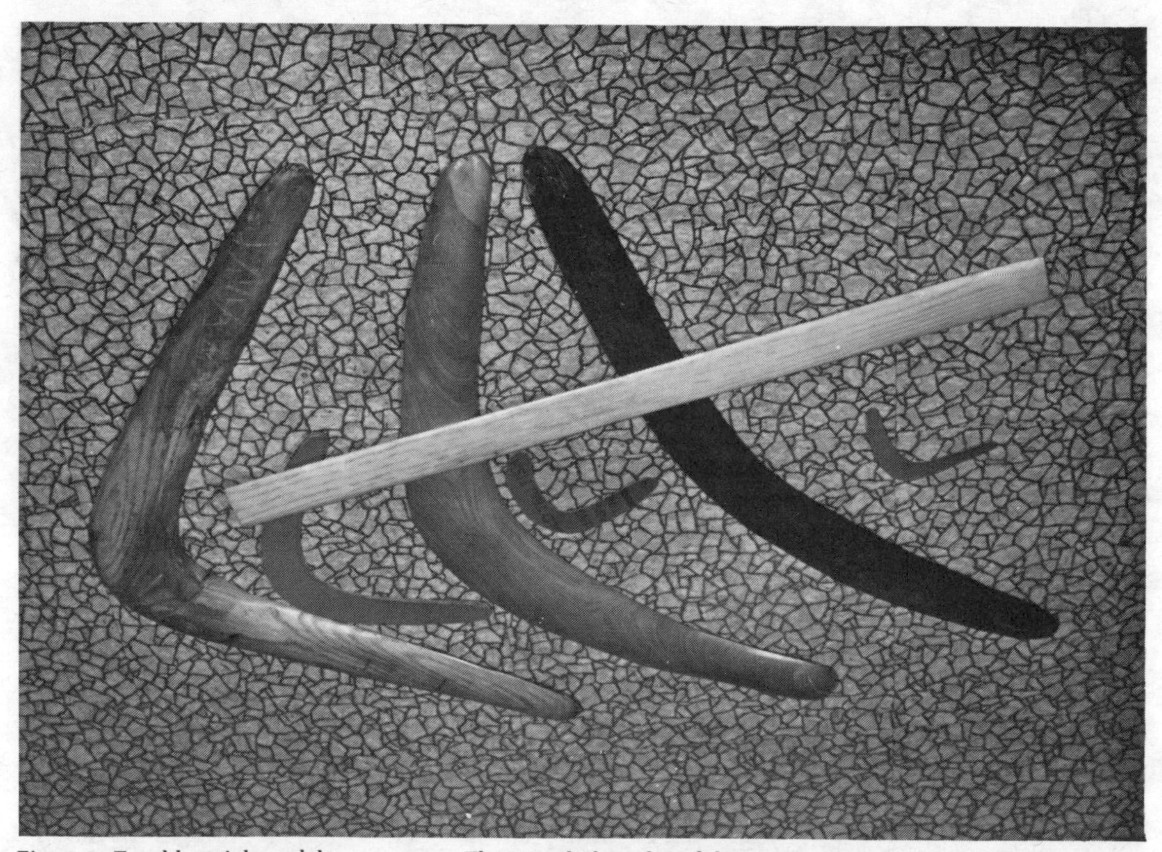

Fig. 8-3. Tumble stick and boomerangs. The two light-colored boomerangs are Australian return-type boomerangs made by the author from red oak and yellow birch. The dark boomerang is an authentic nonreturn Australian boomerang. The small boomerangs are cardboard.—*Photo courtesy Spaulding Studio, Cortland, N.Y.*

or white), poplar, or basswood, with the straightest possible grain. Keep one side of the stick flat and bevel the other side, planing or whittling off the corners of the edges of the beveled side to make them sharp.

To throw the stick, hold one end of it between the thumb and forefinger of the right hand with the beveled or convex side facing the right side of your head. Make a preliminary swing backward so that the end is behind your shoulder, and then throw it forward and upward above the level of your head. In releasing, turn the wrist sharply downward and give the stick a sidewise twist by twisting the wrist sharply inward (to your left), thus turning the hand over so that when the stick is released the palm of the hand is facing up. Actually, this wrist and finger coordination is similar to that of a baseball pitcher when throwing an "out-drop" to a righthanded batter, making the ball curve away from him and drop low. The only difference is that the baseball pitcher throws forward and downward while the tumble stick thrower starts the throw forward and upward before outward rotation or supination of the forearm followed by the downward twist of wrist and fingers, finishing with palm up.

The throw generally should be made into the wind. If the stick persists in returning to the left of you, throw into the wind but a little to the right of where you have been throwing, and if the stick persistently returns to the right of you, aim your throw a little more to the left. When properly thrown, the tumble stick goes up in the air and circles down and back to you with a humming and whirring sound. Feel like meeting the challenge?

chapter 9

Do-It-Yourself Archery Tackle: Making Your Own Bows and Arrows

MAKING A MODERN BOW WITH WORKING RECURVE TIPS, AND back and belly of sheets of fiberglass glued to a thin core of hard maple, requires more power machinery and other tools than the average person has available. However, beautiful bows from one piece of properly selected indigenous wood can be made with a minimum of hand tools and a maximum of creativity. Admittedly, the modern bow will shoot an arrow farther, and shoot target arrows faster and with less arch at longer distances than the self bows of the past. But the creative craftsmanship involved in making a self bow (one made from a single piece of wood) with hand tools is most satisfying, and a rapidly disappearing art which should not be lost. In making a modern bow, one shapes and forms its limbs by cutting them to match certain predetermined dies, then glues, smoothes, and finishes the bow. When making the bow by hand with hand tools, one studies the stave very carefully to see how and where the best possibilities for making a good bow lie within it, and which shall be the upper end of the bow. Such study will include the shape of the stave, the possibility of shortening the bow to eliminate troublesome knots, or if that would shorten the bow too much, working around the knots and leaving more wood around the knot area, and scraping the entire back of the bow-stave so that it is one and the same annular ring from end to end.

Pin-knots or other relatively small knots located not more than six inches above or below the center of the bow (handle area) will not be harmful in any way but rather will add to the beauty of the finished bow.

BEST WOODS FOR MAKING BOWS

The American Indians used the best bow woods they could find in their particular geographical area. If they lived in Oregon they would probably use yew, although it was and is very hard to find a piece of yew straight and long enough to make a good self bow. (Most of the yew bows made in this country and elsewhere were made from two half-staves glued together at the handle.) In southern California, bamboo would be considered, as it might also be considered in Florida and many of the southeastern states. When the French first came down the Mississippi towards Louisiana and got as far south as Tennessee and Arkansas, they found the Indians using for their bows a very tough and beautiful brown-colored wood we know as Osage orange. The French called it *bois d'arc* (wood of the arch), from which the popular name bodark comes.

In Tennessee, Indians used the juniper or red cedar as well as Osage orange. The best cedars for bow wood came from Lebanon, Tennessee (probably so named because of the cedars there and the biblical reference to the cedars of Lebanon). The cedars in this area grow very slowly because of the limestone rock in the soil. In a single tree there might be counted one hundred or more annular rings in the space of an inch of wood. As regards red cedar, its close relative, yew, and other coniferous woods, the greater the number of annular rings packed into a space of wood the better the bow one can make from the wood. However, if one is making a bow from nonconiferous or broad-leafed woods, just the opposite is true. The broader the annular ring or the fewer the number of annular rings per square inch in the bow-stave, the better the bow that can be made therefrom.

Indians in the northern United States and Canada would choose from the following woods: black locust, shagbark hickory, white ash, and ironwood. Hickory and ironwood make bows that last a long time, but they tend to "follow the string," i.e., take a permanent bend towards the string, thus gradually weakening the bow.

Following, listed in descending order of preference, is the author's rating of the best bow woods to be found in the United States.

Osage orange
Yew
Tennessee red cedar
Bamboo
Black locust
Ironwood
Hickory (shagbark species)
White ash
Sassafras

Some authorities would probably rate yew above Osage orange. Spanish yew gained its long-lasting popularity in the days of British supremacy in archery. The best wood for bows native to England was the English elm. The majority of the longbows of English yeomen were made of this wood. However, the cast and efficiency of bows made of Spanish yew far surpassed bows made from English elm. In fact, the English traded as many as ten to twelve staves of English elm for only one stave of Spanish yew. However, it is likely that had the English known about Osage orange and been able to obtain it, they would have used it, and Spanish yew would not have been given such play. Osage orange would have made a very superior war bow. Some of the advantages of bows made from Osage orange over those made from yew are:

1) Well-seasoned Osage orange bows are much more durable.

2) They are better able to stand moisture.

3) They do not break as easily, and when they do start to break, one hears a warning crack first. If one stops bending the bow quickly and serves the cracked area with good cord or baling wire, the bow will continue to serve quite effectively for years.

4) They do not weaken as much as yew does in the hot sun.

5) Their cast is practically as good as that of yew bows and sometimes better.

6) A bow-stave of Osage orange has wider annular rings, which make it easier to follow the grain while making the bow.

The reader may wonder why lemonwood (dagame) was not mentioned in the list of bow woods. Lemonwood was imported from Cuba and has not been available since Castro took over. If it were available, the author would rate it about sixth, almost on a par with black locust.

The procedures for making a simple self bow described herein apply to all native bow woods, especially those from broad-leafed trees (Osage orange, black locust, iron-wood, hickory, white ash, and sassafras). The trees to be used for bow-staves should be cut in the fall, when they contain the least amount of sap. The logs should be straight, at least 5 or 6 inches in diameter, 5-1/2 to 6-1/2 feet long, and split into 4 or more bow-staves, depending on the diameter of the tree. Occasionally 6 to 8 or more staves can be secured from a single log.

The staves should be split out immediately after the log has been cut so that in the seasoning or curing process each stave will bend toward the bark (because of evaporation of water from the sapwood), making the bark surface of the stave concave. This concavity on the bark or back surface of the stave will make a bow that has more cast than a bow made from a straight stave. Strip off the bark of each stave to prevent beetles and other insects from boring under it into the sapwood. Next, coat each stave with a heavy layer of shellac, varnish, or paint, which will help to prevent checking at the ends and sides of the stave. Then stand the staves up against the wall bark side out and heartwood side in towards the wall in a shed, barn, or garage where the seasoning can take place with the temperature the same as it would be outdoors. Season all bow woods at least nine months before using them. The longer the seasoning process the better the cast of the bow in most cases.

Incidentally, when splitting out a stave, one should start at the upper (smaller-diametered) end with the line of the cut keeping in the pith or middle of the log from one end to the other. After the first split one should have two half-logs each with a semispherical cross-section. Then split each of the half-logs into quarter-logs, always splitting through the pith all the way down. If the quarter-logs are four inches wide or more, split through the pith of each quarter-log, again all the way down, making two staves each at least 2 inches wide on the back surface. Splitting it this way will bring out the beauty of the medullary rays on both sides of the finished bow. The medullary rays in oak furniture are what make it so beautiful. They certainly add to the beauty of an Osage orange bow.

TOOLS NEEDED

Tools needed for making the bow include the following: axe, sledge hammer, iron wedges, ruler, pencil, chalk line, soft chalk, tiller, drawknife, pocketknife, scraper, wood rasps (rough, medium, and fine), a small rat-tail file, sandpaper (rough, medium, and very fine), steel wool size 00 or finer, and a finish.

The best scrapers can be made from the back edges of hacksaw blades. Bend a blade into a U shape, hold the back surface of the bent blade tightly against a flat carborundum stone, and give it many circular motions until the two edges of the blade are very sharp—like a skate. With this kind of scraper one can scrape two ways, forward and backward.

For the fine wood rasp an iron file can be used. The rat-tail file is used to make the upper and lower nocks or notches on the bow, into which the string loops fit. The finish may be two coats of clear spar varnish, a French finish, or whatever you prefer.

MAKING THE BOW

After selecting a well-seasoned stave, the first step in making a bow is to decide which surface will be the back. This is easy since the back should always be what used to be the outside of the log or bark side. If split immediately after cutting and allowed to season long enough (one or more years), this side will be concave.

A few bow woods—particularly Tennessee red cedar, Oregon or Washington yew, black locust, and Osage orange—have a marked color difference between the sapwood and the heartwood. Red cedar, for example, has red heartwood and white sapwood; yew has a light amber tan or brownish heartwood and white sapwood, while Osage orange has a beautiful brown heartwood and a whitish tan sapwood. Incidentally, the longer one keeps an Osage bow or stave the darker and more beautiful it becomes on the surface exposed to air. These contrasting colors enable one to use the white or light sapwood for the back of the bow and the heartwood for the belly or face of the bow. Osage orange bows are usually made of heartwood alone since these generally have a slightly better cast than if made with both sapwood and heartwood, and are plenty durable. However, cedar and yew bows with some white sapwood left on the bow for backing do not break so often as they would if made entirely from heartwood. In bow woods the heartwood stands up better under the strain of compression, and the sapwood better withstands the strain of stretching.

Place the bow-stave in a large wooden vise back side up. The vise should be well anchored to the floor so it will not be jerked about while you work with a drawknife or rasp. The first step is to decide how much, if any, of the light sapwood is to be left on the back of the bow, and therefore how many, if any, annular rings of wood must be scraped off. If you want as much sapwood as possible on the bow's back, carefully scrape the varnish or paint off the back, not taking any of the sapwood except a small part of the outer annular ring. If you want only two rings of sapwood on the back of the bow, take off with drawknife or spokeshave all sapwood down to the annular ring which will be the outside of the back of the bow (the spokeshave is safer but slower than the knife). Do not dig too deep. The last annular ring above what is to be the back should be sparingly removed (all but a paper-thin layer). Remove this last thin layer or patches of it from one end of the back of the bow to the other by a scraper, to save going too far with a drawknife.

The next step is to block out the bow with chalk and pencil. See that the ends of the stave are unchecked and square. If not, square them by cutting off the smallest amount necessary with a hacksaw. Measure to find the middle of the stave and draw a line across the back at the exact center. Draw additional lines across the back at the following points: five inches below the center line, three inches below the center line, one inch above the center line, three inches above the center line, and five inches above the center line. The ten inches in the middle of the bow should not bend at all. The area from one inch above the center line to three inches below it will be the site of the handle, and the upper two inches of this area will be the location of the arrow rest, the arrow plate, and the window when the bow is complete.

Place a line down the center of the back of the stave from end to end. This is the reference line which is essential in making a straight bow. *If* one had a perfectly straight and square stave six feet long, two inches wide, and two inches deep, the sides of the bow at every point along its length would be exactly one inch from the center reference line (see Fig. 9-1). However, when making a bow from native woods, this will rarely be the case. Therefore the center reference line must be made with a chalk line (use the dark-colored chalk so it shows up well against the wood). First use a trial unchalked line in order to determine where on the back at the ends of the stave the chalk line ends must be tightly held. Hold the trial string tightly roughly parallel to the long axis of the stave but so that it crosses the exact middle of the first line made. At the same time this trial string should also cross the edges of both ends of the stave at points which will yield the greatest amount of wood on both sides of the center line of reference for a straight bow. Then mark

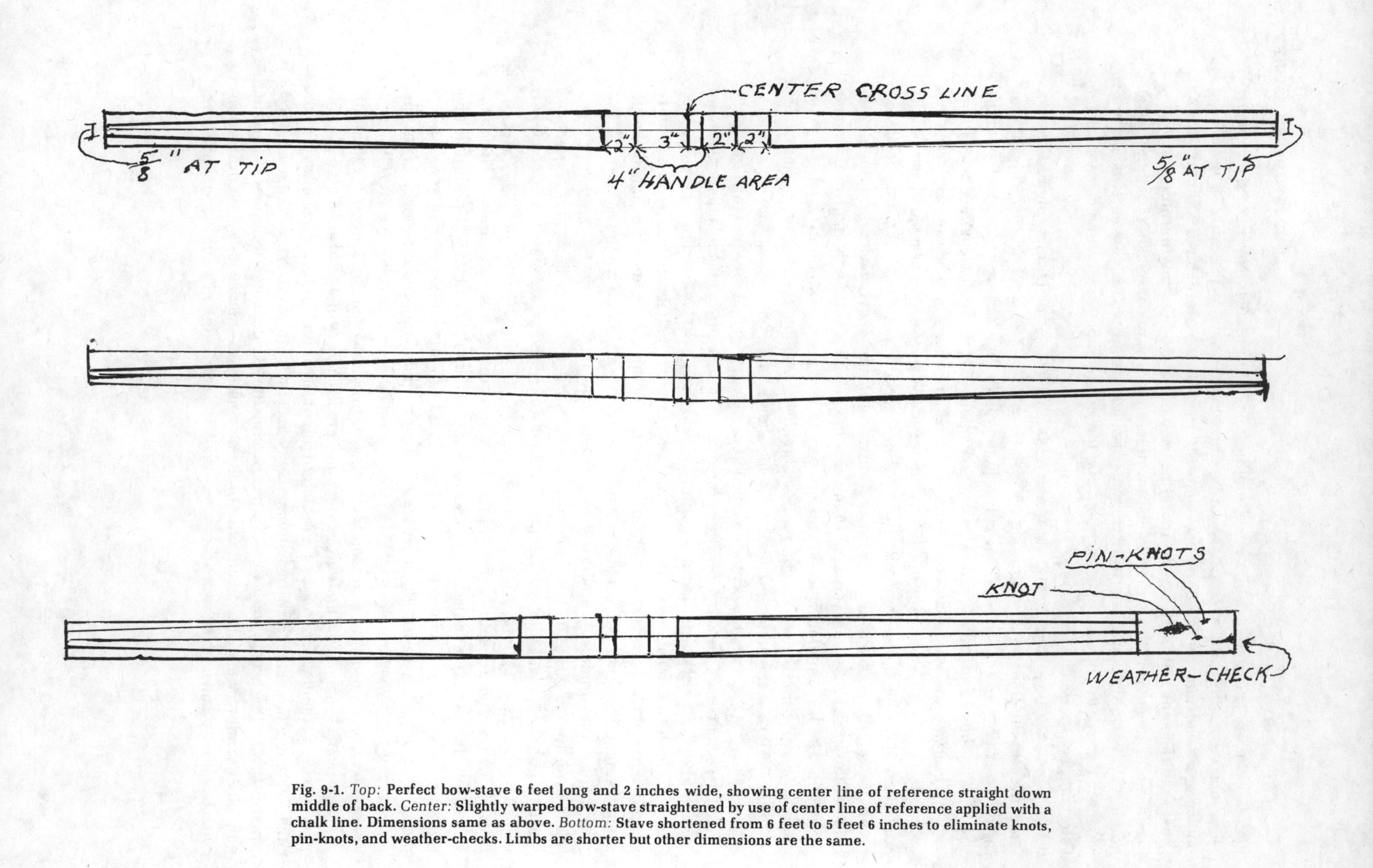

Fig. 9-1. *Top:* Perfect bow-stave 6 feet long and 2 inches wide, showing center line of reference straight down middle of back. *Center:* Slightly warped bow-stave straightened by use of center line of reference applied with a chalk line. Dimensions same as above. *Bottom:* Stave shortened from 6 feet to 5 feet 6 inches to eliminate knots, pin-knots, and weather-checks. Limbs are shorter but other dimensions are the same.

with pencil a dot at the edges of both ends of the stave where the trial string crosses them. Now, holding a well-chalked line tightly over these three points (middle of center line of bow and the dots at each end of the bow-stave), have someone carefully pull the chalk line at its middle a few inches away from the back of the stave and let it snap back onto the stave, leaving a perfectly straight line down the back of the bow which is the reference line from which all other lines must be measured outwards (see Fig. 9-1).

At the ends of the 6-inch central section of the stave measure out from the line of reference 1/2 inch each side of the line and make a dot. Connect these dots with horizontal 6-inch lines, making a rectangle in the middle of the stave 6 inches long and 1 inch wide. Moving out from each end of this rectangle, measure 2 inches (or 5 inches from the cross center line) and make dots 3/4 inch outwards from the line of reference at both the spot 5 inches above the cross center line and the spot 5 inches below the cross center line. Then proceed as follows for both halves of the bow. On both sides of the line of reference draw 2 slanting lines connecting the last dots made with the dots at either end of the 6-inch rectangle. This will make the width of the embryonic bow a total of 1-1/2 inches for both the upper and lower limbs at points 5 inches up and down from the cross center line; from these points the width tapers inward to the corners of the 6-inch rectangle, which has a width of 1 inch throughout. (see Fig. 9-2).

Now, at each of the two ends of the stave, measure out from the center line of reference 5/16 inch on both sides and place dots (a total of 4). With lines connect the two dots on one end of the stave with the two dots representing the widest part of the limb on the corresponding half. Similarly draw these tapering lines on the other half of the bow (see Fig. 9-2). The total width of the ends of each bow limb will be 5/8 inch. In making the four long tapering lines, it is best to use the convexly bowed edge of a slightly warped yardstick, if you have one, as it makes for a bow of more graceful lines. If the yardstick is perfectly straight on both sides, you can make the sides straight.

The major outline of the bow is now complete. The next step is to remove the excess wood outside the lines. In doing this do not approach the guidelines too closely, but rather leave a 1/16-inch layer all round the outline which can later and more safely be removed with a wood file or rasp (medium rough first and then fine). The best tool for taking off large amounts of the excess wood is a sharp drawknife with the bevelled side down. Remove the wood on the sides of the limbs first, working from the broadest part of the limbs down to the tips. To take off the wood on each side of the central 10-inch section of the bow, start with a hacksaw or hacksaw blade and make the following cuts across the grain and at right angles to the horizontal lines of reference: a cut from the outside edges of the stave to each of the four dots which were placed 3/4 inch out from the line of reference and 5 inches up and down from the cross center line (this makes 4 cuts approximately 1/4 inch long). Make 4 more cuts from edge of bow-stave to corners of the 6-inch rectangular section 1/2 inch away from line of reference. These cuts are approximately 1/2 inch long (see Fig. 9-2). In removing the excess wood from one side of the 10-inch central area, place it in the vise with the other side down. Place the drawknife with bevel side down close to the far end of the 6-inch rectangular section in middle and

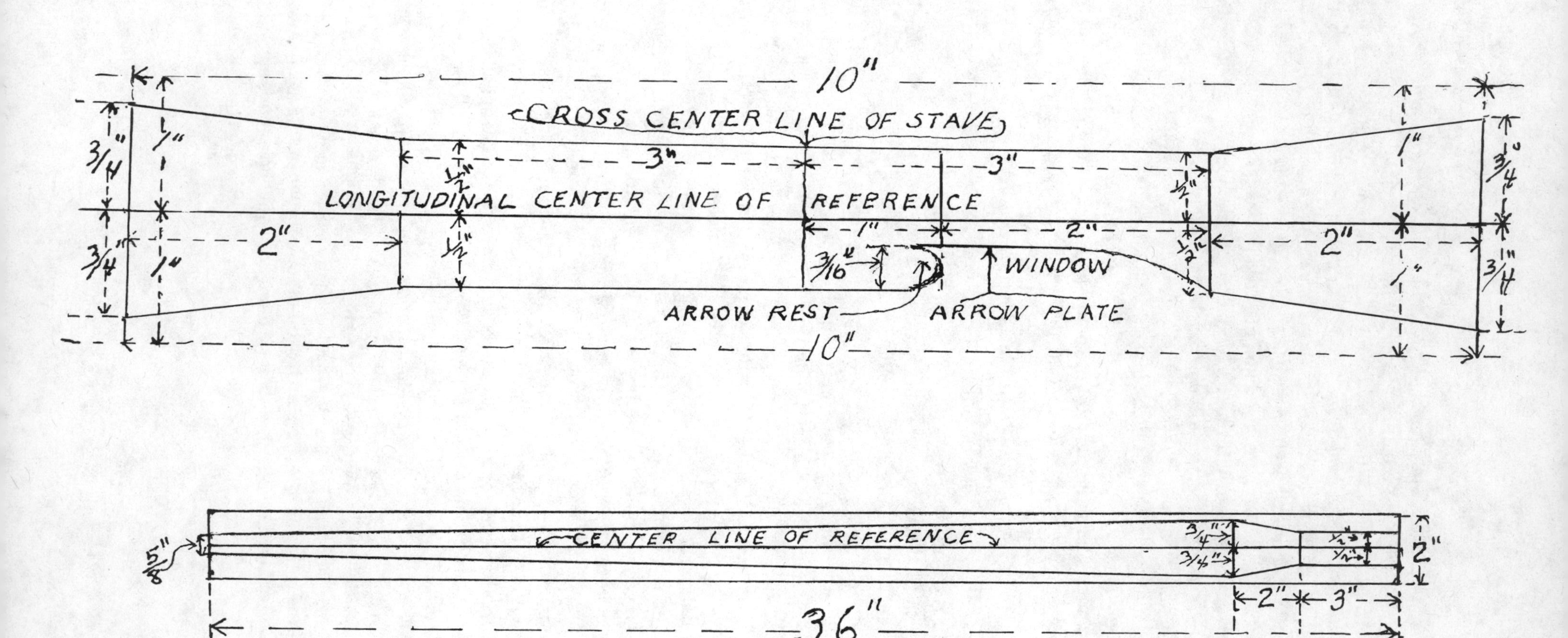

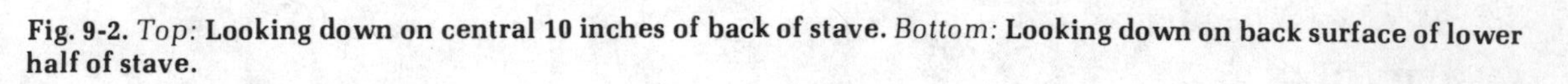

Fig. 9-2. *Top:* **Looking down on central 10 inches of back of stave.** *Bottom:* **Looking down on back surface of lower half of stave.**

draw the knife toward the near saw cut of this section, taking out a good slice of wood. Be careful that the knife stops at this near cut. Make continued slices of wood until you reach the base of this cut. Then reverse the stave end for end and remove slices of wood from the center 6-inch area until you reach the base of the other cut at the other end of the 6-inch area. It is difficult to remove the wood in this area close to the guideline in the middle; so finish this wood off with a medium wood file or rasp so the surface from the base of one cut to the base of the other in this 6-inch area is flat and smooth. Turn the bow-stave over in the vise, and remove wood on the opposite side the same way. Next remove the excess wood outside the lines going from the dots 3/4 inch from the line of reference and 5 inches from the cross center line, to the base of the near cut of the 6-inch rectangle. Start the drawknife, slicing slender chips of wood off from the far end of the 10-inch area (which will be the widest part of the future bow), drawing the knife towards you. Continue this removal of wood until you are right on the guideline going to the near cut of the far end of the rectangle, or within 1/16 inch of the line (so you can smooth down to this line with a file). Reverse bow-stave end for end and in same manner remove wood from the other end of the 5-inch area to the base of the cut at the now near end of the 6-inch rectangle. Turn the other side of bow-stave up and remove the wood with drawknife and file as was done before. The stave begins to look a bit more like a bow now. The next step is to take off the excess wood on the face or belly sides of the upper and lower limbs (parts of bow outside of the 6-inch rectangular area). First, place the bow on its side and sketch some guidelines (see Fig. 9-3). With bow lying on its left side, measure 2 inches out (both left and right) from the bottom ends of the 6-inch rectangular area and put dots on the base line. From each of these dots measure upwards and perpendicular to the base line a distance of 5/8 inch and place dots. From these dots make curved lines up to the top ends of the 6-inch rectangular area. These curves represent arcs with a radius of 4-3/16 inches.

At each end of the 6-foot bow-stave and on both sides measure upwards 1/2 inch from its base line and place a dot. Now connect each of these dots with the dots at the lower ends of the curves which are 5/8 inch from the base line. The wood above this line is excess and should be removed with a drawknife, spokeshave, or plane. This surface after the wood has been removed becomes the belly or the face of the bow, and the curved parts above and below the 6-inch handle area are called the dips. The part below the lower or lefthand dip will be called the lower limb. Likewise, the part above or to the right of the righthand dip will be called the upper limb. The bow is beginning to take more shape now, but it still has to be scraped on the face (never the back) to bring it down to the bow strength that the user of the bow can handle effectively; then it must be tillered properly, and finally finished (sandpapered, steel-wooled, and given two coats of clear spar varnish).

The scraping should be done one limb at a time with the face or belly surface up. In removing the wood above the curves or dips the drawknife should be used carefully, taking only a very little wood at a time. Follow this with a fine wood rasp to round the sharp edges. For scraping wood from the long straight upper surface or face use the back

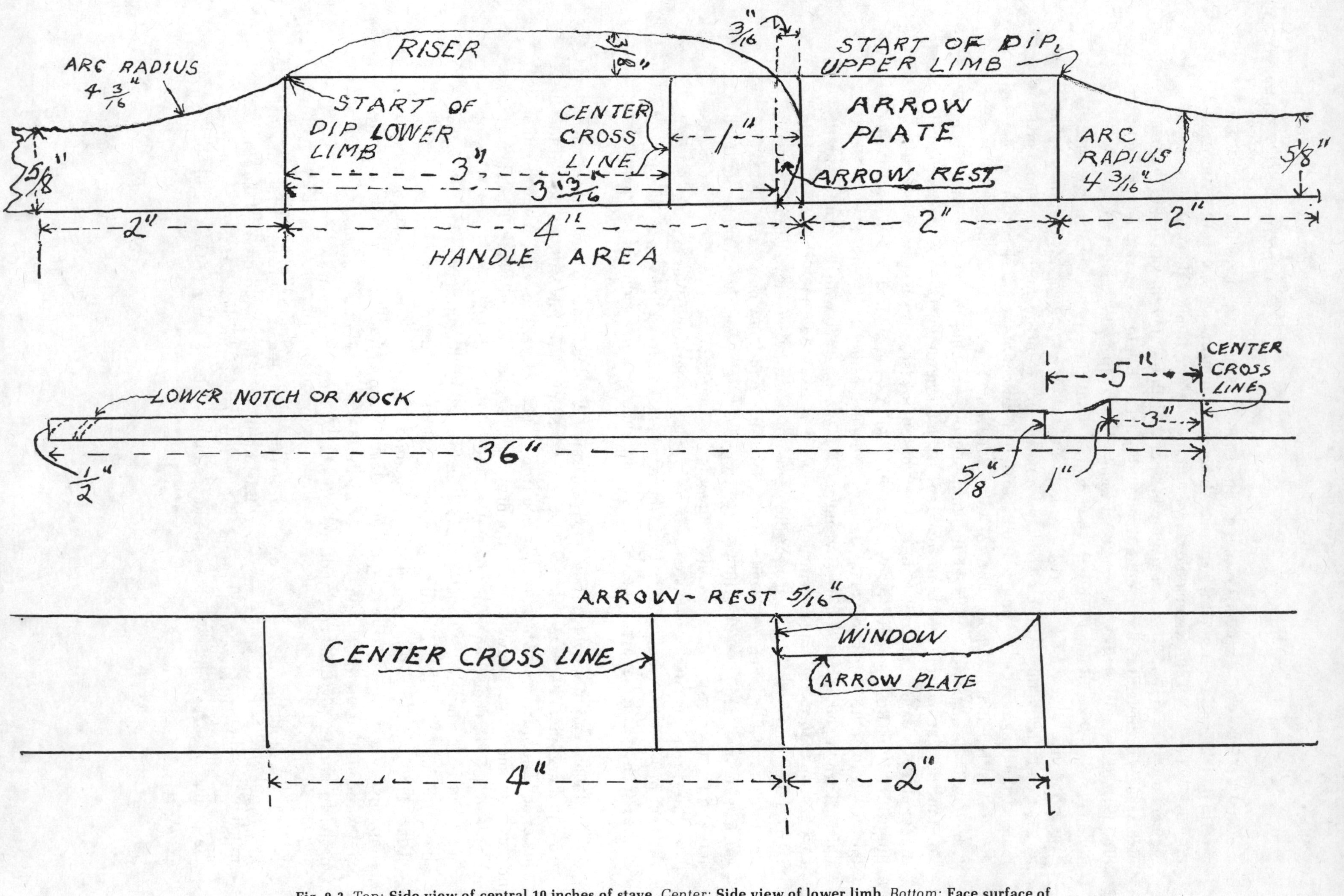

Fig. 9-3. *Top:* **Side view of central 10 inches of stave.** *Center:* **Side view of lower limb.** *Bottom:* **Face surface of handle area of righthanded bow.**

surface of a hacksaw blade which has been sharpened like the undersurface of a skate, so that there are two sharp edges rather than just one as in the case of a knife. One way to sharpen the hacksaw blade is to bend it into a **U** shape and, holding it back down against and perpendicular to a large flat carborundum stone, move it around on the stone in circular fashion. Then with long downward and upward strokes of the blade, take long shavings of wood off with each stroke. Before taking too much wood off the face of the bow, make notches, one at each end of the bow to hold the loops of the bowstring in place, so the bow can be tillered.

The size and design of the tips and notches at the ends of a bow are really a matter of individual creativity. However, a satisfactory design for the tips and notches will be suggested. From the end of a limb on the face surface draw a cross line perpendicular to the long axis of the bow one inch from the end of the bow. On the corner edge where the back and side surface meet, measure 5/8 inch from the end of bow on each side and place a dot. On the sides of the end of the bow draw lines between this dot and the near edge of the cross line one inch from the end of bow. Place on this slanting line a small rat-tail file and rub back and forth exactly on the line until a straight groove is made at a depth of half the diameter of the round file. Duplicate this process and groove on the opposite side of this end of the bow, and in the same manner make grooves or notches at the other end of the bow. It also helps to file (with the same file) grooves on the face surface extending from the side grooves which may almost meet like an arrow or **V** neck. These grooves should not be deep except where the upper parts of the side grooves swing over the edges onto the face of the bow. A small amount of the end of the bow on the face surface may be cut off with a hacksaw, filed with a fine flat file, and rounded or perhaps pointed, according to the wish of the bowyer (see Fig. 9-4).

Now that the notches have been made, a superstrong tillering string can be placed on the face side of the bow connecting the two notches, but with little or no tension on the string. Tillering is the process of gradually getting both limbs of the bow to match in pattern, when bent under various tensions, and to get each limb to share equally in the work at all points. A simply made tiller aids this process. Take a piece of wood about a yard long, 4 inches wide, and 2 inches thick. Square both ends. In one end cut out a semicircle about 1-1/4 inches in diameter. On one side cut triangular notches an inch apart, making the first one 12 inches from the end with the semicircle, and the last one 28 inches from this end. The upper surface of all the notches should be flat and perpendicular to the long axis of the stick or tiller (see Fig. 9-5).

On the upper end of the tiller on the 2-inch-wide sides mark downward from the end a heavy vertical line about 2-1/2 inches long exactly in the middle. Now to use the tiller. Place the middle of the bow, face surface down and back up, in the semicircular hole at top end of tiller so that the cross center line of the bow coincides exactly with the vertical line marking the center of the upper end of the side of the tiller. Now grasp the center of the tillering string with both hands and draw it down and place it under the first notch in the tiller. If the limbs on either side of the tiller seem stiff (as they probably will) and with little if any bend, take the bow out of the tiller, remove the string, and, using

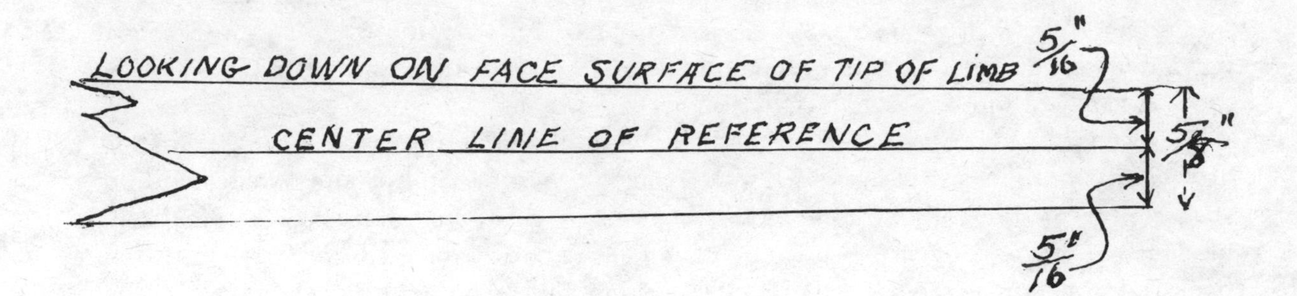

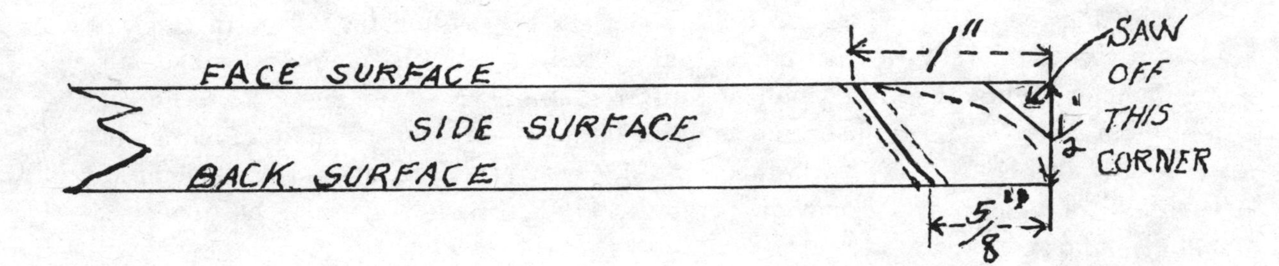

SIDE VIEW OF FINISHED TIP AND NOCK

1/2"

FACE VIEW OF FINISHED TIP AND NOCK

Fig. 9-4. Details of tip end of bow limb.

wooden vise and scraper, take off 15 or 20 long shavings from the face surface. Then put the bow on the tiller again and see how the pattern has changed and how much weaker the limbs may have become. This tillering process is a very long and tedious one involving constant scraping and tillering. As the bow gets weaker, gradually pull the string down to lower notches, and pay particular attention to getting the pattern of bend or arcs of both limbs to match. There frequently will be a stiff part of a limb on one side and a spot on the other limb that bends too much. In this case mark the surface of the stiff area with pencil, take it out of the tiller quickly so the weakness in the other limb will not get worse, and take more long strokes with the scraper on the the stiff pencilled area. Eventually you must get both limbs to match with each carrying the same amount of strain. If there is a noticeable bend or weak spot in one limb and not in the other, the bow will eventually break at that spot. When you are able to hook the tillering string under the 25- or 26-inch notch and find the limbs matching properly, you have nearly finished the bow. Now put on a new string of proper strength, and draw it back several times at only half or three-fourths of the full draw (which for most adults would be 28 inches) in order to break in the bow gradually, and see whether it is about the strength it should be for the user. When this point is reached, take the string off the bow, slightly round all sharp edges of the bow, and remove all file marks made by coarse files with finer files. Follow this with medium sandpaper, then very fine sandpaper, and finally the finest steel wool. The steel wool will remove very small slivers of wood on the surface of the bow almost too small to see or feel. These should be rubbed with the finest sandpaper until no fibers of steel wool catch in them.

One other additional process is recommended; that of putting a window on the bow with special arrow rest and arrow plate. If a person is righthanded, the window should be placed on the left side of the bow (lefthanded archers should place the window on the right side of the bow). To block out the area to be removed in making the window place the bow in the vise back side up and sketch the following guidelines on what is now the right side of the edge of the back of the bow near the center. On the cross line one inch above the center cross lone (which marks the upper end of the handle area) make a dot 5/16 inch in from the righthand edge of the back of the bow. From this point run a vertical line upwards a distance of 1-3/8 inches and place a dot. From this point make a gradual curved line upwards and out to meet the righthand edge of the back of the bow at a distance two inches above the upper end of the bow handle. To remove the wood in the window, cut with a hacksaw the righthand edge of the back of the bow on the cross line at the top of the handle area the outlined distance of 5/16 inch. Then with bow in vise with window side up, starting on the outside edge two inches above the handle and at the top of the curve, use the drawknife most carefully to remove wood in this window area a little at a time. Rather than cut too close to the guideline at the inner edge of the window, leave about 1/16 inch of wood to be taken off with files that are flat on one side and rounded on the other (to make the curve at the top smooth). Then finish as before with sandpaper and steel wool to bring out the beautiful medullary rays, etc.

Any desired finish can be used on the bow. Some bowyers might prefer to stain it a

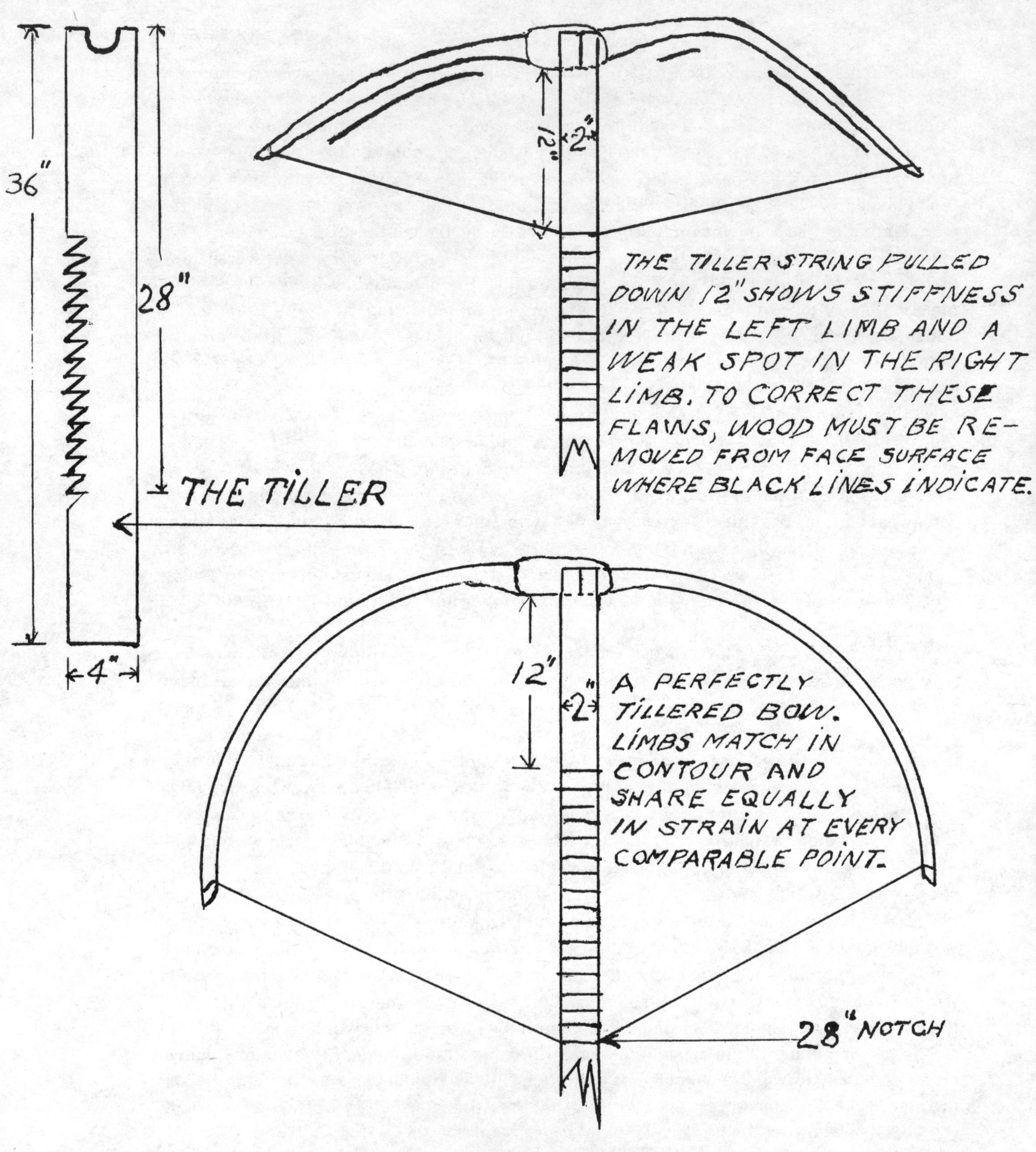

Fig. 9-5. Use of the tiller.

particular color before finishing with French finish or varnish. The author, however, prefers no stain if the wood is as beautiful as Osage orange, red cedar, or yew, but recommends using two coats of clear spar varnish, with a light application of the finest sandpaper between coats after the first coat is perfectly dry. On the shelf representing the arrow rest you can place one of several varieties of commercial arrow rests, or with contact cement glue on a small fitted piece of animal fur, with the hair lying forward in the direction the arrow will be shot.

To complete the handle, you can serve the 4-inch handle area with plain or colored cord or hand-laid basswood or other Amerindian cord, not over 3/16 inch in diameter; or you can shape a small piece of softwood 4 inches long and 3/8 inch in diameter with the outside end and side corners rounded, and the flat side glued to the back side of the handle area of the bow. This piece of wood is called the riser. A small piece of top-grain plain or colored leather can be neatly glued over the whole handle area as one type of bow-handle finish. Another type can be made by gluing and spirally wrapping a long strip of good leather 1/4 to 1/2 inch in width over the handle area.

THE SINGLE-LOOP BOWSTRING WITH FLEMISH LOOP

There are two kinds of bowstrings: the single-loop string and the double-loop string. The latter is most often used at the present time, and is probably more efficient in a target bow. However, the single-loop string is easier to adjust to a new bow, and easier to tighten when stretched. Both types will be described, beginning with the single-loop bowstring.

Materials Needed

From an archery tackle supplier purchase a quarter-pound spool of dacron bowstring thread. From a farmer raising bees and selling honey buy a pound or more of pure beeswax. If you cannot locate a bee farmer, go to a drug store and purchase six or more cakes of beeswax and a pint or quart box of powdered rosin. If you can only get lump rosin, get that, and with a hammer, pound it into roughly powdered form. The last two items are essential to make a good quality of bowyer's wax for dressing the bowstring and keeping it in good condition.

Making Bowyer's Wax

Get a clean empty tin can (size no. 10 or a little smaller). Break up the beeswax into pieces the size of sugar cubes or smaller (use an old screwdriver or ice pick) and put into the tin can. Then pour into the can the powdered rosin in an amount one-fifth as much by bulk as the amount of beeswax already in the can. Place the can of wax and rosin on a hot-plate heater down in the cellar or in the garage, where the fumes will not smell up the kitchen. As the material gets hotter both the wax and rosin will melt. After they have melted, mix them together well with a small stick. Then arrange six or more small wax-paper cups in a line on some old boards or plenty of newspapers, and, using a pair of pliers to grip the upper edge of the very hot tin can, pour the melted material into the paper cups, filling each cup only a third full. If it is wintertime, place the cups outdoors in the snow if present; if not, place the cups in the coolest possible place to speed up the hardening process. When the material is hard, tear off the paper of the cup completely, and you will have little cakes of top-quality bowyer's wax—enough to make or dress scores of bowstrings.

Strengths of Bowstrings

Bowstrings are of different strengths and diameters according to the different purposes they serve. If the string is to be used on a target bow, it should be of medium weight and strength (the bow should have a drawing weight no more than thirty-five pounds at a draw of twenty-eight inches). If it is for a roving and hunting bow, a bow with drawing weight up to fifty pounds or more at a twenty-eight-inch draw, it should be heavier and stronger. If the string is to be used on a flight bow, designed to shoot a flight arrow the greatest possible distance, the string should be much lighter in weight and weaker in tensile strength, so that it creates the least possible amount of wind resistance when it is released. Also, this light string means that all the power possible to muster from the bow is used in propelling the arrow, rather than moving a heavy string.

Making the String

Using the rough wooden wall of a garage or barn, or a rough board eight or more feet long, drive two large nails into the wall or board separated by a distance of twelve inches more than the tip-to-tip length of the bow for which the string will be used.

There are different diameters of threads used for bowstrings, and generally printed directions are included with each 1/4-pound spool of dacron bow-thread to tell one how many thread diameters are needed for bows of different drawing weights (the drawing weight of a bow is the number of pounds pressure registered on a scales when the latter is hooked onto a strung bowstring and pulled out to a distance of twenty-eight inches). If the above directions are not included, the following procedure for determining the correct number of thicknesses of thread for any given bow will prove quite satisfactory.

Take an eight-foot length of bowstring thread and double it back at the middle (making two thicknesses four feet long). Double the two thicknesses back at the middle and you have four thicknesses of thread two feet long. Double the four thicknesses back at the middle and you have eight thicknesses one foot long. Double the eight thicknesses back at the middle again, and you have sixteen thicknesses six inches long. Hold one end of this bunch securely with thumb and index finger of the left hand (lefthanded readers should follow these directions in reverse). With right thumb and index finger grasp the other end of the bunch of sixteen thread thicknesses and twist up tightly clockwise into the semblance of a smooth, round cord. If this section of cord fits easily into the groove or nock of the arrows you will be using, you have the approximate correct number of thread thicknesses for the bowstring. However, since in making a single-loop string one needs a number of thicknesses that can be divided by three, take one thickness away from the sixteen, leaving fifteen, which, divided by three, is five; so you can make a bowstring with three strands of five thicknesses each. If you desire a larger and stronger string, add two more thicknesses of string to the sixteen to make eighteen; in this case, the string made will contain three strands each with six thicknesses. A satisfactory bowstring for a target bow can be made from twelve thicknesses, and one for a flight bow with nine thicknesses. To make the bowstring fit the nock of the arrow properly, serve the string with more thread over the four- to six-inch area which will contain the nocking point until the diameter of the string is large enough to fit the nock so tightly that it will hold the weight of the arrow suspended therefrom.

How to Make a Bowstring of Fifteen Thicknesses

Coming back to the two big nails driven into the board, tie the end of the dacron thread from the spool to the nail on the left. Then carry the thread to the right and wind it over the nail at the right, go over it and around back under and on top of the left nail and take it back over and around the right nail and then back once more around the left nail and back finally to the right nail; then tie it off with three or four half-hitches to hold all of these five thicknesses of thread together. With a cake of bowyer's wax rub the whole length of the five thicknesses into one strand.

With a sharp knife cut off this strand flush with the lefthand nail, and let it hang down from the righthand nail. Make two more waxed strands of five thicknesses each just as was done to make the first one. Next cut off all three strands flush with the righthand nail. Then taper one end of each of the three waxed strands as follows: with left hand hold one strand so that two inches of it protrudes out to the right; place this on a cutting board. With the right hand place the sharp blade of a pocketknife on the strand about one and a half inches from the end. Bear down with the blade lightly but with pressure enough to hold strand on board snugly. With your left hand draw the strand to the left under the knifeblade; a certain amount of fuzz from the threads and some wax will be scraped off. With right thumb and index finger grasp the scraped area of the strand. Stretch it out and, with added wax, twist it out to a point to see if it is tapering nicely. If not, put it under the knifeblade again and carefully draw off some more fuzz. Straighten the end out again to see if it tapers gradually. Continue drawing off fuzz and molding the waxed end of string until a good taper is secured. Taper each of the other two strands in the same way. Now put the three strands together so that the tapered ends are flush with each other. Measure back from the tapered tips a distance of eight inches; hold all three strands tightly together at this point, while you start what is called the hand-laying process of making a Flemish loop.

Maintaining a tight hold with left thumb and index finger on the three waxed strands at the point 8 inches from the tapered tips, with right thumb and index finger grasp the top or first eight-inch piece of strand you come to at a point 1/4 inch or less from where the left fingers are holding all three strands. Give the strand one good clockwise twist, and lay it down on top of the other two strands into the pinch of the left fingers and tucked snugly under the tip of the left thumb. At the same time the upper tip of the left index finger is pushing up the next strand in sequence, which is then grasped by the right thumb and index finger 1/4 inch or less from the grip of the left fingers, twisted clockwise, and laid down on top of the other two strands and snugly under the tip of the left thumb while the upper end of the left index finger pushes up the next or third strand. The process is repeated with the third strand and then with all three strands in the same order as before. As this hand-laying process continues, an ever lengthening twisted cord appears under the left hand and to the left of the pinching fingers, and the three strands keep getting shorter. When the cord attains a length of three inches, stop and bend the three-inch area at its middle back on itself 180 degrees to make a loop. Hold this loop under the left hand, and with the thumb and index finger tightly hold the two ends of the three-inch corded area so that protruding out to the right of the pinching fingers are six strand tips: three very short tapered end tips and three very long ends, which are very nearly six feet long. Now with right hand place each short strand with a different long strand. Pinch and stroke them together as one with the wax that is on them; use more wax if needed. You now have a loop on the left end, and at the base of the loop three larger strands extend out to the right. Now, holding the base of the loop, where the three strands begin, with index finger and thumb of the left hand, grasp the top strand close to the left fingers with right thumb and index finger. Pinch the strand, give it one good clockwise twist, and, as before, lay it on top of the other two strands and tuck its base under the tip of the left thumb as the upper end of the left index finger pushes up the next strand to be grasped by the right fingers for a good clockwise twist. This hand-laying process continues taking the strands in proper sequence, resulting at first in a large even cord but then tapering gradually to a smaller-diametered cord as the three tapered tips disappear into the main body of the cord with the same diameter as the loop part of the string. Continue hand-laying these three long strands for at least two inches beyond the point at which the ends of the three short tips disappeared (see Fig. 9-6).

Next place the loop over one of the nails (if it is in a solid stable position, as on a wall), and wind a piece of tape 2 inches long and about 1/8 inch wide several turns tightly around the last 1/8 inch that was hand-laid, to keep the strands from unwinding. Now take hold of the ends of the long strands and pull them out straight to secure equal pressure on each of the strands. Holding this tension with the right hand, grasp the string with the left thumb and index finger at a point one foot from the end where the right hand holds the

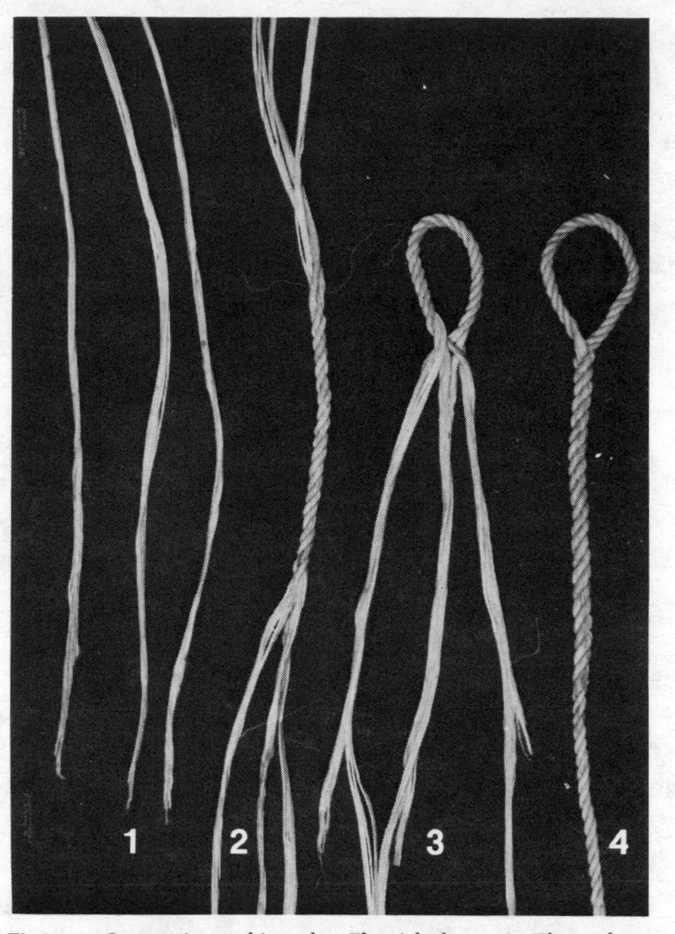

Fig. 9-6. Stages in making the Flemish loop. 1. Three long strands, waxed and tapered. 2. Three-inch section hand-laid into cord toward the tapered ends, starting 8 inches from tapered tips. 3. Three-inch corded area bent in loop, with each of the 3 short tapered strands pressed onto each of the 3 long strands with bowyer's wax. 4. The 3 enlarged long strands hand-laid into the finished Flemish loop.—*Photo courtesy Spaulding Studio, Cortland, N.Y.*

tips of the three long strands. Now start the hand-laying process again and continue it throughout the rest of the string to its end. This results in an even hard-corded area for later adjustment to the nock on the lower end of the bow's lower limb. Keeping tight hold of the end of the string, and with the loop still on the nail, twist the entire string from its lower end about twenty to twenty-five clockwise turns. If righthanded, let the left hand replace the right in holding the string tight, and, with a small piece of medium-soft leather protecting the right fingers, rub the bowstring briskly up and down to heat the wax so it permeates the entire string, rounding it, weatherproofing it, and taking off excess wax. Now release the string and let it hang a few moments from the nail. The surface will slightly harden and you will have a beautiful bowstring with a Flemish loop. To prevent possible but unlikely unravelling, tie a simple overhand knot at the end, or serve the end (the last quarter-inch) with small thread and apply Duco or other cement. The bowstring is now complete except for adjusting to the bow, serving the grip, and establishing the nocking point.

To adjust the string to the bow, place the loop over the upper tip of bow and lower it until the upper or far end of the loop measures five inches from the top of the side and back edge of the upper notch. Now, holding the upper loop steadily at this point, straighten the bowstring out and downward toward the far end of the lower notch in the lower limb of the bow. At this exact point on the string tie a timber hitch (see Fig. 9-8) and tighten it around the lower nock. Also twist the knot around so that the string comes from the knot at the center of the face surface of the end of the lower limb of bow. With the timber hitch tight around the lower notch, string the bow and the string will be in approximately the right place. Let the strung bow rest for five or ten minutes while it stretches slightly. This will bring the center of the string closer to the face side of the bow handle. This distance should always be the same. It used to be called the "fistmele," and in the old days was measured by an archer who would make a fist out of his hand and stick his thumb upwards. Then he would place the bottom of his fist on the face surface of the bow handle, and if the tip of his extended thumb just touched the bowstring, his string was at the proper distance from the face of his particular bow, or he had the proper fistmele. This would also be the proper distance for the above-described self bow. However, for a modern, working recurved bow, the proper measurement would start from the back of the bow and the proper distance to the string would be seven to ten inches depending upon the manufacturer's recommendation. With either type of bow, here is a quick way to bring the string up to the proper fistmele. Take the upper loop off the upper notch and let it slide down around the upper limb several inches. Then take the lower timber-hitched loop off the bottom notch and tip (without disturbing the timber hitch) and twist the bottom end of the string clockwise to shorten and tighten it. Then replace the lower timber-hitched loop, tighten it up around the lower notch, restring the bow, and again measure the fistmele to see whether it is correct or not. An archer always checks his string this way before a tournament so that his arrow flights will be consistent in cast. Of course, another way to tighten the string and lengthen the fistmele would be to retie the timber hitch closer to the upper notch.

The bowstring should now be served, or built up in the middle, to protect it. One good way of doing this is to place the strung bow in the vise with the string side out facing you. Extend a line from the middle of the bow handle and perpendicular to the string and mark the spot where the line crosses the string. Take a nine-foot piece of button thread or a nine-foot length of bowstring dacron or, if that is too thick in diameter (as it is likely to be), untwist this two or three counterclockwise turns so it is divided into two nine-foot strings with a smaller diameter. Wax each of these smaller strings so they will better hold together. Take one of these strings and place the two ends together and the bend or loop will be in the middle of the string. Hold the loop against the bowstring at the mark just made above so that the loop at the middle of the string sticks up above the middle an inch or less. Take the two ends of the string down, under, and up from behind the string and stick them through the loop and pull them through and tight right on this spot. Now wind the double string over back and around the bowstring five or six times to the left; then continue winding tightly but going back to the right over the five or six winds just made to the left to keep the string from unravelling on the left end of the serving. Continue wrapping this double thickness of thread neatly and tightly to the right until only five or six inches of the serving thread is left. Now make four half-hitches one after the other, pull each one tight, and cut the end of the serving string off flush with the end of the last half-hitch. Now add two or three drops of Duco or other quick-drying cement to the half-hitches and to the five or six overwraps at other end of serving. This should keep both ends of the serving from coming apart. There remains but one more task to do in order to complete the bow; that of establishing the nocking point (place to put notched end of arrow) on the string.

While the bow is still strung and fastened in the vise with the string side out toward you and the window side up, the arrow should rest on the arrow rest. From this point of contact with the bow, place the nock of the arrow on the bowstring at the place where the arrow is at right angles to the string. Now shift the nock 3/16 inch to the right or towards the upper end of the string. Place ink marks on either side of the nock of the arrow, for this is the place every arrow shot in the bow should be nocked. It is called the nocking point. You can mark it several ways. One way is to paint the area between the two ink marks clear around the string with black India ink; this would be an area about 1/4 inch long. Probably the best way is to wind two little lumps of fine thread on the string, one at either edge of the nocking point, so that the nock of the arrow rests securely on the nocking point between the two lumps on the string and does not slip off. The bow and string are now complete and ready to use. But do not use it with full draws of twenty-eight inches yet. Draw it many times as much as eighteen to twenty-one inches several times a day for a day or two, but do not hold it long at any of the distances drawn. This breaks the bow in gradually without breaking it. With this beautiful homemade self bow the age-old statement "a bow fully drawn is nine-tenths broken" is true. Another point to remember is that the bow should always be unstrung when not in use.

DOUBLE-LOOP BOWSTRING

The double-loop bowstring is most often used for target bows and is simple and quick to make. As to the length of the bowstring, make it the same length as the old one that was on the bow (if it was the proper length). If you do not have the old string to measure by, use the distance from the lower nock of the bow to the top of the nock on the upper limb of the bow minus five inches. Drive two nails close together at one end of a sizeable old board. Drive two other nails close together at a distance from the first two nails which is exactly the same as the length of the bowstring-to-be. Drive another smaller nail eight to ten inches from the last two nails driven and off to the left of them (see Fig. 9-7). This will allow ample distance for tying off the two ends of dacron thread together

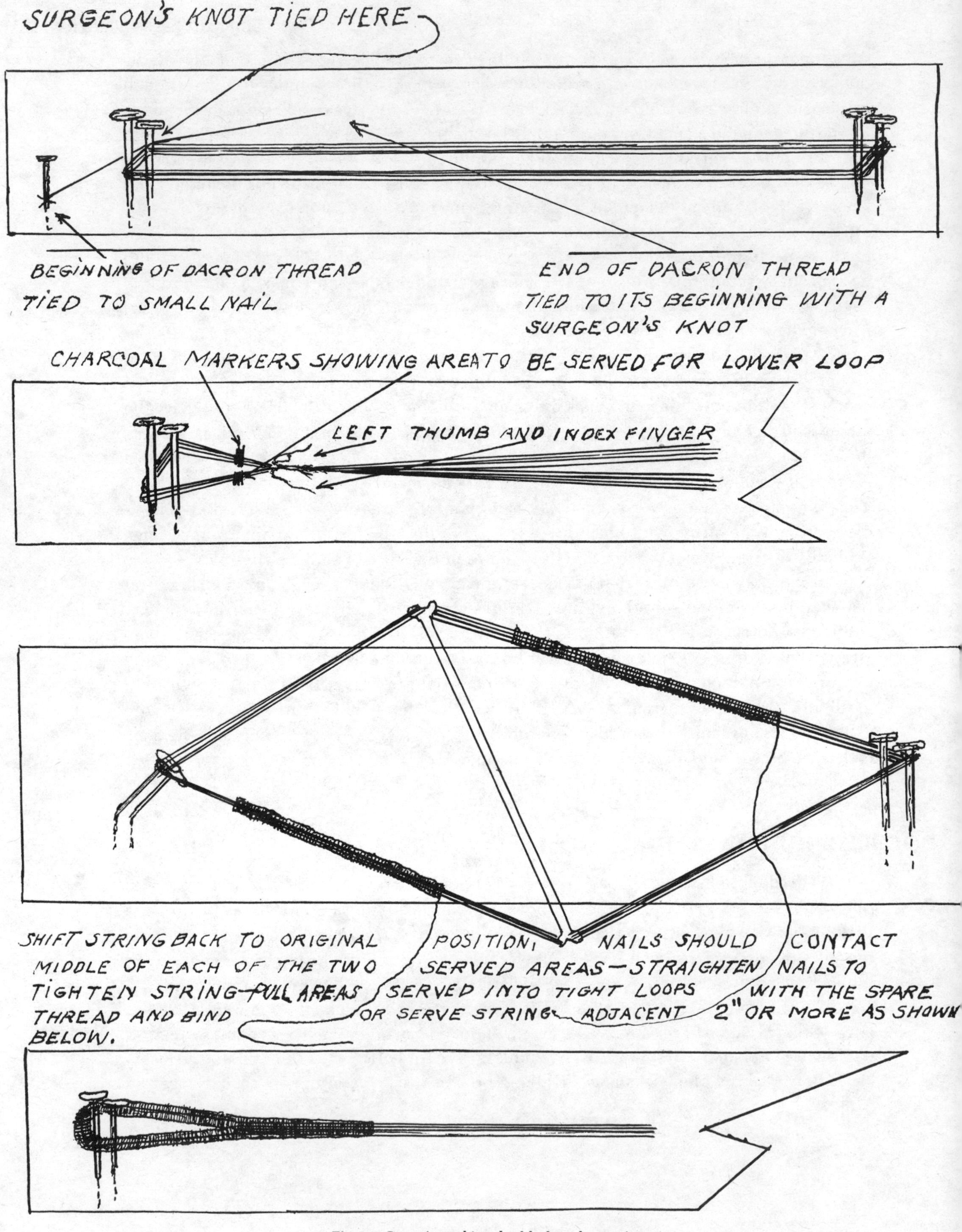

Fig. 9-7. Steps in making double-loop bowstring.

later on. To this nail tie the starting end of the dacron thread to be built into a bowstring. Having secured the starting end of the dacron thread on the small nail, carry the long end of the thread (which is wound around a spool*) in a clockwise direction down and back around the outside of the two nails at each end of the embryo bowstring. Continue circling the thread in a clockwise direction down and back around each of the two nails at the ends. It will look like two parallel lines of thread about half an inch apart. Each time the thread is carried down and back, it will lay down two thicknesses of thread. Continue this circling of thread down and back until the desired thickness for the bowstring is reached. Assuming one wants a bowstring of sixteen thicknesses of dacron thread, this would necessitate circling the thread down and back eight times. The two ends of dacron thread must then be tied together, and a tight tension of all sixteen threads should be maintained. This requires a knot that does not slip. A square knot is not good enough, as with tension this knot may change to a double half-hitch, slip and come apart. Use the surgeon's knot (see Fig. 9-9), as it holds better than the square knot and is also small enough to be hidden and covered by the serving of the lower loop in the finishing of the bowstring. This knot should be trimmed so that each side of the knot has a half-inch of dacron thread left.

The lower loop of a bowstring should always be smaller in diameter than the upper loop so it will be just large enough to slip over the lower tip into the groove of the nock of the bow, and will stay there. The upper loop of a bowstring should always be larger than the lower loop so it can be slid up and down the upper five inches or so of the upper limb of the bow and lodged in the upper nock during shooting.

Having tied the ends of the thread together with a surgeon's knot tightly against the outside of one of the two nails at the end where the original end of thread was tied to the small nail, pinch with left thumb and index finger the two eight-thickness strands of the bowstring together, forming a loop around the two nails at the knot end which you estimate should become the smaller loop at the lower end of the bowstring and hold tight. At the upper edge of the pinched fingers and lower boundary of the lower loop, with the right hand mark with black charcoal or crayon a line visible on all sixteen threads. Now move to the other end of the bowstring and, facing the two nails at that end, estimate the distance from the nails that would represent the upper loop. Pinch the two strands of eight dacron threads at this point and make black lines across all sixteen threads as was done above.

When free and unpinched, the distances between the black marks at either end of the bowstring represent the circumferences of the two loops to be; and each loop must be protected by wrapping or serving the loop areas with additional thread, preferably the strongest cotton button thread one can secure of a color different from white. To do this easily without interference from the two nails at each end, the two marked loop areas must be shifted temporarily from their contacts with the nails. To loosen the tension of the

*Spools of 1/4-pound waxed dacron thread for making bowstrings can be found at most archery supply stores. Browning Company's Super B-43 is one of a number of good ones. A 10-thread string is strong enough for strings for bows of 25 to 35 pounds drawing weight, and a 12-thread string for bows 35 to 45 pounds drawing weight.

sixteen threads slightly, bend the two nails on one end slightly toward the two nails at the opposite end by use of hammer or fingers. Now, near the middle of the string, tightly pinch the strand of eight strings farther from you with the left thumb and index finger, and pinch tightly the nearer strand of eight threads with the right thumb and index finger. Shift the position of the marked areas on the string by moving the left hand (still pinching tightly, of course) to the left about twelve inches and the right hand the same distance to the right. The pinching during this operation must be tight enough so no individual threads can shift either way. The marked areas are now in a position to be served.

To make the serving process still easier, separate the two strands of eight threads by inserting between each of these strands a stick ten to twelve inches long with grooves on each end. Take about six feet of the button thread and tie one end of it around the left-hand black mark of the area containing the surgeon's knot with a simple overhand knot, leaving the short end of the button thread with a spare of two inches. Lay this two-inch spare out to the right along with the marked area threads and start serving or winding the long end of the button thread (over, down, under, up and over, etc.) neatly and tightly around the eight dacron threads and short end of the button thread out to the right until the righthand black mark is reached. End the serving with one or two half-hitches, and allow the rest of this serving thread (hopefully three or four feet) to hang down loose at this point for future use. Of course, while wrapping or serving the above, one approaches and covers the surgeon's knot and the half-inch trim on each side of it. Now move to the opposite area marked out for the larger upper loop. Use a longer piece of button thread, about eight feet for this serving. As was done above at the other end, tie an overhand knot at the beginning of the marked area and lay the spare 2 to 2-1/2 inches out to the right along with the eight thicknesses of dacron thread, and wrap or serve this until the other end or black mark is reached. Then stop and tie off with one or two half-hitches, leaving five or six feet of spare thread hanging down free.

The next step is to shift the position of the bowstring back to its original position behind the two nails at each end. The two nails which were bent inward to loosen the string can now be pounded or bent back straight. These nails should now be right in the middle of the served area with the ends of this area directly opposite each other. At one end of the served area at each end of the string three, four, or more feet of button thread should be hanging down free. Grasp one of these free ends of button thread and cross it over the opposite side of the other eight-thread strand and pull it tightly over so the two ends of the served area meet and are pulled together, forming the loop. Continue several wraps around this point to secure this loop. Keep up the wrapping or serving towards the middle of the bowstring around the sixteen thicknesses of dacron thread until the button thread has been used up except for about six inches with which one can tie it off with three or four half-hitches. A drop or two of a fast-drying cement like Duco will hold the hitches from coming undone.

Now go to the other end and grasp the string hanging down from one end of that served area. Wrapping it over the other eight dacron threads at the end of that served area, pull those ends together into a loop and serve from the loop down towards the middle of the string and finish as was done at the other end of the string. The double-loop bowstring is now complete except for the serving area five to six inches long at the middle of the string where the fingers contact it while shooting, and the placement of the nocking point. These items have been described before in the directions for making a single-loop bowstring.

To string the bow with the double-loop string, first slide the upper and larger loop over the upper tip and nock of the bow and down the upper limb far enough so you can attach the lower loop to the lower nock of the bow easily. Then string the bow by sliding the upper loop into the upper nock of the bow. For safety, use one of several bow-stringers now on the market.

Other simple systems for placing the nails to hold the string which obviate the need to bend the nails inward in order to loosen the string are:

1) Pounding two nails in a large wooden packing box and the other two nails in another packing box, with the boxes placed apart the length of the bowstring.

2) Placing two nails in a board held in a vise and the other two nails in a packing box or bench a bowstring length away. Adjust string tension by shifting position of the board in the vise.

3) Placing two one-inch boards about five feet long one on top of the other and overlapping each other about two feet, where they can be held tightly together by a C clamp. Put two nails in each board a bowstring length apart. Slide the boards closer together or farther apart by adjusting the C clamp.

KNOTS USED IN ARCHERY

All of Robin Hood's merry men used longbows equipped with single-looped bowstrings; the loop surrounded the upper limb and tip, and the lower end of the string was tied to the nock in the lower tip of the bow by means of the bowyer's knot, known today as the timber hitch. Actually, this knot was used by all archers up until the time the double-looped bowstring came into use in about the second decade of the twentieth century.

Timber Hitch

The timber hitch holds securely without slipping, and yet is a very easy knot to adjust when tightening the bowstring (see Fig. 9-8).

Perfection Loop

This loop has many uses. In archery it can be used as the upper loop for a single-loop bowstring, when one doesn't know how to make the Flemish loop or other satisfac-

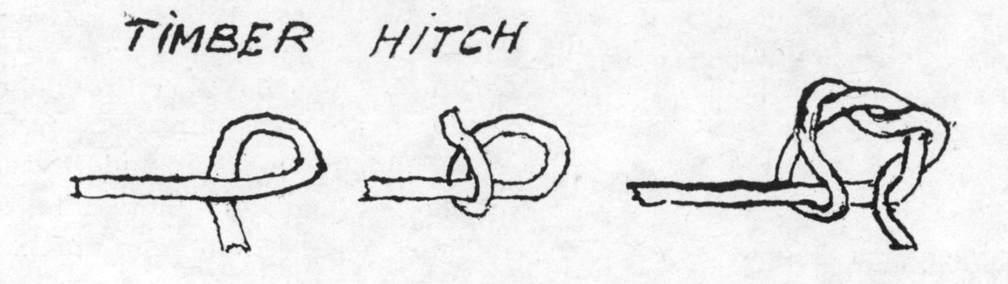

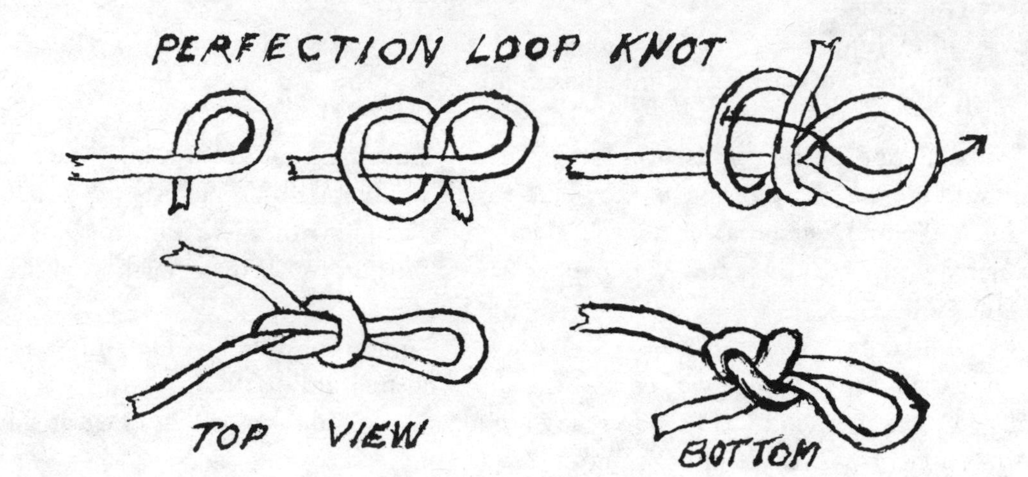

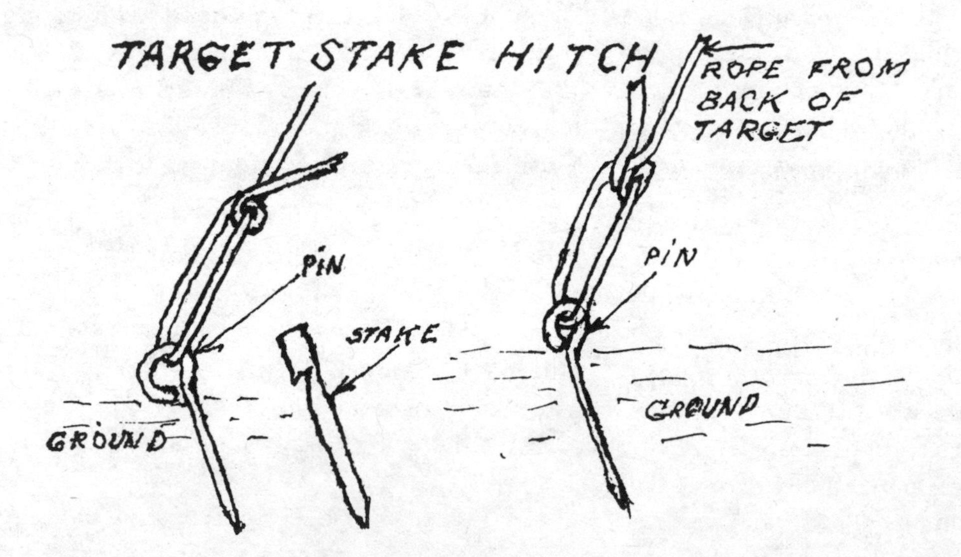

Fig. 9-8. Knots used in archery.

tory loop. It can also be used to adjust long bowstrings to short bows while keeping the serving in the right place.

To tie the perfection loop, hold the string by the thumb and index finger of the left hand (reverse directions, if lefthanded) with about seven inches of the short end out to the right of the left hand and the long end under the palm of the left hand. Take 2-1/2 or 3 inches of the short end with the fingers of the right hand, make an underhand loop (see Fig. 9-8), and hold it securely with the left thumb. Next, take the short end directly over and behind or underneath the base of the first loop, making another loop to the left. Take the rest of the short end and pass it snugly up, over, and on top of, the base of the two loops. Hold this short end up out of the way by placing the left middle finger on top of it, and holding it against the top of the index finger. With the right thumb and index finger, reach up through the righthand loop, grasp the lefthand loop, and pull it down and through the righthand loop. The loop that is pulled through becomes the perfection loop. Before pulling it tight, adjust this loop to the desired size, since once it is pulled tight, it will not slip in any direction but will hold like a bowline knot, which it closely resembles.

The Surgeon's Knot

This knot is used in the early process of making a double-loop bowstring to tie the two ends of dacron thread together after the process of winding the thread continuously around the two posts or nails the correct number of times has been completed. When properly tightened, it will not slip as easily as a square knot, especially since it is supported by the serving on top of it at one of the loops. This knot is for tying together two ends of string or cord (see Fig. 9-9).

The Target Stake Hitch

This knot can be used most satisfactorily for attaching a canoe to the top of a car for a day-long trip, four ropes coming from the ends of two thwarts (a front one and a rear one) and the lower ends of the four ropes tied to the front and rear bumpers with this particular knot. It is also handy while camping out for holding tops of ridgepoles securely to trees, or holding the sidewalls of a tent to stakes. However, the author has used this knot consistently for several years to stake down archery targets in order to maintain the proper slant or tilt for the target boss and to prevent it being blown over by the wind, with the consequent destruction of any arrows that might be in the target. That is why he chooses to call it the target stake hitch.

Secure a 12-foot length of good 1/4-inch rope. Tie one end of rope to the top of the three-legged target-stand on the bolt that holds the three legs together. Next pass the long end of the rope down through three or four of the tight cord bindings on the back of the

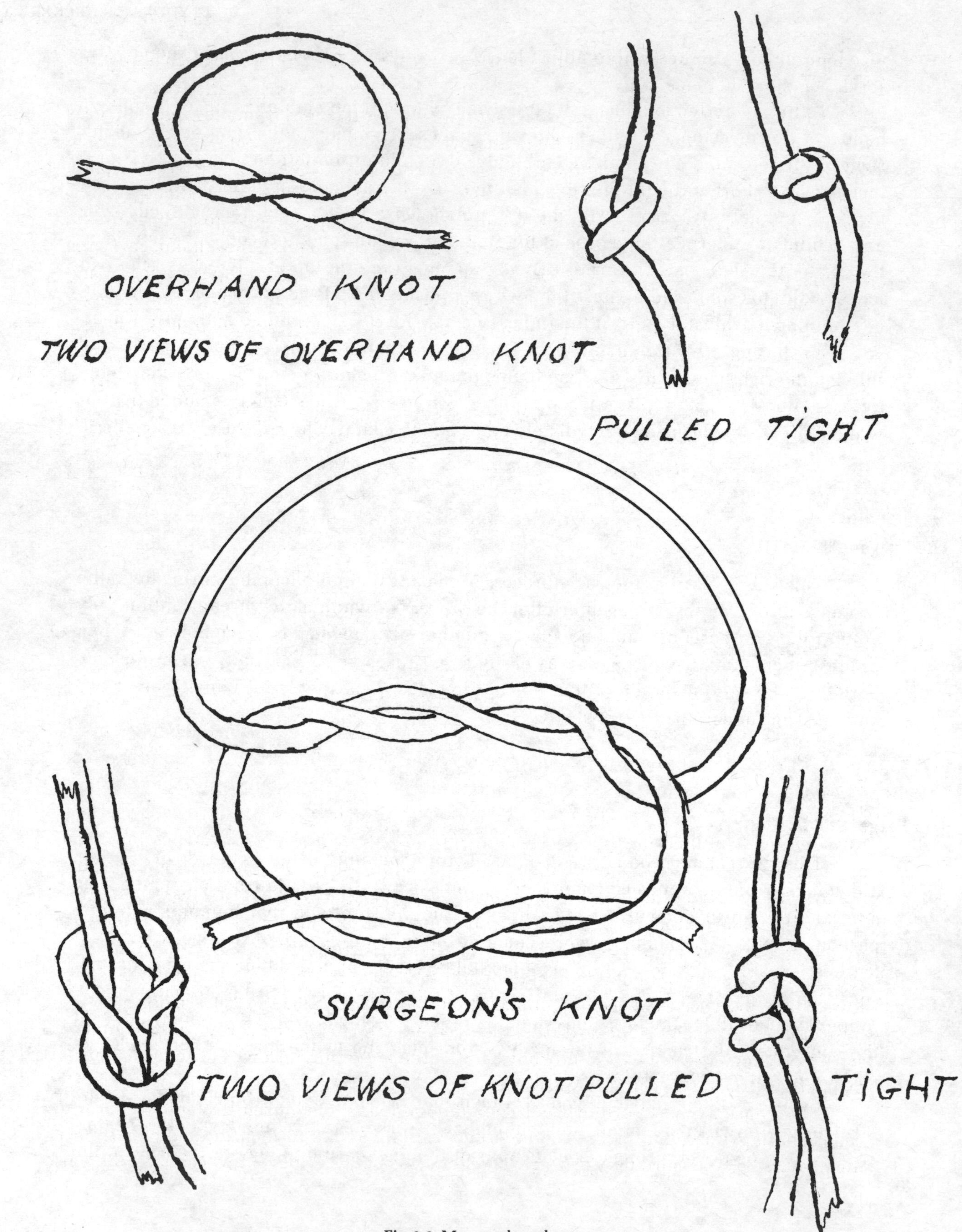

Fig. 9-9. More archery knots.

target, and then secure it tightly to the wooden stake or 1/4-inch iron pin, which is about 18 inches long and a few feet back of target stand.

To make the hitch, take the long end of the rope as it comes from the target and pass it around the top of the stake or through the eye of the pin (see Fig. 9-8). Make the rope to the stake or pin very tight by applying body weight downward on the rope with the palm surface of the right hand (reverse directions, if lefthanded). Maintaining the pressure (tightness) already gained, with the left hand raise the remaining rope up and parallel to the down-rope for a foot or more. Still holding the pressure with the left hand, carry the free end of the rope with the right hand across and over top of down-rope, around it, and up between the two ropes. Keep applying a tight pressure with the thumb and index finger of the left hand now pushing the overhand knot upwards. Again carry the free end of rope up and over the outside and upper surface of the overhand knot, down under the knot, and up through the long narrow loop below the knot, and pull upward strongly, if necessary, with a strong jerk. This pulls the last turn of the rope up so that it lodges tightly between the short up-rope (from stake or pin) and the first turn of the rope which made the overhand knot. The hitch is now complete. If the left hand has done its work in maintaining tightness while the right hand makes the knot, the rope at the finish will have the same degree of tightness with which it started. To undo the hitch, simply jerk the rope-end down. If you still have extra rope, make a half-hitch above the knot on the long down-rope, possibly with a slip loop in it so that it will still come undone with one downward pull on the end of the rope.

ARROWS

Making arrows does not afford as much scope for creativity as making bows. Also, although it is fascinating to make arrows of the highest quality, to do so requires many expensive pieces of equipment. For these reasons the author recommends that the beginning archer purchase a set of 12 arrows. Select the straightest Port Orford cedar self arrows (all made of the same piece of wood) you can get that have been matched in weight and spine for shooting in a bow of about thirty pounds drawing weight. You should be able to purchase a dozen of these for from $6.00 to $7.20 and up. If you pay any less for arrows, they will be warped and crooked. Of course, one can purchase much better arrows as follows (prices are approximate): Port Orford cedar arrows footed (front part of shaft reinforced by hardwood) and matched for spine, $8.00 to $14.00 a dozen; tubular glass arrows, $16.00 to $24.00 a dozen, and tubular aluminum arrows $25.00 to $30.00 a dozen.

There are certain basic skills required for repairing an arrow which anyone starting archery as a hobby should know, and perhaps the simplest way to acquire them is to make a set of simple self target arrows.

Purchase from a sporting goods shop the following: one dozen straight Port Orford cedar shafts with round cross-section 30 inches long and 5/16 inch in diameter (select them yourself to be sure they are straight even if you have to pay a few cents more), one dozen parallel-sided steel target tips to fit 5/16-inch shafts, one dozen plastic nocks with indicators to show where the cock feathers are, and three dozen primary wing turkey feathers, all having grown on the same side of the turkey. Two dozen feathers should be regular gray, and the other dozen should be white, black, or some color other than gray. One can purchase the feathers in the natural gray color (exactly as they would be if just pulled from the turkey's wing) or cut and ground. The latter means that excess parts of the quill have been cut off and that the quill part has been ground off to a smooth flat surface finish at right angles to the broad feathered side of the feather.

It is more fun to secure turkey feathers from several poultry farmers who raise turkeys. Make arrangements with them to allow you to visit their farm when they are dressing turkeys before Thanksgiving or Christmas. Ask them to save for you several of the primary wing feathers. There are only nine or ten such feathers on each wing, and they have a very broad feathered area only on one side of the quill (see Fig. 9-10). The farmers may feel that it is too much work for them to separate out just the primary feathers. If so, ask them merely to save all the wing feathers and tell them you will come out and separate them. Get a lot of them while you have a chance as they can be used in other ways as well as for feathering (fletching is the proper term). When you get the feathers home, clean and dry them if necessary and then separate them, putting the left wing feathers in one box and the rights in another. When making a set of arrows, use only those from a particular box (use only all rights or all lefts).

Cut feathers are practically always used in the fletching of commercial arrows as they are supposed to last longer; however, this matter could be debated, and since cut feathers require fairly expensive equipment, we shall use stripped feather vanes (a vane is one of the three pieces of feather generally used in fletching an arrow). To strip a primary wing feather, hold the base of the quill between the knees or in a vise with a flat side towards you. In looking at one of these primary wing feathers, note that the barbs on one side of the quill reach out from the quill at a slight angle as much as an inch or more (see Fig. 9-10). On the other side of the quill barbs reach out only a quarter of an inch or so but at a very acute angle. Place turkey quill vertically in vise one-fourth inch from bottom, small barbs to left. Hold onto the upper soft small end of the quill and the barbs coming out most acutely with the left hand (reverse directions, if lefthanded). Grasp with right hand (thumb and index finger) a half-inch or more of the long barbs on the other side. Holding the left hand and upper quill stationary, give a slight jerk outward and downward with the right hand and the broad material will start stripping off the right side of the quill. It may split the quill first at the top, but continue gently pulling off a little at a time, emphasizing the downward pull a little more. If the feather breaks off the quill, start again where it broke and eventually it will all be stripped off. Try to strip so carefully that you get all the material off in one piece. The part of the quill that was stripped off will be a rounded concave section that will perfectly fit the rounded shape of the arrow shaft, thus offering more gluing surface which will hold longer, without wearing out as soon as the cut feather surface frequently does.

Use thirty-six stripped feathers, each preferably eight or nine inches long.

Fig. 9-10. Primary turkey wing feather. The middle section of feather is best for fletching target arrows; the other 2-1/2-inch sections will do for ordinary arrows. The middle 5-inch section is best for vanes on hunting arrows.

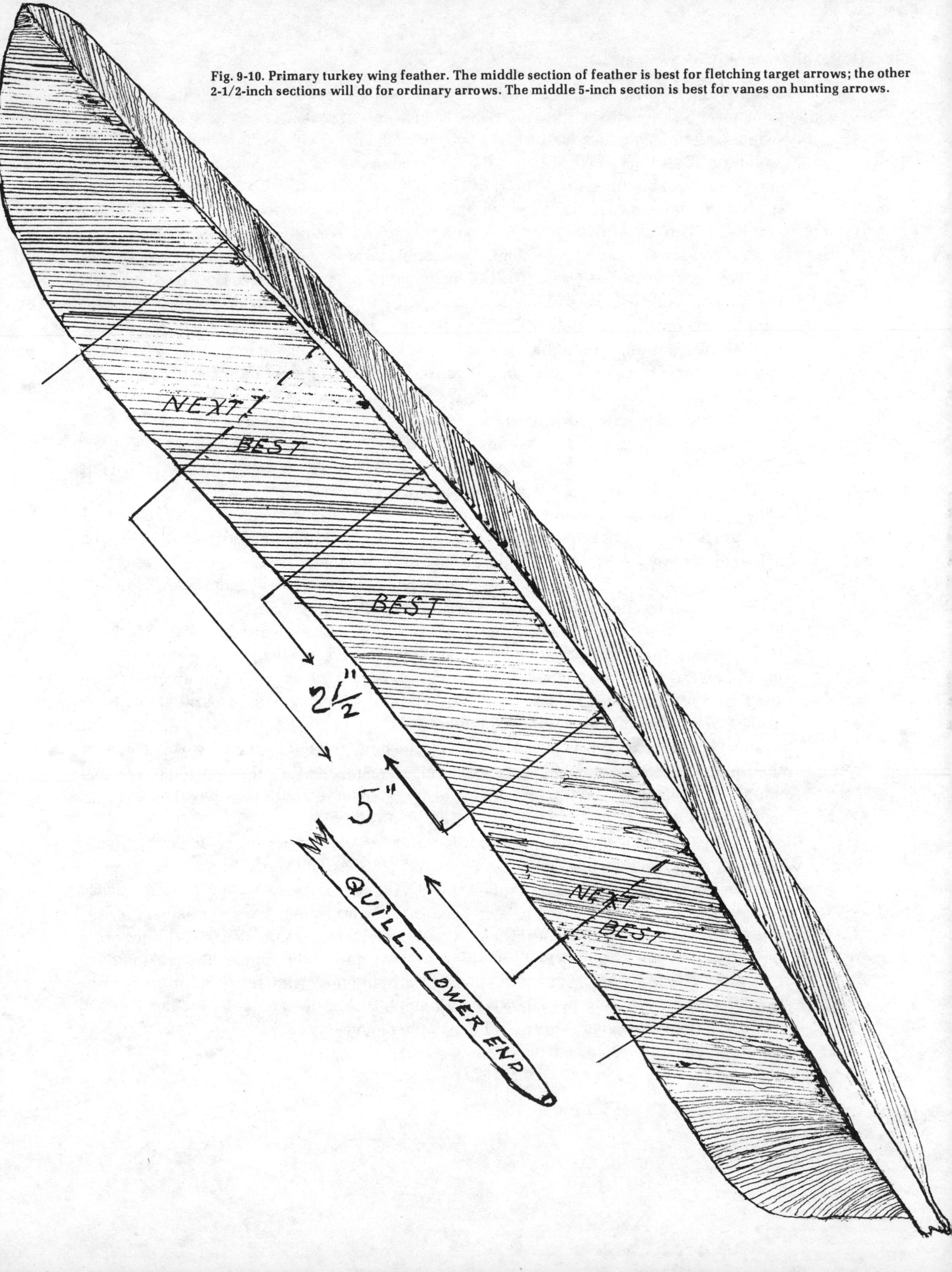

Twenty-four of them should be gray and twelve white or some other color. Starting at the top end of one (where quill is narrowest), measure 2-1/2 inches; cut at this point with scissors and place this 2-1/2-inch section on your left in a small box or bag. Measure another 2-1/2 inches (starting where the first section was cut off), cut this middle section, and place it in a small box right in front of you. Then cut a third 2-1/2 inch section from the stripped feather, measuring from the end where the last section was cut, and put this section in another box or bag on the right of you. Continue cutting all thirty-six of the stripped feather sections and place all of these in their proper boxes or bags. Arrows can be made by using feathervanes from any of the boxes (three to an arrow). However, the best, most hardy, and straightest-shooting arrows will be made by using only vanes from the middle box, for these represent the toughest and strongest vanes from the middle of the feather. Use only these middle sections for your first and best arrows. Vanes from the other boxes can be used for inferior arrows you might use for practice and throwaways.

To construct an arrow, first take a parallel-sided target tip or point. Measure its depth by inserting a small straight piece of small-diametered wire or end of small nail inside the tip. Mark this distance at one end of the arrow-shaft. At this spot, with a sharp pocketknife gird the shaft completely with a shallow cut. The cut should be only as deep as the thickness of the sidewall of the target tip. Make shallow minute knife-cuts starting about halfway between the end of the shaft and the girding cut, and toward the base of this cut all around the end of the shaft. Now reverse the direction of the knifeblade and make shallow cuts outwards off the end of the shaft, taking very slim slivers off to the end of the shaft, parallel to its long axis and no deeper than the cut girding the shaft. This will be the end where the tip will fit up against a shelf where the first girding cut was made. Take off too little wood rather than too much so the tip will fit tightly rather than loosely. If there has been so much wood left on at this place so it is too tight to get started, place a medium-sized fine flat iron file on the area to be fitted with its left side up against the shelf marking the first cut to gird it, with the flat side of file touching it parallel to the top of the bench. Now draw or roll the shaft towards you under the file. This will round out this surface so it exactly fits into the tip with some pressure. Put a drop or two of cement in the tip, force tip on, and then, using a steel pin, pound it into the tip on three places just enough to indent the steel wall of the tip into the wood underneath, which will hold the tip on for keeps.

Nocks for the other end of the arrow can be easily secured from any archery supplier and from most sport shops and hardware stores. Get the size that best fits the diameter of the arrow you are making (5/16 inch for most self target arrows). One can also purchase an old-type manually twisted pencil sharpener, which when applied to the rear end of the shaft and twisted clockwise will give just the right slant to exactly fit the inside of the nock. If you cannot locate one of these sharpeners, mold some malleable material like plasticine to fit the inside of the plastic nock, and then with knife and file, shape or form the end of the shaft to imitate it and fit the inside of the nock snugly. Glue the nock on with fletching cement; a type sold by suppliers and some sport shops, Duco, or some other good fast-drying cement will do.

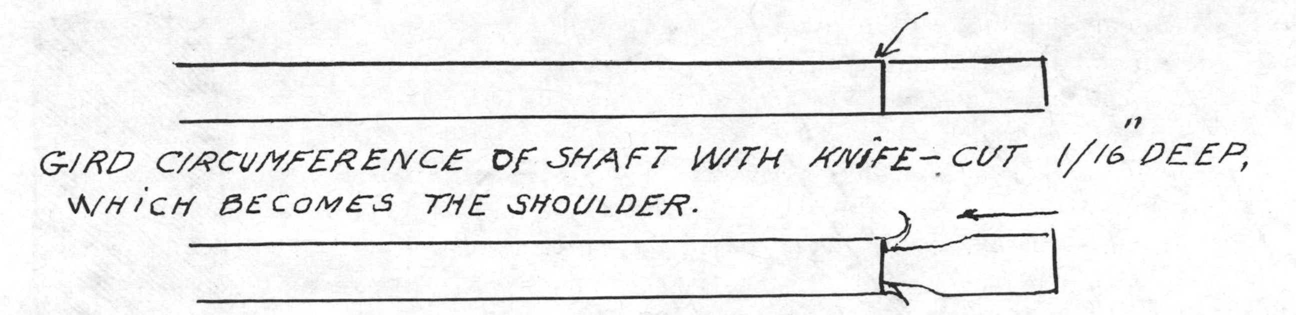

MAKE SHORT KNIFE-CUT CHIPS AROUND SHAFT TO BASE OF SHOULDER.

WHITTLE CHIPS OFF IN OTHER DIRECTION.

SMOOTH AND ROUND OFF THIS END WITH FILE TO FIT TIP. SEE OTHER SKETCH.

TIP FITTED TO END OF ARROW.

Fig. 9-11. Fitting tip to end of arrow-shaft.

In fletching the arrow, glue onto the shaft the cock vane or guide vane first. This will be the odd-colored feather, or black one if the other two feathers or vanes are gray or white. This should be glued on so that its rear end is exactly in line with the indicator on the nock, a slightly raised ridge of plastic in a straight line 1/4 inch long on the lower open end of the nock. This, when arrow is finished, indicates to the archer where the cock or guide vane is by feel as well as by sight. The rear end of this guide vane is glued to the shaft 1/2 inch from the near edge of the nock. The other two feathers or vanes are called

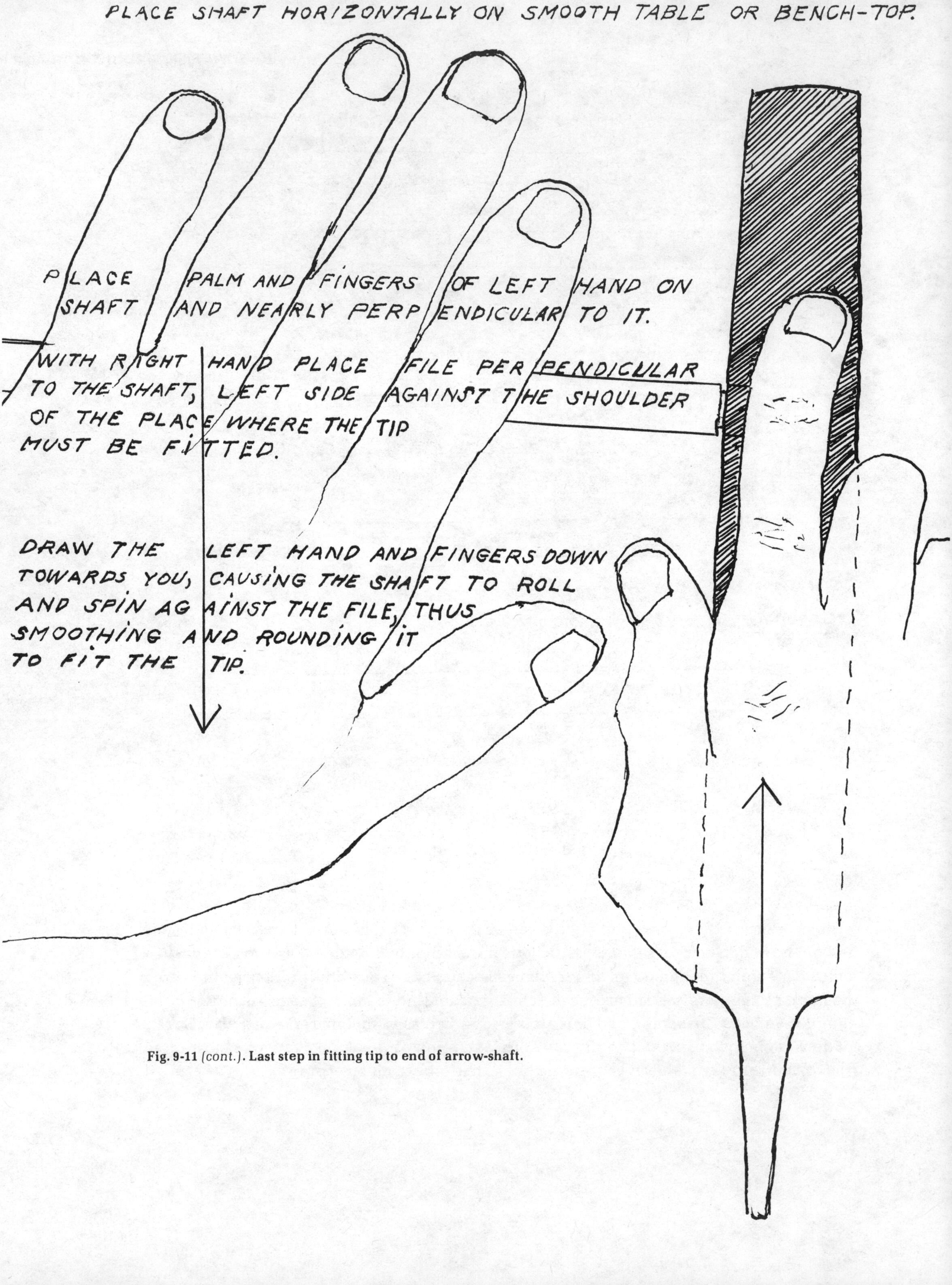

Fig. 9-11 *(cont.)*. **Last step in fitting tip to end of arrow-shaft.**

the hen vanes and are glued on the shaft at the same distance from the nock, but each one is 120 degrees from the other; so the distance between the vanes is equal (see Fig. 9-12). There are fletching devices which will place and glue the vanes on the shaft correctly, or one with practice can apply glue to the concave quill surfaces of the vanes and pin vanes on the shaft by careful sighting to get them equidistant. Of course, the vanes should be placed on the shaft so the fibers slant backwards rather than forwards. After the glue is set and thoroughly dry, one can shape the vanes as desired with sharp scissors, or burn feathers to uniform design in an electric feather trimmer.

Next one may paint the arrow any way desired, but should certainly paint on the shaft forward of the fletching rings around the entire shaft with two or more colors and widths. This combination or design of colored rings is called the crest of the arrow. Each archer has his own crest, which identifies the arrow as his own. The arrow is now complete except for a final coat or two of clear spar varnish, with light sandpapering between coats.

The length of an arrow is measured from the base or bottom of the groove in the nock of the arrow to the far end of the parallel-sided tip, but does not include any part beyond this which slopes to the point. If one wants an arrow to be 28 inches long, he should cut the 30-inch shaft so it measures 27-3/4 inches in length; after the nock and the tip have been put on, the arrow will measure 28 inches.

American Indian Arrow Shafts

For the shafts of their arrows, the North American Indians preferred to use either of two closely related species of viburnum: *Viburnum acerifolium* (leaves shaped like maple leaves) and *Viburnum dentatum* (leaves with serrate or sawtoothed edges). The common name for both of these shrubs is arrowwood, for the young shoots of both plants are unusually straight. *Viburnum acerifolium* tends to grow in rocky wooded areas and may grow as high as five feet. *Viburnum dentatum* may sometimes grow as high as fifteen feet. Its young shoots have smooth ash-gray bark. Its leaves are opposite, broadly oval, and have sharp, sawtoothed edges. This plant grows in many habitats but is generally more often found in damp places not far from lakes, streams, and swamps. One can sometimes find shoots from the latter shrub straight enough and long enough to make spears for use in a spearthrower. These viburnums, particularly the *dentatum*, generally grow in close clusters of twenty-five or more shoots. To prepare the shafts for arrows or spears, select three or four of the straightest shoots from two or three different clusters. Check each shoot for straightness, since there will generally be one or two slight curves not noticed until cut. Heat the curved areas in very hot ashes, hot water, or steam and straighten them out. Then wrap them tightly together, all of the shoots exactly parallel to each other, from one end to the other. The cord used for wrapping should be long enough to wrap the bundle of shoots spirally up and down the bundle, with the distance between spiral wraps of the cord being about one inch. If you allow these shoots to season a few weeks, they will remain quite straight until it is time to make them into arrows or spears.

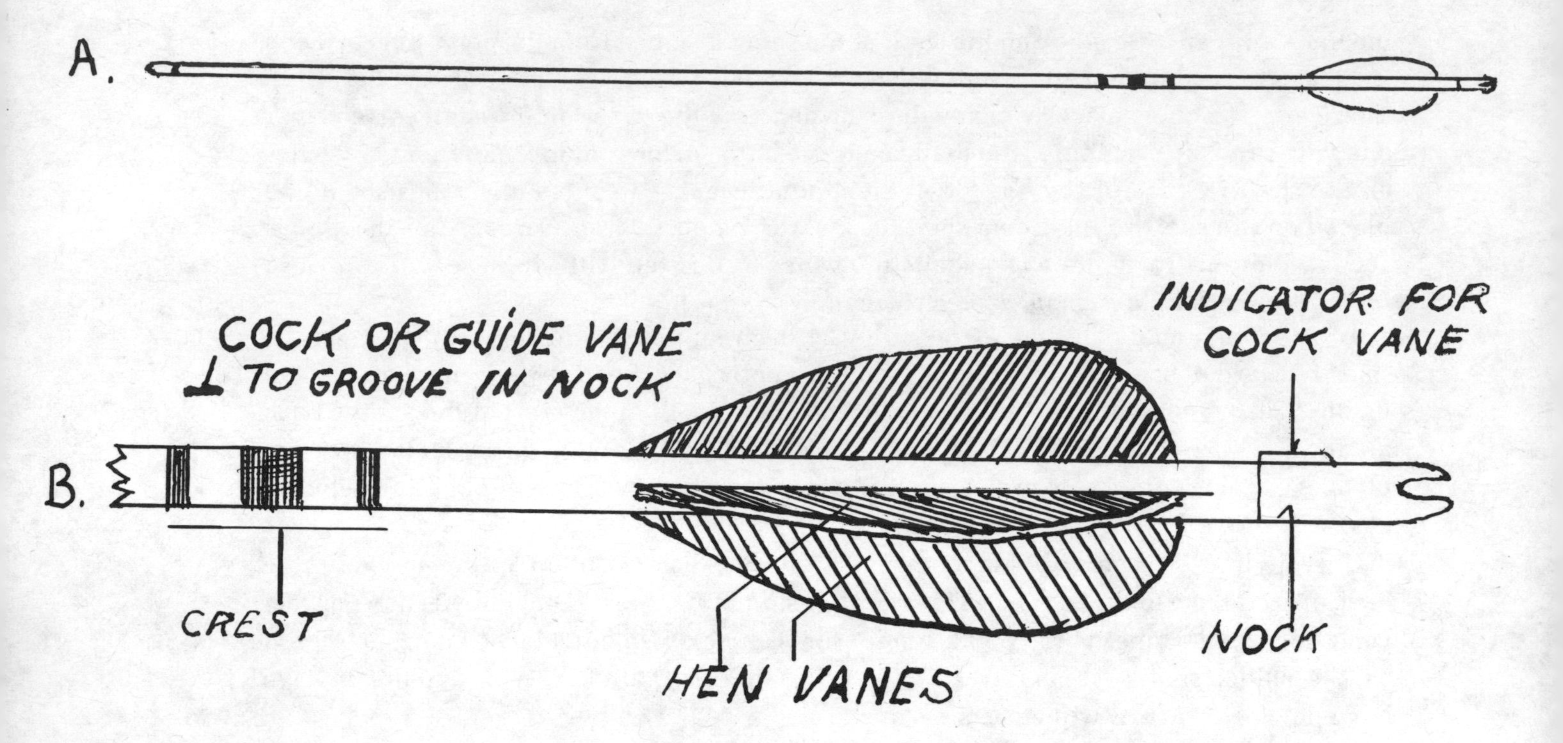

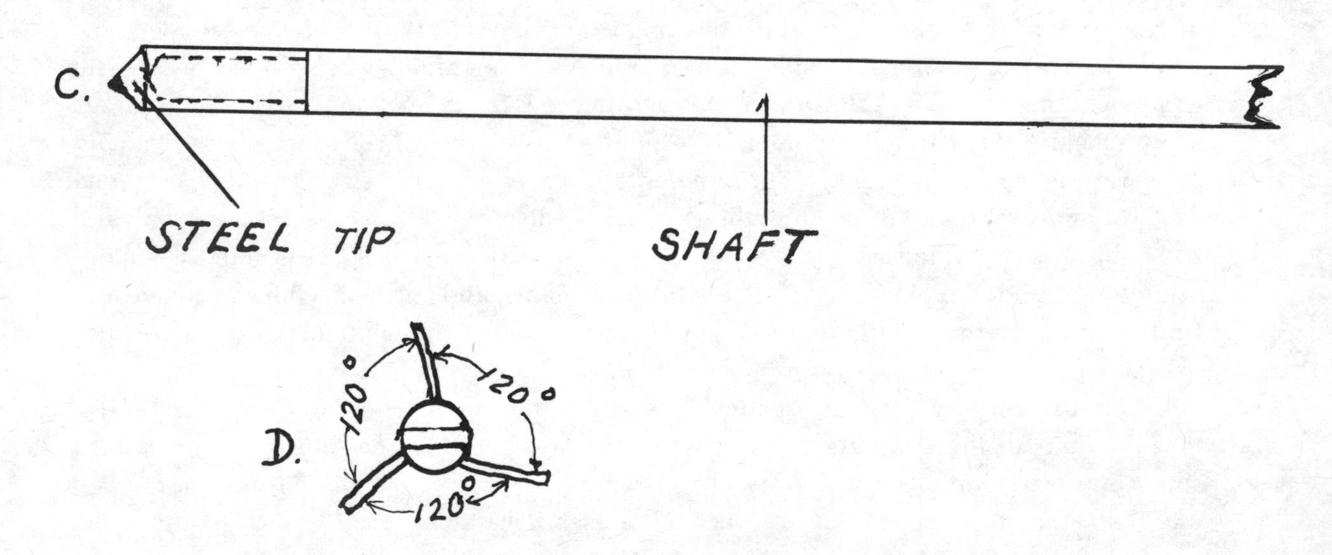

Fig. 9-12. Arrow. *A.* **Overall view.** *B.* **Close-up of rear end.** *C.* **Close-up of front end.** *D.* **Nock-end view, showing vanes spaced 120° apart.**

chapter 10

Walking Sticks: An Outlet for the Creative Imagination

COLLECTING WALKING STICKS MAKES A FINE NATURE CRAFTS hobby because of the infinite variety of native materials that can be found, and the creativity that can be used in finding handles that look like heads of animals, birds, or fish, or can be carved with pocketknife to simulate them.

Wood from the two hornbeams—the American hornbeam or blue beech (sometimes called musclewood because of its smooth, rounded ridges which look like contracted human muscles) and hop hornbeam (often called ironwood because of its exceptional hardness)—make good walking sticks. How one of Robin Hood's men would have treasured a six-foot length of either of the hornbeams for a quarterstaff for rapping heads on a narrow bridge across a stream. A straight, seasoned 1-1/2-inch diameter piece of this wood makes an ideal Boy Scout stave.

Many species of poplar, particularly small-toothed aspen, make excellent walking sticks with built-in handles, since the roots generally are not deep but grow outward just a few inches under the surface of the ground perpendicular to their main shoots. Look for a grove of young aspens 7/8 to 1-1/4 inch in diameter crowded close together and in need of trimming. Select a good shoot and loosen it at the bottom by sideward-upward pulls from all sides. When you find the side from which the shoot's main or thickest root extends, pull the trunk of the young aspen outward in that direction to secure it. Then wash the root, trim off excess rootlets, and carve or shape the root as your creativity suggests. In loosening the roots, digging and thrusting upward with a small round-pointed spade six to eight inches out from the base of the desired sapling and on four sides of it will save much energy.

In nearly every hardwood forest saplings or shoots of sugar maple will be found crowded so close together that most of them will not grow to maturity unless they are thinned out, so that selecting a 3/4- to 1-1/2-inch diameter sapling once in a while for use as a walking stick is good ecology.

Another fine lightweight walking stick can be made from the lower 3-1/2 feet of the stalk and roots of a mullein plant, collected in the fall. The stalk should be straight and seven to ten feet tall. Also, its diameter should be at least 7/8 inch at a point 1 foot from the ground, in order to be strong enough for a walking stick.

The mullein plant takes two years to mature, as it is a biennial. At the end of the first year it will have developed a rosette of velvety leaves about 1 to 1-1/2 feet in diameter growing flat to the ground. In the fall of the second year look for the tall stalks strong enough for walking sticks.

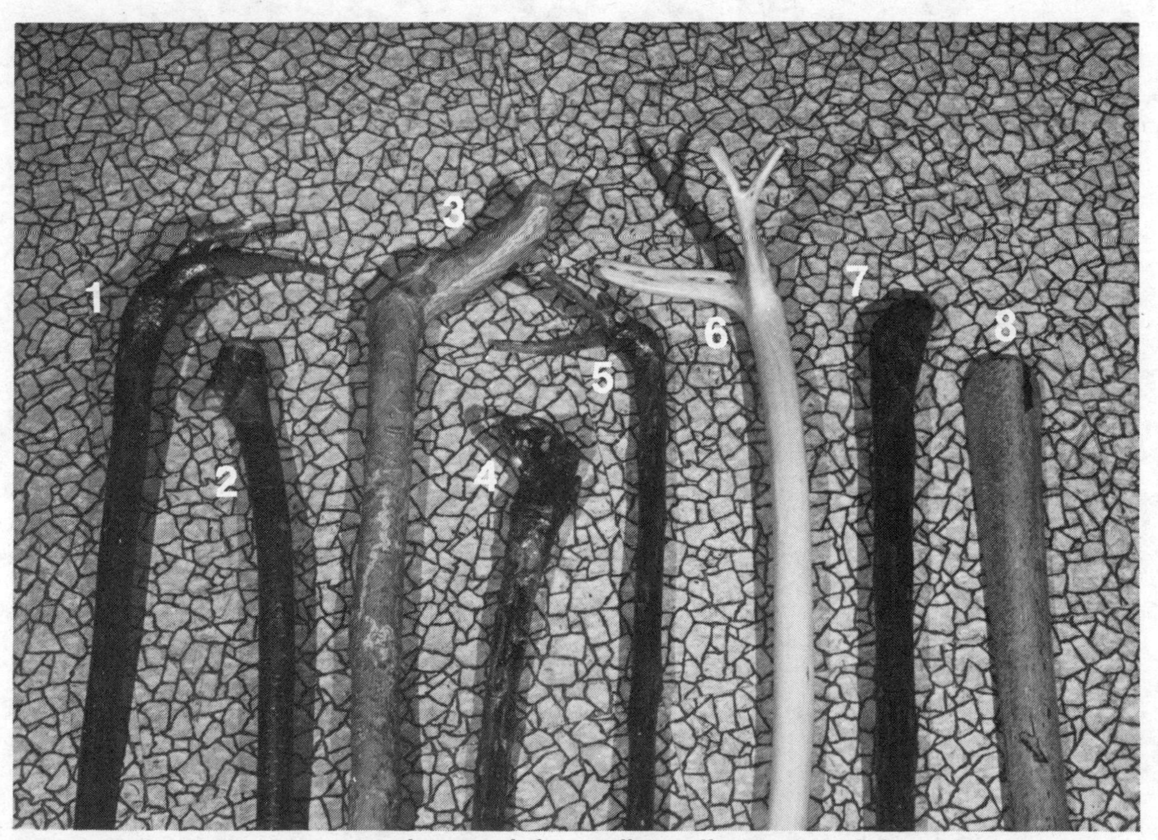

Fig. 10-1. Walking sticks. Nos. 1, 4, 5, and 7 are made from mullein stalks. No. 2 is made from yellow birch. No. 3 is white ash. The handle is the start of the root. No. 6 is quaking aspen *(Populus tremuloides)*. **The handle is the root. No. 8 is the leaf stalk of a cabbage palm.**—*Photo courtesy Spaulding Studio, Cortland, N.Y.*

It is amazing what a great variety of shapes and growth designs can be found in young shoots of trees and branches that are suitable for unusual canes and walking sticks. One treasured walking stick of the author bears a scar on its side caused by a young buck deer rubbing the velvet fuzz from its antlers in the early fall. Another has a beautiful spiral groove for its whole length, where a poison ivy vine entwined itself. Honeysuckle vines will do the same thing. Again, one frequently finds a young shoot pressed down to the ground by a tree or large dead limb. In many cases the young shoot didn't give up but continued growing straight up on the far side of the restraining tree or dead branch, making a fine curve for a cane handle where it had been held down. Keen observation and imagination are all that is required for building this kind of a collection. If you collect a large enough variety of walking sticks, it is fun to share them with friends. See Figure 10-1 for examples of walking sticks.

Rubber crutch bottoms make excellent bottoms for walking sticks. They can be found at all hardware stores.

chapter 11

Simple Fishing Ways: How to Catch Fish Without Modern Tackle

FISHING IS FUN FOR PEOPLE OF ALL AGES WHETHER ONE USES the most modern fly-casting gear or an improvised tin-can reel and homemade fishhooks. There is much to be learned from fishing with simple implements one makes oneself—self-reliance and survival skills, for instance. Of course, for primitive peoples fishing was a necessity for survival. They devised many ingenious and successful fishing techniques which are described in this chapter. Some of these techniques are illegal in certain states, and the reader should inquire of his state fish and game department which of the methods described herein are permitted in his state. Everyone should be familiar with these methods, however, as a knowledge of them may very well avert starvation in an emergency.

FISHING WITH HOOK AND LINE

Most fishing today is done with hook and line. Primitive peoples, including the American Indian, used these implements too, often in exciting ways not familiar to most people today. Following is a discussion of some of the many fishing methods employing hook and line.

Fishhooks

Fishhooks of various shapes and from different materials have been used for centuries. The first fishhooks were made of hardwood or bone; later metal was used. The earliest type of fishhook had two small sticks lashed together at the lower or closed end, making a 30-degree angle. The upper end of the hook, or the shank, had a slightly longer stick with an expanded knob for attaching the line. The smaller stick would be whittled or ground down to a very sharp point. Landing a fish with one of these hooks required great skill; the line had to be kept taut at all times since, with any slack in the line, the fish could easily throw the hook and escape. Because of this, barbs were eventually cut into the lower end of the bottom stick a fraction of an inch from the point. The principle of barbs had already been used on spearheads. Some Indians made fishhooks from one of the toe bones of deer. They halved the bone and ground it down with infinite patience using various pieces of sandstone.

The Gorge Hook

The gorge hook was widely used by many Indian tribes. It was made from a small piece of hardwood or bone one-half inch or more long (depending upon the size of the mouth of the fish to be caught), with both ends sharpened to a fine point. In the middle of the stick there was a groove completely circling the stick to which the fishing line was attached. When this baited stick was taken into the mouth by the fish, and pressure applied by the fisherman, one sharp end would stick into the side of the fish's mouth, and increased pressure from the string on the center of the stick would immediately bring the other pointed end of the stick across the inside of the fish's mouth and block it so it could not be pulled out (see Fig. 11-1).

Skittering

Skittering was undoubtedly practiced by Amerindians and American pioneers and is still done in areas where it may be hard to get modern fishing tackle or where people cannot afford to purchase it. It is a thrilling way to catch fish. It is done with a long cane pole, a line about twelve feet long, and a medium-sized hook (no. 1). Bait the hook with a perch head or strip from a perch belly. Swing the baited line out and skitter it along the edge of lily pads, weedlines, and logs. Skittering means to drag the bait along the top of the water fast enough to make it bounce and splash in an unpredictable manner so as to catch the attention of a pickerel or bass. The pickerel is the most likely to respond with a tremendous lunge; when it is hooked, a battle-royal takes place.

Jugging

Jugging is another fascinating method of fishing. It requires a rowboat or canoe, and four or more empty jugs tightly corked so they will float. Equip each jug with a fishline six

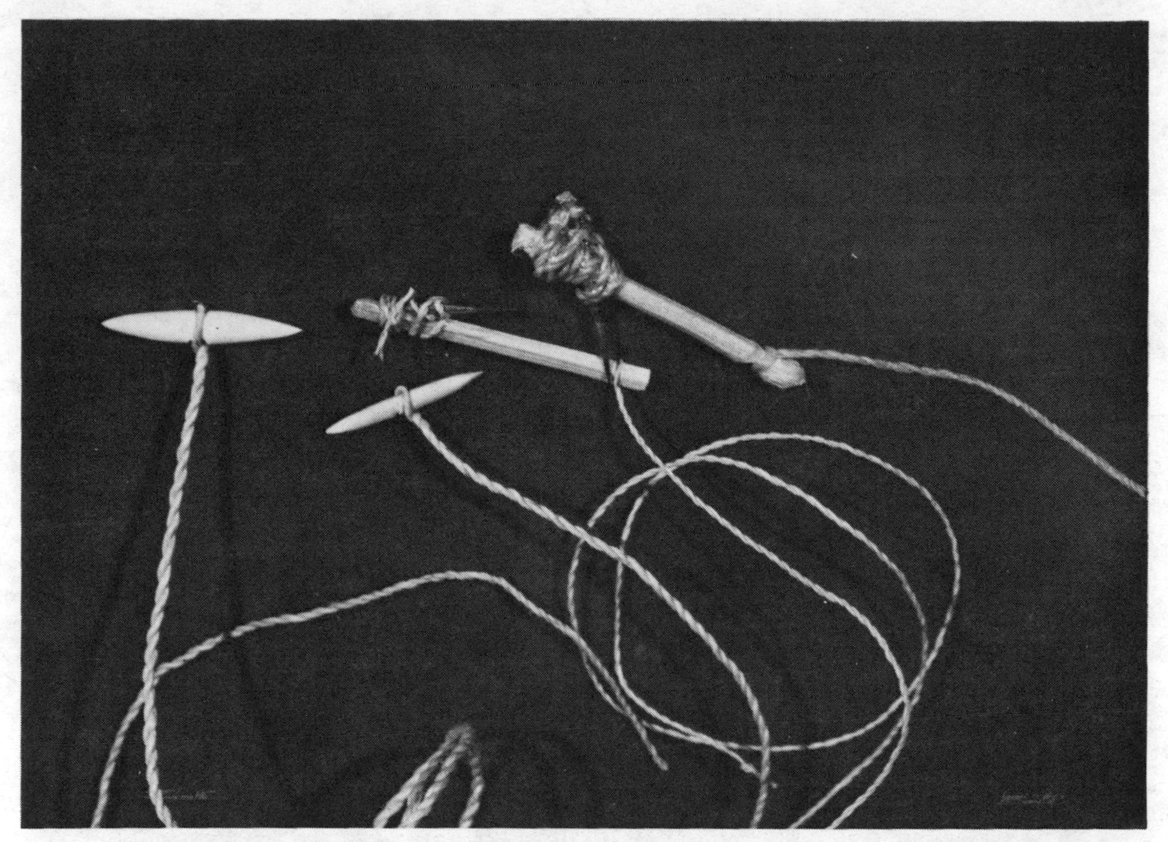

Fig. 11-1. Fishhooks. *From left to right:* **Two gorge hooks and two fishhooks made by splicing thorn from honey locust tree to small piece of bamboo.**—*Photo courtesy Spaulding Studio, Cortland, N.Y.*

to ten feet long and a sinker and hook baited with nightcrawlers, chicken wastes, and other choice tidbits for river fishing. Row the boat to the middle of the river and put the baited jugs overboard so that the boat and the fleet of jugs will all float down the river together. When the fish begin to bite, one or more of the jugs begins to bounce, dive, splash, and travel in a most erratic fashion. The fisherman immediately rows or paddles to the wayward jug. Hopefully, he puts a fish on his stringer, rebaits the hook of the jug, and replaces it in the water. By this time possibly one or more other jugs begin to signal their need for attention and, since the jugs are now farther apart than they were at first, the fisherman soon becomes as busy as the proverbial one-armed paper hanger. At any rate, this kind of fishing tends to promote physical fitness. In place of jugs, which are hard to come by now, one can use maple syrup cans, Clorox cans, or chunks of dry softwood cut in one-foot lengths six inches or more in diameter. If the latter, screw into the middle of one side of the chunks eye-screws 2 to 3 inches long and 1/4 inch in diameter, for tying on the line with sinker, hook, and bait.

Tin-Can Reel

As this system is described and illustrated, one can readily see how it might well have been the origin of the spinning reel. Certainly the tin-can reel is a reasonable one that any fisherman can well afford.

Secure a clean empty no. 10 tin can or larger one. From a stick of wood with a diameter about 1 to 1-1/2 inches, cut a small stick whose length is the exact inside diameter of the can. Each end of this stick should be flat and perpendicular to the stick's long axis. Place the stick inside the can about two-thirds of the way from the open top to the closed bottom (see Fig. 11-2). Both flat ends of the stick should be in close contact with the opposite sides of the can. At the middle of each of these contact points drive a small flat-headed nail through the tin can and into the center of the stick of wood. This being done on both ends of the stick makes a stable handle for the reel. To this inside handle tie one end of a 50-yard spool of 10- to 15-pound test casting line. Wind all of this line around the outside of the tin can which now becomes the spool of the reel. On the free end of the line, tie on a small snap swivel with which to snap on and off different lures weighing about 5/8 ounce. The handmade tin-can spinning reel is now complete.

Fig. 11-2. Tin-can reel, with practice plug hanging from end of line. The two pieces of wood glued to the top of the can have slots sawed in them to control the line. Note handle inside reel.—*Photo courtesy Spaulding Studio, Cortland, N.Y.*

To get the feel of operating this reel properly, first snap on a 5/8-ounce practice plug (a teardrop-shaped plug with no hooks). Place the left hand (reverse directions, if lefthanded) inside the can and grasp the handle. Now strip off from the tin-can spool about seven feet of line from the plug end. Then with the thumb and index finger of the right hand grasp the line at a point 3 to 3-1/2 feet from the plug and swing the plug forward and upward in continuous circles with considerable wrist motion. This gives one the feel of the weight of the lure and the method of gaining force and impetus for the cast. To make the cast, first see that the long axis of the tin can or spool of the reel is facing in the direction you want the plug to go and start swinging the plug in circles with a radius of three or more feet, swinging forward, upward, back and downward, etc. with constant acceleration and keeping the circles in the plane of the direction of the cast to be made. Maximum speed can ordinarily be reached after four or five complete swings. To make the cast, release the plug and line on the forward upward part of the swing. The plug will sail out at about a twenty- to twenty-five-degree angle with the surface of the water, with the line spinning off the tin reel following the lure. To stop the plug, simply flex the left elbow; this brings the long axis of the tin reel perpendicular to the line, which immediately stops all forward motion. To retrieve the lure, bring the right hand down on the line a foot or so out from the reel, grasp the line, and wind it back onto the spool with downward, under, upward, forward, and downward movements, incorporating into the retrieve varied movements—pops, pauses, fast reeling, steady reeling, and change of pace—as necessary to entice the game fish to strike. Remember, to make a cast straighten the reel arm out so the long axis of the reel is pointed toward the target. To stop the plug and line, just bend the elbow of the reel arm, grasp the line with the right hand so as to play the fish when it strikes, and wind up the line on the tin-can spool.

KNOTS USED IN FISHING

Knowing one's knots is certainly a big help in fishing with hook and line. Knots are used to tie ends of leader material together, to tie flies onto leaders, to tie leaders to flylines, and to attach bobbers to fishlines. Instructions for tying the knots most often used in fishing follow.

Fisherman's Knot

This knot was used in the days when good fishing line was hard to come by, and one had to save pieces of string and tie them together whether they were used for kite-string or fishing line. It is still a good knot to use if the diameters of the two pieces of string are the same or nearly so. It is very easy to tie. Lay the two butt ends of the string parallel but facing in opposite directions; have each end overlap the other by five or six inches. Take one end and tie an overhand knot around the other string. Then take the end of the latter string and tie an overhand knot around the first string. Now take the long end of one string in the right hand and the long end of the other string in the left hand, pulling outward with both hands. As this is done, the two overhand knots will slide together until they meet in the middle. This completes the knot (see Fig. 11-3).

Barrel Knot, or Blood Knot

The barrel knot, or blood knot, is used for tying the two ends of nylon leader material together. It is particularly used for tying leader material of slightly different diameters in order to make a tapered leader. If the variation in diameters of the two leaders is great (more than .015 inch), the Stu Apte improved blood knot (see below) would be more suitable. The blood knot is tied as follows. Cross the two ends of leader material with three or four inches of each extending out from the cross. Cross the leader end of the left hand under the leader end from the right hand and, holding the cross spot with thumb and index finger of the right hand (reverse hands, if lefthanded), take the short end which is sticking out from the cross at the left with the left thumb and index finger and bring it down and around the long end of the other leader three or four times. Place the rest of this short end across to the right and down over the original cross between the angle made by the other short end of the leader and the other long leader. Change fingers so that the fingers of the left hand now hold the cross with the short end of the leader pinned down. Now with the right hand take the short leader sticking out to the right and wrap it down around the other long leader sticking out to the right three or four times. Then bring it back to the left and put it down or up through the hole or space just to the right of the original crossing. Both short ends are through this same hole. Now, grasp all four leader ends and gently pull them outward to tighten the knot. If you do not grasp a short and a long end in each hand and pull carefully, one of the two short heads may pull out from the center and the knot will be lost. After you have pulled all four ends out a safe distance, pull only on the two long ends. The knot will become very small and look like a miniature barrel. Now with sharp knife or shears cut off the short ends close to the knot, which is now complete.

The Stu Apke Improved Blood Knot

This knot is used when one thickness of leader material is so great in comparison to the other it is not possible to tie the regular blood knot. To tie this improved knot take the thinner of the two leaders, and at a point 6 inches from the end bend it back on itself 180 degrees. Now use the doubled thickness end as one of the short ends to be crossed and from here on proceed as for tying the regular blood knot.

The Perfection Loop, and Looping the Loop

This knot has already been described and illustrated (see Fig 9-8), but it also has many uses in fishing. In most cases it is a matter of looping one loop to another loop, at-

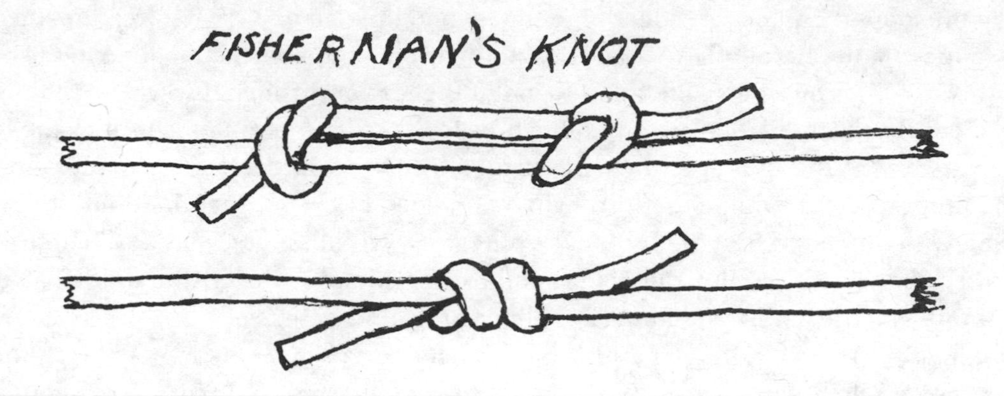

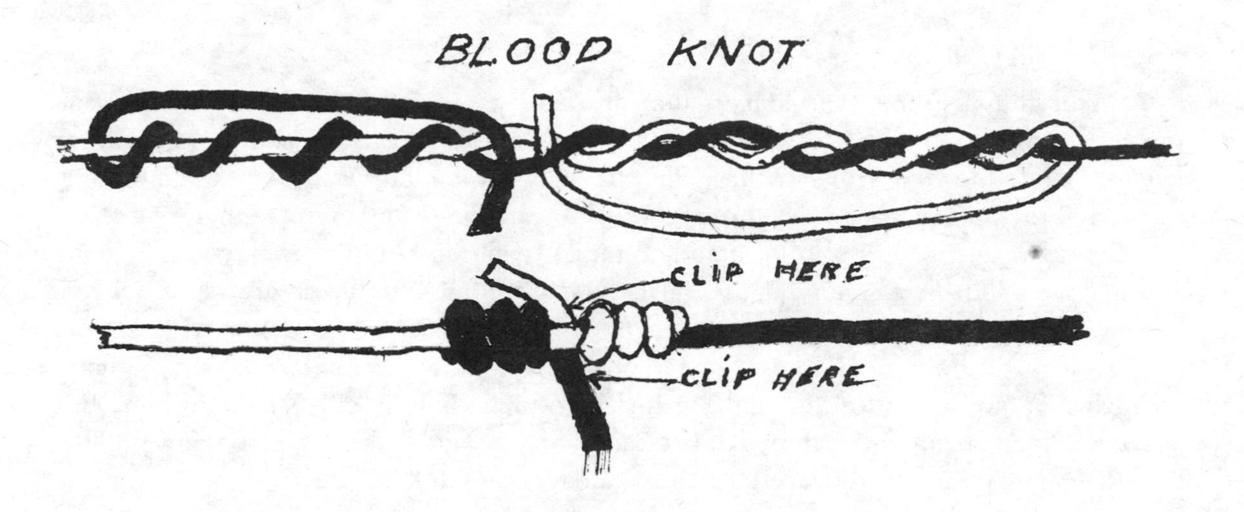

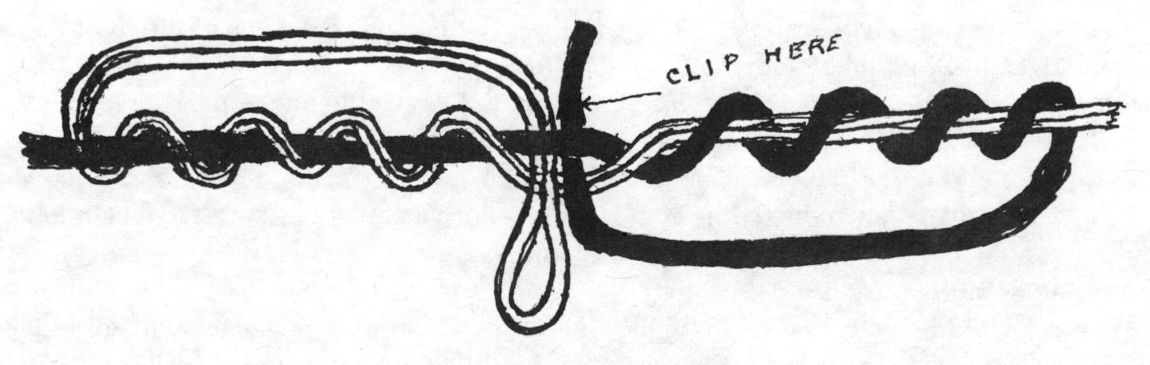

Fig. 11-3. Knots used in fishing.

taching the looped butt end of a leader to the loop in the end of a fly-fishing line. Push the small loop from the butt end of a leader partially through the perfection loop in the end of a flyline, and then put the small tapered end of the leader through its own small loop and pull it clear through. Another way of doing the "loop the loop" would be to stick the larger loop on the end of the flyline through the small loop on the butt end of the leader and then put the tapered end of the leader through the big loop of the flyline; then pull the leader one way with one hand and the flyline the other way with the other hand. When the lines are pulled together tight, the knot where the leader joins the line will look like a square knot. If one is bait-casting, spinning, or spin-casting, and breaks or loses the snap-swivel, by making a perfection loop about four inches long he can push the loop through the eye of the plug and then open up the loop in the line and pull the whole lure through the loop in the fishline and it will tighten up, having looped the loop with the eye of the lure.

The Improved Clinch Knot

This knot is probably used more than any other by fly fishermen to tie their flies on the ends of their leaders; it certainly is the easiest to tie. Hold fishhook in left hand with eye of hook to the right (reverse these directions, if lefthanded). With right hand holding the end of the leader thread this through the eye of the hook and out the other side of the eye about two inches. With left thumb and index finger still holding the eye of the hook and the threaded short end, wrap the short end back and around the long end four or five turns with right thumb and index finger. Then bring this short end back over the turns and stick it through the loop between the eye of the hook and the first of the turns. Stick it through this loop no more than half an inch and immediately with left hand bend this short end back up and down through the larger loop just made (see Fig. 11-4). Now pull the long thread tight for a beautiful clinch knot that will hold for keeps.

Nail Knot

This knot is a fairly recent one in the long history of knot-tying. The author recommends it for tying a leader to the end of a flyline. To tie it, place the end of the flyline out to the right and with the left thumb and index finger grasp it about four or five inches from the end of the line (reverse directions, if lefthanded). Place the butt end of the leader so that it faces in the opposite direction, or out to the left. Place this leader into the grip of the left thumb and index finger under the flyline with seven or eight inches hanging down loose. Now add on top of the flyline at the point of pinch a nail about 2 to 2-1/2 inches long, with pointed end to left. With right thumb and index fingers take the free loose butt end of the leader and wrap it around the nail, line, and leader to the right of where the left fingers are pinching it all together for about five wraps. Carefully remove the nail, and stick the butt end of the leader back 180 degrees through all of the five loops where the nail was

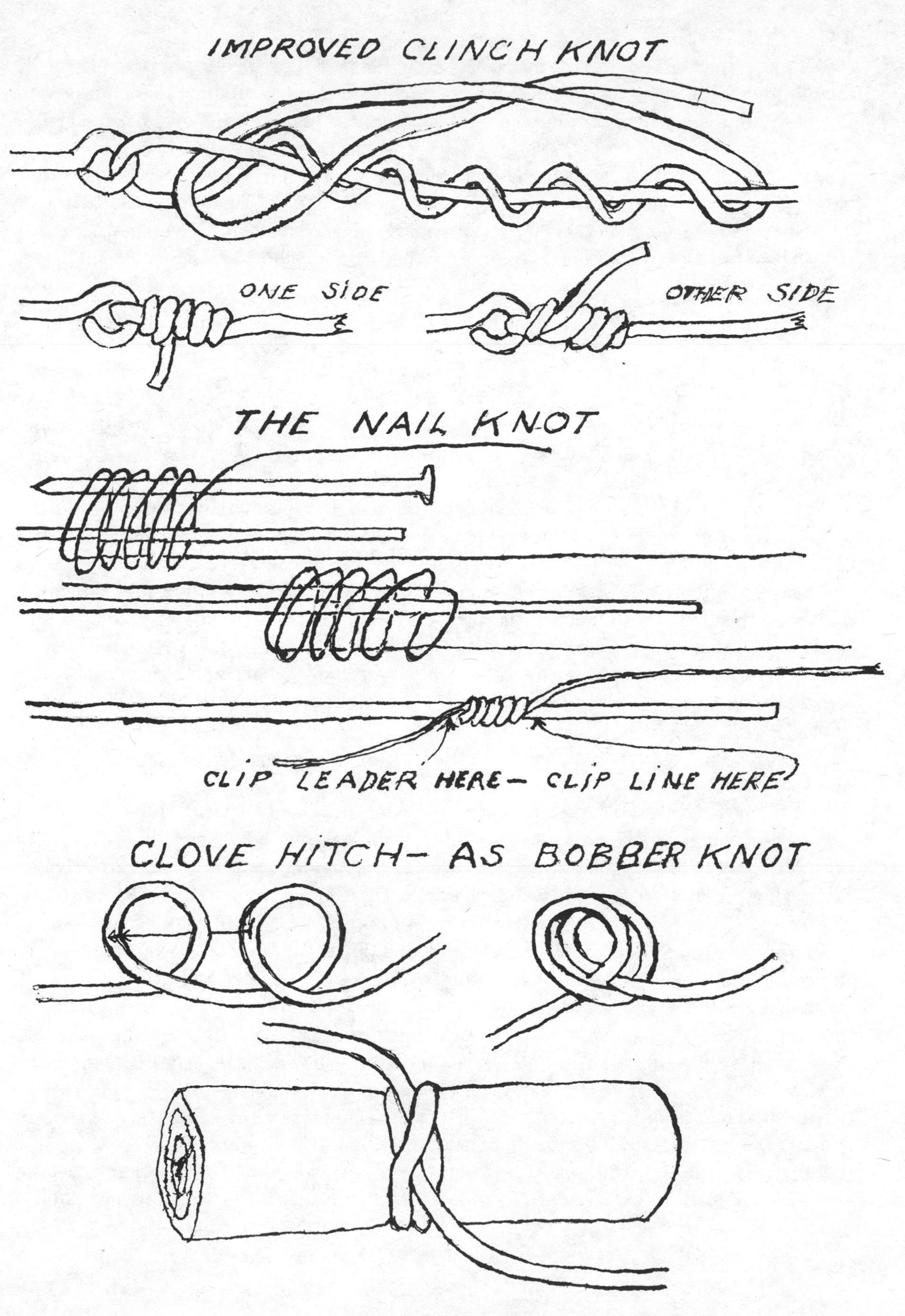

Fig. 11-4. More knots used in fishing.

(see Fig. 11-4). Continue pulling this short end of the leader to the left and the long end of leader to the right so that the loops gradually tighten around the flyline. Be careful not to let the flyline slip out from the loops. Before final tightening of the five or so loops of leader, collect the loops together in a close compact group (if they are not so arranged already) and then pull very tightly so that the leader bites so hard on the flyline it does not slip. Now grasp the long end of the leader in one hand and the long end of the flyline in the other and pull the two lines tightly in opposite directions. If it does not slip, the nail knot is complete. With scissors, knife, or clippers, cut off the short ends of leader and flyline close to the knot.

Clove Hitch

In fishing the clove hitch is used to attach a bobber to a fishline. Most fishermen carry a bobber or two in their tackle box. However, if you want to still-fish with a bobber and you do not have one, you can make a very satisfactory one with a dry stick or large cork and a clove hitch. With a pocketknife cut out a shallow groove completely around the middle of a dead dry stick about two or more inches long and one inch thick, so the knot will not slip off an end of the stick. Now to tie the clove hitch. With left hand (reverse directions, if lefthanded) grasp the fishline at a point about four or five feet above the baited hook and sinker so that they are just off the bottom where the fish can see them and go after the bait. With the right hand grasp the fishline about six or seven inches above the left hand and make an overhand loop a little larger than the circumference of the stick. Hold this loop with thumb and index finger of the left hand. Now make another overhand loop with the right hand the same size as the first one, and place it underneath the first loop. Now place the stick inside of both loops and, by pulling on the ends of the line, tighten up the clove hitch around the middle of the stick in the groove.

Suppose you are fishing for bluegills off a dock with a rod, a small sinker, and a size 10 hook on which a piece of worm about one inch or less long is fastened. As the line with hook and bait is lowered so that the bobber can float, you note that the sinker and hook are resting on the bottom of the lake. The line from the bobber down should be shorter by eight to ten inches so that the bait is up where the fish can see it. This is no problem. Withdraw the line; put the stick in one hand, and the line above the bobber in the other. By rolling the bobber-stick downward and with the string tightly pulling on the rolling stick, you will be able to adjust the stick so that it holds the bait and sinker the proper distance off the bottom to catch fish. The tight clove hitch will hold in this position. Now suppose you are fishing from a boat with a no. 1 bass-size hook baited with a live minnow and the water is ten feet deep. If you are using the same line and the bobber where it was for bluegills, the bobber will be too low so that the hook rides too high for the bass to see it. Simply roll the bobber-stick up the line while holding the line below the bobber tight with the other hand. Roll the bobber upward on the string to a point where the line under the stick is about 8-1/2 feet. Now it is in the water with the bait 12 to 18 inches above the bottom of the lake, where the bass will be more likely to see it and strike. The point is that with a clove hitch around your homemade bobber, you can adjust the bobber easily to any desired height.

BOWFISHING

In recent years shooting rough fish has become a very challenging branch of archery. Archers should check with their state conservation department to see in what waterways it is legal to shoot fish with bow and arrow, and what rough fish can be taken. In most states it is legal to shoot carp, suckers, and alligator gars.

For retrieving fish after they have been hit, bowfishing reels and special fishing arrows have been developed and are available in nearly all sports shops selling bowhunting tackle.

A fairly satisfactory homemade bowfishing reel can be made by finding an empty salted nuts tin can, 3-1/4 inches in diameter by 3 inches high, or a short coffee can 4-3/4 inches in diameter by about 3 inches high. With 2 small nails, nail the bottom of the smaller can to the middle of a stick of white pine, basswood or poplar 7 inches long, 1 inch wide, and 1/2 inch thick. Place this stick on the back of the bow with the open end of the can facing outward. The lower end of the stick should be 2-1/2 to 3 inches above the arrow rest (see Fig. 11-5). With Scotch filament tape fasten the upper and lower part of the stick above and below the tin can to the bow. If you are using the coffee can, use a stick 9 inches long. Drill a hole 1-1/2 millimeters in diameter through the arrow about 1-1/4 inches from the feathered end. Tie one end of a level, floating flyline no. 9 through the hole drilled in the end of the arrow. Fasten the other end of the line onto the bow or to the stick supporting the can. Wrap the level flyline, which should be at least 45 feet long, from the bow end of the line around the tin-can reel. If you are using the larger tin can, you could use an entire level line 90 feet long.

Carp are frequently close enough to the surface of the water so that one can see their dorsal fins above water. This would make a fairly easy shot. However, if a fish is one or more feet under the surface of the water, it looks closer then it really is because of the angle of refraction. Shooting from different distances at small sponge rubber targets submerged at different depths is fun, challenging, and productive in developing skill in bowfishing.

SPEARFISHING

Fishing with spears was practiced by most primitive people everywhere. Certain tribes in Africa successfully took fish by throwing spears. Later they took fish by shooting spears from bows. Even today some African tribes use this method. They stand on the bank, edge of stream, or overlooking rock and shoot fish. They use extremely long bows

Fig. 11-5. Homemade bowfishing outfit.

eight or more feet in length. Their spears are five feet long or more. The length and weight of the African fishing spear make it possible to fish in much deeper water and assure better penetration of the fish. The Eskimos, of course, originally used spears for taking seals and other Arctic wildlife for their survival. Sometimes they would use a thrusting movement, if they were close enough, and sometimes they would throw the spear. Their need to secure seal at a distance naturally led to their development of the harpoon, which was a spear in which the handle could be dislodged; the spearhead would remain in the animal and could be retrieved by a cord made from seal sinew which was attached to a hole in the base of the spearhead.

Some tribes of American Indians adept at spearfishing used small decoys carved from pieces of dead seasoned wood to attract big fish close enough to spear them. These decoys were carved life-size to look like minnows or small frogs. Each decoy was attached by a small cord six to ten feet long to the end of a stick three or more feet long. With this stick the Indian could jiggle the decoy at the other end of the cord, giving the decoy lifelike action.

CATCHING MULLET

Mullet can easily be taken with spears, whether thrown by hand or with the aid of spearthrowers. They are an excellent saltwater food fish found in surf, bays, and estuaries in southern waters of the United States. Mullet are particularly plentiful in Florida coastal waters, where the annual catch is about 35,000,000 pounds. They travel around in closely packed schools from which an individual mullet will leap out of the water a foot or more and hold its pose in the air until it falls back into the water with a splash, whereas most fish after leaping from the water dive back in head first, making very little noise. As a rule mullet grow to a length of twenty-four inches. Any size mullet makes good food for humans, and live mullet up to twelve inches long are excellent bait for large game fish. The author singled out this fish because it is often caught by methods akin to those described in this chapter.

The most common means of taking mullet is by the use of various nets such as cast nets, gill nets, trammel nets, and seines. They can occasionally be caught on a flyrod, using a no. 10 or 12 hook baited with a piece of compact white rubber foam, or a section of a fish-worm about the size of a round shot used in an air rifle.

Snagging Mullet

For snagging mullet use a saltwater spinning reel, a stiff saltwater rod, and a ten- to fifteen-pound test line, either monofilament (would be best) or regular bait-casting line with a large treble hook tied on end. This treble hook should be large enough to cast easily. The procedure is to cast the hook just beyond the middle of a school of swarming mullet, allow it to sink about a foot downwards, and then as vigorously and fast as possible swing the rod-tip back in reverse direction from the cast. Reel up the slack line as fast as possible while allowing the rod to swing back towards the mullet school, and then again execute the fast swingback of the rod; repeat this procedure three or four times. Hopefully, you will snag a mullet from the school on the swingback. The first or second swingbacks are most likely to hook a fish, for the fish will disperse very quickly after the first snatch or two. If the rod is not stiff enough, but soft and flexible like many bait-casting rods, the snatch will come too late as the fast jerking pull will be delayed by the flexing action of the rod.

Spearing Mullet

Mullet are quite common in the shallow waters of all of the various bays and inlets of the Gulf of Mexico. Frequently schools of them will come within five or six yards of the shore or seawall, crowded so closely together that a well-thrown spear can hardly miss one. Spears commonly used for this purpose should be about eight or nine feet long, floatable, and heavy enough to penetrate fairly deep in the water. Attached securely to the front end of each spear should be a metal spearhead with three, four, or five sharp barbed points similar to a frog spear but larger. The other end of the spear should be rounded and have a hole a quarter-inch in diameter driven through it one inch from the end. Through this hole, pass the end of a small-diametered piece of nylon rope about thirty feet long and tie it securely to the end of the spear. At the other end of the rope make a loop for the fist (preferably with the perfection loop knot).

Practice from the shore throwing the spear at spots in the water; retrieve it with the throwing hand and coil the rope neatly in the other hand in coils approximately one foot in diameter. This practice should help you judge how much below the fish in the water to aim in order to compensate for refraction. When not in use the spear should be placed horizontally high on a rack (two hooks or nails six feet apart), and the pointed and barbed end sheathed in heavy leather to prevent accidents.

Throwing Mullet Spear with Spearthrower

Since seven or eight yards is about the greatest distance at which one can effectively throw spears to get mullet, the author has been studying ways in which mullet might be taken at longer distances such as twenty to twenty-five yards from shore. While trying out various experiments in Tampa Bay from the seawall in St. Petersburg he was finally successful in mid-April 1973. To reach mullet at these longer distances one needs only to use the same skill used in throwing spears with a spearthrower (see Chapter 4). Take one of your best spears which you have made for use with your spearthrower and attach a metal mullet spearhead on the front end. Then about 3/4 inch from the rear end, bore a hole transversely through the spear. Through the hole, tie one end of a level, floatable flyline of the thickest diameter (L 12 F). Tie the other end of the flyline to the handle on the inside of a tin-can reel (described earlier in this chapter). Now wind all the rest of the line on the outside of the can, starting at the open or near end (top of tin can) and wrapping the line clockwise (when facing the open end of can) except for about four feet of the end of the line, where it is attached to the spear. This much line is needed for play. Lay the spear on the spearthrower, pointing out in the direction of the swarming school of mullet. Fit the hook of the spearthrower securely and tightly into the depression made for it on the end of the spear. Now stretch the throwing arm straight back, keeping the entire length of the spear in the same plane with the direction of the throw, and with the spear slanted upwards at about an angle of twenty-five degrees from horizontal, make the throw. The line spins off smoothly and the mullet spear pierces the water where the fish are. One then retrieves the spear (with or without a fish) with the throwing arm and winds the line back on tin-can reel with clockwise turns. In winding the line onto the reel do not overlap on line previously wound but try to wind the line evenly; each circular wind should be close to the previous one. The single winds should be close enough so that the entire line is contained on the reel except for the four or five feet at the rear end of the spear. Each time you throw the spear, check to make sure the hook on the end of the spearthrower is tight up against the socket or concavity on the end of the spear. Also make sure that the long axis of the tin-can reel is pointing in the direction of the throw to be made (see Fig. 11-6). In general, the tin-can reel used in throwing the mullet spear with a spearthrower should be made with a tin can bigger in all dimensions than the one used for bass.

PRIMITIVE FISHING METHODS

Fishing with gear one makes oneself is certainly a lot of fun and challenges the adventurous spirit of young people everywhere, but there are fishing methods, employing means more primitive than those so far discussed, which require a good deal of initiative, ingenuity, and even daring. These methods, though illegal under ordinary circumstances, may save lives in an emergency.

Fish Trapping

Various methods of trapping fish have been used from earliest times by the American Indians and other primitive peoples. One method was for several natives to form a semicircle at one side of a likely looking pool and drive across it into shallow water at the other side where they and others waiting would scoop up the fish with hands or crude scoop-nets. The natives doing the driving would keep their arms and legs flailing and splashing to scare the fish. They would also have a crude net spread on the bottom in shallow water which two or more natives would raise to capture the fish after the splashing drive was completed.

Such nets were made from native plants. For instance, there is in parts of Florida and some other tropical areas a species of palm tree that has a broad fibrous, perforated

Fig. 11-6. *Top:* **The author with mullet spear poised on spearthrower ready to be thrown.** *Bottom:* **The mullet spear thrown and on its way.**

netlike structure which completely enfolds the trunk of the palm just below the start of each leaf stalk, for a foot or more. Several of these fibrous leaf stalk bottoms sewed edge to edge with inner bark fibers of other plants made good nets and were used as such.

At times in the spring when certain fish, particularly suckers, were running in streams where there were rapids alternating with holes, a small group of natives would start at the lower end of a hole and splash-drive the fish towards the upper end. The fish driven upstream would stop against the rocks, confused and sometimes wedged between them, and were not difficult to catch by hand and throw up on shore.

A practical fish trap used by American Indians can be made with straight green sticks averaging 1/2 inch in diameter and lashing materials, plus some wythes of flexible wood that can be bent into circles of three different sizes. The circles should have diameters of twenty-one, fifteen to sixteen, and six inches. The best kind of wood for making the circles is shagbark or bitternut hickory. If hickory wythes are not available, use long slender branches of yellow birch or purple willow. Use long branches of green wood. To make a branch more flexible, grasp a stiffer area with hands about six inches apart and twist the wood in different directions several times. Wherever this is done, it will become quite flexible. To make it easier to form circles with the branches, remove with a pocketknife several long slices of wood from the butt ends of the wythes, on the insides of the circles. In order to have the wythes overlap sufficiently and still have diameters of the proper size, the total length of the wythe for a particular circle should be about three feet or more greater than the circumference of that circle. This applies particularly to the two larger circles. The small circle does not, of course, need so much length for overlapping. Serve each circle in the overlapping area with inner bark cordage to prevent slipping.

The next step is to make two cones: a big one 4-1/2 feet long with the small end closed at the apex, and a small cone about 12 inches long. Approximately 83 sticks each 4-1/2 feet long will be needed for the big cone and about 63 sticks 14 inches long for the small cone. To make the large cone, lash the butt end of each 4-1/2-foot-long stick to the outside of the big circle, so that about 1-1/2 inches of each butt end sticks out beyond the circle. Each stick should be lashed with a continuous piece of cordage so that all sticks are parallel, close to each other, and perpendicular to the circle. The small ends of these sticks are all brought together at the end opposite to the circle and tied tightly with cordage; this end becomes the apex of the cone. In like manner lash the butt ends of the sixty-three sticks fourteen inches long to the outside of the circle sixteen inches in diameter and their small ends to the outside of the small circle six inches in diameter. However, since the smallest circle does not have room to lash each stick separately as was done with the butt ends, you must lash the small ends to the small circle in bundles of three or four sticks at a time. The small cone is now complete; place it inside the large cone so that the two larger circles are close together. After these two circles are securely tied together the fish trap is complete (see Fig. 11-7). Tie an adequate length of 1/4-inch nylon rope or rope made from basswood cordage around the two larger rings at the open end of the trap. Attach the other end of the rope to a dock, a tree on the shore, or a buoy (only in a lake). If placed in a stream, the trap should be lowered into a deep hole with the open end facing the current. Place bait in the trap appropriate to the fish to be caught and hanging from cordage or a wire about six inches inside the trap from the six-inch diameter opening in the smaller cone. Fish pass through the six-inch hole but get confused about escaping from the trap. They get caught either at the closed apex or in the space around the small cone up towards the front where the two large rings are fastened together.

Grabbling

One of the most primitive methods of catching fish, and also a dangerous one and therefore not used very often, is called grabbling. In this activity one wades slowly and quietly in a stream along its banks where they overhang and make little caves. This is a favorite place for fish to hide. To catch fish by this method, reach both hands under the bank very slowly, feeling for fish. When one is felt, slowly and carefully slide your hands along the side of the fish toward the head. After your hands have passed the middle of the fish and your fingertips are about to the edge of the gills, suddenly grab the fish with both hands and throw it as far up on the shore as possible; then quickly climb out on shore to catch the fish before it rolls back and flops into the stream. One would think this to be impossible, but it is not; the slow fingers feeling their way up the sides of the fish do not seem to disturb it particularly. The author has caught fish this way but recommends it only if fish are needed for one to survive. Beware especially of attempting to grab catfish using this method. A catfish will turn its head instantly and spike your hand deeply and painfully with one or both of its dagger-sharp lateral spines. This wound, being a puncture type, is most susceptible to serious infection.

HOW TO FIND NATURAL BAIT

Part of the fun of fishing for youngsters of all ages is finding the bait, if natural bait is used. It's educational too.

Earthworms

Certainly the most universally used freshwater fish bait of all time is the common earthworm. It can easily be dug with a four-pronged or sharp-pointed spade. Look for earthworms in damp, dark, rich ground, not far under the sod. As a boy living in the country, the author always looked in two places: behind the barn, and the area adjacent to the place where the drain from the kitchen sink entered the earth. One can also always find worms by turning over a flat board or rolling a log that has been lying on the ground undisturbed for some time. Turning over large stones ten to eighteen inches in diameter

Fig. 11-7. *Top:* **Side view of fish trap, with Chippewa Indian kitchen in background.** *Bottom:* **Front view of fish trap. All the lashing is done with basswood cordage.**

that have rested in the same position for several weeks is also productive. In this rolling or turning over process, one frequently will find a bonus of a large nightcrawler or two. If a board, log, or stone is particularly productive, take care to replace it in the same position since after a few days other worms will be found there. It is like tending a trap-line for muskrats.

Nightcrawlers

Probably the most effective, enjoyable way to collect nightcrawlers or nightwalkers (largest species of earthworm in the United States) is to stalk them with a flashlight at night on a lawn of closely cropped grass or a golf green. Walk slowly to prevent vibrations which will alert the nightcrawlers and cause them to slip back into their holes and escape. Hold the lighted flashlight one to two feet from the ground and shining on it. When you find a nightcrawler, check to see whether it is out of its hole free so it can be readily picked up and put in the container (large tin can), or whether part of it is out and the rest inside the hole. If the latter is the case, quickly pinpoint the location of the hole. Next, place the fingers of one hand on the worm tightly just a fraction of an inch from the hole, bearing down on the worm with pressure enough to prevent it from slipping back into the hole. Then, holding the worm tightly against the ground near the hole, securely grasp the part of the worm outside the hole and start to pull the worm out of the hole carefully. You will feel the worm contracting and pulling backwards as hard as it can. Do not try to pull it out at this time. Wait until it stops or relaxes a part of a second, then pull. You will gain an inch or two before it contracts to pull back in. Then hold what has been gained until the worm again relaxes, and pull again. You may gain the entire worm on this pull, or possibly only another inch or two. Continue this alternate pulling and holding and you will eventually win the worm. If you pull tightly while the worm is pulling, you are likely to gain only half the worm at most.

Nightcrawlers and earthworms can be kept fresh and in good fettle until time to use them by keeping them in cool, damp earth, leaves of grass, or fronds of ferns. The best thing to keep them fresh is damp sphagnum moss from a natural swamp area.

Hellgrammites and Nymphs

A hellgrammite is the larval stage of the Dobson fly. It is carnivorous, approximately two inches long, and has pincers at its head end; it must therefore be carefully handled. It is one of the favorite baits of smallmouth and largemouth bass and can be collected in shallow waters by hand or with a small meshed net.

Perch bugs, aquatic flying insects in the nymph stage of development just previous to maturity, are favorite foods of most all fish, particularly trout, perch, and bass. These can be caught by hand or small meshed net in thick water weeds along shallow shores of streams and lakes.

Grubs

While digging for earthworms with a spade, keep your eyes open for grubs. They are small white caterpillars about 3/4 to 1 inch long and generally found curled up in a circle. They might be in soil similar in texture to that of the earthworm, or they may be in rotted-out stumps and logs. They are the larval from of the scarab beetle, and are good bait for trout, perch, and other pan fish.

Grasshoppers

Grasshoppers and crickets can also be used for fish bait, and can be caught in hands or with butterfly nets. The first time the author used a grasshopper for bait he caught a large dark-phased crappie or calico bass.

Frogs

Frogs are one of the best baits for all kinds of bass. They can be caught in mid and late summer on banks and shores of lakes and streams with hands, but more successfully with nets because of their long jumps. At certain times in the summer when not quite full-grown, they will be found in great abundance in marshy regions among cattails and saw-grass. You can purchase hooks with a frog harness which permits frogs to swim without injury from the hook. There are, of course, other ways to attach them to the fishhook. Passing the hook up through both lower and upper lips is the most common way.

Crawfish or Crayfish

Crawfish, often called crayfish or crawdads, are excellent bait for bass and pickerel. This is especially true of soft-shell crawfish (only found once in a long while, having just shed their hard shells). Crawfish are found under flat rocks in the shallow waters of streams and lakes. They come in many sizes, from about 3/4 inch long to 5 or 6 inches long. They are shaped exactly like lobsters, and are various shades of tan and brown.

To collect crawfish, it is best to protect the feet by wearing sneakers, hip boots, or waders. Also wear a bathing suit or old pants rolled up above the knees. All children will likely insist on going barefoot.

Wade slowly in water ankle-deep to ten inches or so until you spot a flattish rock with one or more sides and edges overlapping miniature concavities about 1/2 to 1 inch from the ground. Slowly and carefully lift the rock or turn it over. Wait for the murky water to clear, and then look for one or more crawfish. Try to catch the largest first; it will probably be of medium size, about two inches long. Cup the catching hand or net and slowly place it close to the bottom a few inches from the tail of the crawfish. Since the crawfish swims backwards and upwards with a downward flap of its powerful tail, you are in a good position to catch it. Keep trying and success will come. Of course, it's easier with a net, but it's more fun bare-handed.

Crawfish 1-3/4 inch long and longer will try to pinch one with their clippers. To prevent this hold the crawfish with thumb and index finger around the hard thoracic or chest shell just behind and between the pincers. Place caught crawfish in a pail with a few inches of water, and add a little sand and a few stones.

Crawfish, like lobsters and crabs in salt water, are scavengers; so adding a small amount of fish cleanings in water close to shore once in a while helps to maintain crawfish in the area for future collections. Do not overdo this practice as it will make an objectionable shoreline. Try baiting the shallow shore with a little at night and see how much and what kinds of refuse are left on the shore the next morning.

Minnows

Live minnows are always an acceptable bait for all game fish (bass, pickerel, perch, crappies, pike, wall-eyed pike, and muskellunge). Check with your regional or local department of conservation to see what are the legal methods of catching minnows for bait. In some states nets of various types and specific dimensions are legal and in other states they are not. One method legal in most states is as follows.

Locate a pool in a small stream or lake area where minnows are observed to be plentiful. Make a fishing rig consisting of a very flexible stick or pole about five to six feet long (a fresh shoot of willow would be best). Tie to the small or top end of this pole some strong thread or string about five or six feet long. On the end of the string tie a bent pin or a regular hook, preferably size 12 or 14 and no larger than size 10. To be more sporting, pinch off the barb with pliers. Bait the hook with a piece of earthworm about 1/8 inch long or a goldenrod gall (see below). Now dangle the baited hook in the pool of minnows and the fun will begin. The bait will be attacked by minnows from every direction, and soon one minnow will start to run off with it. This is the time, of course, to set the hook and play the minnow in earnest with the aim of eventually swinging it out of the pool and into the minnow pail. In this process, and with a very flexible shoot of willow for the rod, one experiences all the fun and excitement that is present when playing a two-pound bass on a regular casting outfit.

Blunt-nosed minnows (*Pimephales notatus*), sometimes called stonerollers, are a particularly delectable treat for small-mouthed bass, which like to roam shoals of lakes.

These minnows lay their eggs on the bottoms of rocks six to ten inches or more in width, in close flat patches of fifty to one hundred eggs each.

Collecting these blunt-nosed minnows is fascinating fun. It requires special but simple equipment. Since these minnows are found in water 1 to 2-1/2 feet deep, wear hip boots, waders, or a swimming suit, and something to protect the feet from stone bruises.

The net one uses has an open bottom as well as open top. The close-meshed netting hangs straight down from the hoop like a cylinder about one foot in diameter and two feet long. Some link chain about 1/3 inch or slightly more in diameter should be sewed or tied into the bottom edge of the cylindrical net. Now with a minnow pail with cover, tied around the waist or over the shoulder, you are all set to start. First, wade in water 1-1/2 to 2 feet deep; do so slowly so as not to roil the water or scare the fish. Look for rocks no longer or wider than 12 inches, whose bottoms are concave enough to allow minnows to enter and hide or lay eggs. When such a rock is noted, carefully lower the open bottom of the net around the rock and pack the chain closely around the outside edges of the rock on all sides of it. Then, holding the hoop of the net with one hand, reach into the net with the other hand and take out the rock. Turn it over and carefully observe its bottom surface. If it does not have a bunch of eggs clustered together in one or more flat patches throw the rock to one side, pull up the net, and move on to another promising rock. Repeat the previous steps. If an egg patch is found on the bottom of the rock, you can be nearly sure that there is a stoneroller swimming around in the net. When the murky water clears, catch the minnow in your hand by crowding it up against the side of the net and put it into the minnow pail. Then move on to the next likely stone.

The Goldenrod Gall

During the latter part of the summer a round ball-like growth approximately one inch in diameter develops on the upper part of the stalks of many goldenrod plants. It is the same color as the rest of the stalk and is generally formed within six to ten inches of the top of the plant. This is a gall. It is caused by an attack on the upper stem of the plant by a parasitic insect. This attack irritates the plant, causing certain fluids and materials to collect at the attack area and producing a spherical swelling. At the time of attack one or more eggs are implanted which, when hatched into the larval stage, feed on the accumulated swollen material from the center outward. Generally only one of the larvae survives. If at the proper time in the fall one rests the gall on a hard wooden surface and cuts it open carefully with a sharp knife, a small grub-shaped worm will be found in the center of the gall. This worm is excellent fish bait, especially for trout.

Some Thoughts on A Viable Lifestyle

DURING THE AUTHOR'S UNDERGRADUATE LIFE AT OBERLIN, HE had the rare opportunity of having as a teacher Dr. Henry Churchill King, president of Oberlin College for over thirty years. He was loved and respected by students and faculty alike and knew the names of all the students, their family backgrounds and their interests. President King was a gentleman "for all time," and his teaching was of the best because he sincerely lived what he said and wrote. To us as seniors in his class in ethics, he gave a bit of his personal philosophy in a statement his students will always cherish, try to practice, and want to share with others: "Stay persistently in the presence of the best, in the sphere in which you seek attainment, and make an honest response". Since the author wholeheartedly believes this philosophy, accepts it, and tries to live it, it has become a part of his own philosophy which he recommends to his readers.

Theodore Roosevelt was the first president of the United States to realize the values of wilderness and the preservation of our natural resources. He set aside as national parks many of the best and most beautiful unspoiled natural areas in the country. It was one of his ways of "making an honest response." Theodore Roosevelt was one of the greatest naturalists of all time. One of his best-loved recreations was the study of birds. His knowledge of ornithology extended not only throughout the United States but included Great Britain, South America, Africa, and many other regions of the globe. One of the author's adopted thoughts comes from the following statement by Theodore Roosevelt:

> No man is fit to live who is not fit to die and no man is fit to die, who shrinks from the joy of life or from the duty of life.

Roosevelt placed the joy of life on the same plane as the duty, and his greatest joy or recreation was nature-recreation with particular emphasis on birds.

A famous poet once wrote: "Life is not so short but there is always time for courtesy." The author accepts this thought and adds a few others:

Life is not so short but there is always time to point out (especially to children) the beauty and mystery in life in all facets of nature.

Life is not so short but there is always time to stop and listen for a while to the sounds of nature day or night.

Life is not so short but there is always time to show respect for the personalities of children by answering their questions truthfully, appreciating the expression of their sense of humor, and recognizing and appreciating their interests as important.

Life is not so short but there is always time to take a child fishing, or help him or her fly a kite.

As a final challenge or perhaps a prayer and probably both: may we be instrumental in helping people, especially children and young people, to develop an increasing respect and reverence for life—all life, plant, animal, fish, and human life—and to realize as did Albert Schweitzer, the great physician, musician, and teacher, that the only way to teach or influence others is through one's personal example. Help us to believe and know that the Creator of us all planned an environmental place, a purpose, an ecosystem, and active program for every living plant and animal including man, and that through research, experimentation, and practice we must make our way of life ever increasingly one of living in harmony with the natural resources of the biosphere and with all people the world over.

Selected Bibliography

GENERAL CRAFTS

Couch, Osma Palmer. *Basket Pioneering*. New York: Orange Judd Co., 1947.

Di Valentin, Louis, and Di Valentin, Maria. *Practical Encyclopedia of Crafts*. New York: Sterling Publishing Co., 1970.

Eaton, Allen Hendershott. *Handicrafts of the Southern Highlands*. New York: Russell Sage, 1937.

Gilley, Wendell. *Bird Carving*. Princeton, N.J.: Van Nostrand, 1961.

Griswold, Lester, and Griswold, Kathleen. *The New Handicrafts Processes and Projects*. 10th ed. Minneapolis, Minn.: Burgess Publishing Co., 1969.

Hils, Karl. *Crafts for All*. Newton Center, Mass.: C. T. Branford Co., 1960.

Ickis, Margaret. *Arts and Crafts*. New York: A. S. Barnes, 1943.

———. *Handcrafts and Hobbies*. New York: Hawthorn Books, Greystone Press, 1948.

Mason, Bernard Sterling. *Primitive and Pioneer Sports*. New York: A. S. Barnes, 1937.

Newkirk, Louis V., and Zutts, Lavada. *Crafts for Everyone*. 2 vols. Scranton, Pa.: International Textbook Co., 1950.

Pluckrose, Henry. *The Book of Crafts.* Chicago: Henry Regnery Co., 1971.

Reeves, Robert. *Make It Yourself Games Book.* New York: Emerson Books, 1962.

Rich, Frank M. *Dictionary of Discards.* New York: Association Press, 1952.

Zechlin, Ruth. *Complete Book of Handcrafts.* Boston: C. T. Branford Co., 1959.

NATURE CRAFTS

Angier, Bradford. *Living off the Country.* Harrisburg, Pa.: Stackpole Books, 1966.

Hammett, Catherine, and Horrocks, Carol M. *Creative Crafts for Campers.* New York: Association Press, 1957.

Ichinoto, Tatsuo. *The Art of Driftwood and Dried Arrangement.* New York: Crown Publishers, 1951.

Jaeger, Ellsworth. *Nature Crafts.* New York: Macmillan Co., 1951.

Lyford, Carrie A. *The Crafts of the Ojibwa (Chippewa).* Washington, D.C.: U.S. Government Printing Office, for Office of Indian Affairs, 1942.

Mason, Otis Tufton. *Aboriginal American Basketry.* Annual report of Smithsonian Institution Historical Museum, Board of Regents. Washington, D.C.: U.S. Government Printing Office, 1902.

Musselman, Virginia. *Learning About Nature Through Crafts.* Harrisburg, Pa.: Stackpole Books, 1969.

Thompson, Mary. *The Driftwood Book.* Princeton, N.J.: Van Nostrand, 1960.

Underhill, Ruth. *Pueblo Crafts.* Washington, D.C.: U.S. Government Printing Office, for Education Division, Office of Indian Affairs, 1944.

Van Der Smissen, Betty, and Goering, Oswald H. *A Leader's Guide to Nature Oriented Activities.* Ames, Iowa: Iowa State University Press, 1965.

Whiteford, Andrew Hunter. *North American Indian Arts.* New York: Western Publishing Co., Golden Press, 1970.

Wright, Dorothy. *Baskets and Basketry.* Boston: C. T. Branford Co., 1959.

NATURE GUIDES

Brown, Vinson. *Amateur Naturalist's Handbook.* Boston: Little, Brown & Co., 1948.

———. *Reading the Woods.* Harrisburg, Pa.: Stackpole Books, 1969.

Cobb, Boughton. *A Field Guide to the Ferns.* Peterson Field Guide Series. Boston: Houghton Mifflin, 1956, 1963.

Gray, Asa. *Gray's New Manual of Botany.* New York: American Book Co., for Harvard College President and Fellows, 1908.

Grimm, William Carey. *Home Guide to Trees, Shrubs, and Wildflowers.* Harrisburg, Pa.: Stackpole Books, 1970.

Harlow, William. *Trees of Eastern and Central U.S. and Canada*. Dover, N.Y.: Peter Smith, 1942.

Hottes, Alfred C. *Book of Shrubs*. New York: De Le Mare, 1952.

House, Homer D. *Wild Flowers*. New York: Macmillan Co., 1935.

Palmer, E. Lawrence. *Fieldbook of Natural History*. New York: McGraw-Hill Co., 1949.

Peterson, Roger Tory. *Field Guide to the Birds*. Boston: Houghton Mifflin Co., 1947.

———. *Field Guide to the Wildflowers*. Boston: Houghton Mifflin Co., 1968.

Petrides, George. *A Field Guide to Trees and Shrubs*. Peterson Field Guide Series. Boston: Houghton Mifflin Co., 1958.

Rickett, Harold Williams. *Flowers of the United States*. New York: McGraw-Hill Co., for New York Botanical Garden, 1967.

Swain, Ralph B. *The Insect Guide*. Garden City, N.Y.: Doubleday & Co., 1948.

Wherry, Edgar T. *Wildflower Guide: Northeastern and Midland United States*. Garden City, N.Y.: Doubleday & Co., 1954.

Wyman, Don. *Shrubs and Vines*. New York: Macmillan Co., 1969.

HOBBIES

Anderson, H.S. ("Andy"). *How to Carve Characters in Wood*. Albuquerque: University of New Mexico Press, 1953.

Belash, Constantine A. *Braiding and Knotting for Amateurs*. Boston: C.T. Branford Co., 1952.

Flick, Arthur B. *New Streamside Guide to the Naturals and Their Imitations*. New York: Crown Publishers, 1969.

Knight, John Alden. *The Complete Book of Fly-Casting*. New York: Putnam's, 1963.

McLane, A. J. *McLane's Standard Fishing Encyclopedia*. New York: Holt, Rinehart & Winston, 1965.

———. *The Practical Fly Fisherman*. New York: Prentice-Hall, 1953.

Mulac, Margaret E. *Hobbies, The Creative Use of Leisure*. New York: Harper's, 1959.

Noll, H. J. *A Guide to Trout Flies and How to Tie Them*. New York: Davis-Delany-Arrow, 1969.

Quick, Leland, and Leiper, Hugh. *Gemstones, How to Cut and Polish Them*. Philadelphia: Chilton Co., 1959.

NATURE EDUCATION

Brainerd, J. W. *Nature Study for Conservation*. New York: Macmillan Co., 1971.

Geagan, William. *Nature I Loved*. New York: Coward-McCann, 1952.

Encyclopaedia Britannica. 11th ed. S.v. "Boomerang."

Freeman, Orville. *Outdoors U.S.A.* Washington, D.C.: U.S. Government Printing Office, 1967.

Hammerman, Donald R., and Hammerman, William M. *Outdoor Education: A Book of Readings.* 2d ed. Minneapolis: Burgess Publishing Co., 1973.

Harris, Ben Charles. *Eat the Weeds.* Barre, Mass.: Barre Publishers, 1972.

Ickes, Marguerite. *Nature in Recreation.* New York: A. S. Barnes, 1965.

Kjelgaard, Jim. *Boomerang Hunter.* New York: Holiday House, 1960.

Leopold, Aldo. *A Sand County Almanac.* Fairlawn, N.J.: Oxford University Press, 1947.

———. *Round River.* Fairlawn, N.J.: Oxford University Press, 1953.

Leveson, David. *A Sense of Earth.* Anchor Natural History Book. Garden City, N.Y.: Doubleday & Co., 1972.

Price, Betty. *Adventuring in Nature.* Washington, D.C.: National Recreation Association, 1939.

Reben, Martha. *The Healing Woods.* London: Hammond, Hammond, 1954.

Smith, Julian; Carlson, Reynold; Donaldson, George; and Masters, Hugh B. *Outdoor Education.* Englewood Cliffs, N.J.: Prentice-Hall, 1963.

CORDAGE

Boyce, Sidney Smith. *Hemp.* New York: Orange Judd Co., 1900.

Franklin, Eric. *Knotting, Splicing and Cordage.* London: Cassel, 1952.

Himmelfarb, David. *The Technology of Cordage Fibers and Rope.* Plainfield, N.J.: Textile Book Service, 1957.

Manchester, H. H. "Back to Methusalah in Rope Making." *Cord Age,* June 1922, pp. 52-56.

Palmer, E. L. *Fibers.* Cornell Rural School Leaflet, vol. 38, no. 2. Ithaca, N.Y.: Cornell University Press, 1944.

PRIMITIVE PEOPLE

Gould, Richard A. *Yiwara Foragers of the Australian Desert.* New York: Scribner's, 1971.

Hodge, Frederick W. *Handbook of American Indians North of Mexico.* 2 vols. Westport, Conn.: Greenwood Press, 1912.

Kroeber, Theodora. *Ishi.* Berkeley and Los Angeles: University of California Press, 1961.

Mason, J. Alden. *Ancient Civilizations of Peru.* Rev. ed. Baltimore: Penguin Books, 1969.

———. "Some Unusual Spearthrowers of Ancient America." *University of Pennsylvania Museum Journal* 19 (1928): 290-324.

Nuttall, Zelia. *The Atlatls or Spear Throwers Used by the Ancient Mexicans.* Harvard University Papers, vol. 1, no. 3. Cambridge, Mass.: Peabody Museum of American Archaeology and Ethnology, Harvard University, 1891.

Steward, J. H., and Faron, L. C. *Native Peoples of South America.* New York: McGraw-Hill Co., 1959.

Stirling, Matthew William. *Historical and Ethnological Material on Jivaro Indians.* Smithsonian Institution, Bureau of American Ethnology, bulletin 117. St. Clair Shores, Mich.: Scholarly Press, 1938.

Index

(Note: Page numbers in italics refer to illustrations.)